Lobbying from below

INQUEST in defence of civil liberties

Mick Ryan
University of Greenwich

UCL
PRESS

First published in 1996 by UCL Press

UCL Press Limited
University College London
Gower Street
London WC1E 6BT

and
1900 Frost Road, Suite 101
Bristol
Pennsylvania 19007-1598

The name of University College London (UCL) is a registered
trade mark used by UCL Press with the consent of the owner.

British Library Cataloguing in Publication Data
A catalogue record for this book is available from the British Library.

Library of Congress Cataloging-in-Publication Data are available

ISBNs: 1–85728–225–8 HB
1–85728–256–6 PB

Typeset in Palatino.
Printed and bound by
Biddles Ltd, Guildford and King's Lynn, England.

Lobbying from below

Contents

CONTENTS

Preface

This preface addresses three issues.

First, it will soon become clear that some of the cases discussed in this book will involve men and women with criminal records. In one or two cases they may have been convicted of serious offences. This once prompted a new recruit to INQUEST to observe that:

> It seems to me that the thrust of your campaign is not best placed to get the support of the average person in the country. This is not meant as a criticism, but it is because much of your work seems to be concerned with the criminal fraternity, or those who are in some way linked to such. Now, don't get me wrong, I am not saying that . . . subjects should not be adequately protected, but most of our fellow citizens would look at certain accidents as being a form of justifiable vigilantism.

While those associated with INQUEST would rightly point to a far wider constituency than this suggests, they would not deny this particular strategic difficulty. However, it deserves a sharp riposte. To begin with, the INQUEST archive makes it abundantly clear that many men and women who behave in anti-social ways are not one dimensional; they are often devoted fathers or mothers, dutiful sons or daughters, faithful and loving partners. It is memory of these positive qualities and relationships that drives families and friends forward in their search for the truth and what they often rightly define as their "search for justice".

But beyond this, it is not unreasonable to assume from the evidence of history that once we ride roughshod over the liberties of what some might uncharitably describe as the flotsam and jetsam of our society then our own liberties will surely be at risk. That is what I believe; that is why I became involved with INQUEST, and that is why I have written this narrative.

The second point is about academic objectivity. When I wrote my first book on pressure groups nearly twenty years ago, *The acceptable pressure group. Inequality in the penal lobby* (Farnborough: Saxon House, 1978), a case study of the Howard League and Radical Alternatives to Prison (RAP), I had only a very limited firsthand knowledge of penal politics and was not a member of either of the lobby groups that were the subject of the book. The situation today is very different. In the intervening years, I became very active in the penal lobby and was closely involved with INQUEST, the subject of this book. This was first as a fairly inactive member of a fairly inactive Executive Committee in the late 1980s, and then as its chair during a quite vigorous, and no doubt my critics might argue, managerial period between 1991 and 1993. I have not been closely involved since writing this narrative, but remain a committed member.

It is inevitable that so close an involvement will colour my view of events, both before and during my time as a member of the Executive Committee. It is important that readers keep this in mind and register its disadvantages. On the other hand, this inside view has certain obvious things in its favour. Space does not permit me to elaborate on them here other than to say that while I could certainly have gained an understanding of INQUEST's operating framework from a distance, I could never have fully grasped the dynamics of the group as an outsider, understood the personal and professional compromises that were part of its daily being and that impacted directly on its operations. I would like this plus to be added to the balance sheet, though no doubt conventional British and American social scientists will treat it with a long spoon.

The final point is about my own academic interest in pressure groups. This arose in a contradictory way. In the late 1960s and early 1970s I was a postgraduate student in Bernard Crick's newly created Department of Political Theory and Political Institutions at the University of Sheffield. It was here that I came across Stuart Walkland's general interest in the study of such groups as one way of avoiding the "constitutionalism" that he then felt so bedevilled the academic study of British politics, a critique that others have noted (for example, A. G. Jordan & J. J. Richardson, *Government and pressure groups in Britain* (Oxford: Clarendon, 1987)). Ironically, however, it was Bernard Crick who finally confirmed my interest in pressure groups when he later wrote to me in London explaining that he and Patrick Seyd were putting together a series on "good cause" groups for *The Political Quarterly*, of which he was the editor, and would I care to choose one of the following groups – they gave me a long list – to write on? This I duly did, picking out Radical Alternatives to Prison.

The irony of this was twofold. Any student of politics worth his or her salt will have read Crick's *The American science of politics* (London: Routledge & Kegan Paul, 1959). His disdain of group theorists like A. F. Bentley and D. B. Truman is pretty clear, and he would often remark between gritted teeth that he was more interested in politics and government than mere pressure groups! However, the second irony is that it was writing about Radical Alternatives to Prison that led to my first book on the penal lobby more generally, and that in due course took me away from political science, or political studies as I still prefer to call it, and into criminology or social policy where I now ply my interdisciplinary trade.

I make these points to explain how I lost touch with the academic study of pressure groups. Except for the late Sammy Finer and David Marsh I cannot put a face to any of the leading theorists in the field, though I might recognize Wyn Grant as we overlapped as undergraduates in the politics department at Leicester University in the 1960s, but here again I had no idea that he was developing his influential insider/outsider framework at about the same time as I was independently writing *The acceptable pressure group*. Perhaps I should also mention here that I have kept in touch with Robert Benewick who wrote an early, seminal essay on pluralism/pressure groups before developing other academic interests.

It was therefore with some interest that recently I began to catch up on what had happened in the years in between, the years of the New Right. My impression – and it is no more than that – is that while policy analysts have demonstrated some new insights, I sense an American preference that stresses the primacy of process, community and network above ideology and old-fashioned concerns about government. But perhaps more to the present point, I detect in more general texts on British government and politics the still familiar tendency to draw boundaries around the political system in such a way that it restricts our understanding of how power operates in modern societies and the manner in which some pressure groups, though admittedly not all, contribute to making the exercise of that power accountable. I develop some of these points towards the end of my narrative.

Acknowledgements

A number of individuals associated with INQUEST have given me interviews and information about its activities.

I am particularly grateful to Celia Stubbs, Tony Ward, Deborah Coles, Phil Scraton, June Tweedie, Tim Owen, Mark Urbanowicz and Ken Worpole.

Tony Ward and Deborah Coles were especially helpful in going through the entire manuscript.

Alistair Brinkley has a long political memory and his recollections and opinions were valuable too.

Two MPs, Michael Meacher and Barry Sheerman, also answered questions without reserve.

I should also mention Vincenzo Ruggiero who was for several years an active member of INQUEST. Other academic friends and colleagues have likewise made a very real contribution, most notably Joe Sim, David Downes and Robert Benewick, all of whom commented on my original proposal. Adam Edwards, Simon Hallsworth and Maeve McMahan began a debate in Komotini, Greece, about the nature of social control and the state which is reflected in this text.

I must also mention my colleague, Bridget Leach, who loaned me a draft copy of Tommy Banks's book on Jimmy Kelly. She also put me in touch with Marg Nicol who provided me with the photograph used for the cover.

The librarians at the University of Greenwich were helpful, especially Imogen Forster, and one of my former students, Peggy Stewart, provided me with an excellent press cutting service on the courts and legal matters generally. Pat Rosser-Davies gave time and care to getting the manuscript into its final form.

Joan Ryan's tolerance and intellectual support were significant and valuable, as ever.

List of abbreviations

ALA	Association of London Authorities
CPS	Crown Prosecution Service
DPP	Director of Public Prosecutions
GLC	Greater London Council
HSE	Health and Safety Executive
ILG	Inquest Lawyers' Group
LBGC	London Borough Grants Committee
LBGU	London Borough Grants Unit
Met	Metropolitan Police Force
MIND	national association for mental health
NCCL	National Council for Civil Liberties
PCA	Police Complaints Authority
PROP	Preservation of the Rights of Prisoners
RAP	Radical Alternatives to Prison
SHSA	Special Hospitals Service Agency
SPG	special patrol groups
WEA	Workers' Educational Association
WIP	Women in Prison

Dr John Burton, the Secretary of the Coroners' Society, described
. . . INQUEST, the organization set up by families of people who
died in custody, as an overtly political and self appointed group.
P. Scraton & K. Chadwick, *In the arms of the law*
(London: Pluto, 1986), p. 47.

We canvassed the idea that the body, INQUEST, which holds itself
out to assist – and does so remarkably well – the relations of
those who die in legal custody, should be properly funded. We
suggested that the Government should make a modest contribution annually to INQUEST to allow it to represent such families.
Report of the committee of inquiry into complaints
about Ashworth Hospital (London: HMSO, 1992), p. 213.

Chapter 1

Introducing INQUEST and inquests

It is perhaps one of the most obvious human paradoxes that death is an integral part of life. In the normal course of events the routine death of a member of the family or a friend is a deep, private grief, even resignation in the face of wider, impersonal forces. However, there are deaths that are far from routine and that invoke quite different responses – feelings of anger, recrimination and public disputation. Such deaths are often, although of course not always, the subject of a coroner's inquest and raise wider questions about the culpability of state officials, their political masters or private employers. In other words, they become matters of public concern. The role of the pressure group INQUEST, founded in 1981, is to provide families and friends involved in such inquests with the emotional support and legal expertise they need to help piece together the circumstances that surround the death that has transformed their grief into anger.

This simple description of INQUEST's role requires amplification. First and foremost, the quality of the casework it does with families involved with controversial deaths is greatly hampered by both the legal procedures governing inquests and the manner in which these procedures are interpreted by coroners. Thus, while INQUEST is working with families on a routine basis in cases across the country it is at the same time campaigning at Westminster for changes in inquest procedures, significant changes that require legislative force. Secondly, and more visibly, inquests often reveal inadequacies in institutional procedures, say the administration of suicide prevention procedures in prisons, and INQUEST campaigns in a high profile way to repair these deficiencies. Indeed, it is arguably more associated in the public mind with these campaigns arising out of its casework than with the reform of inquest procedures *per se*. We will therefore return to consider some of these campaigns in later chapters.

1

INQUEST is thus best introduced as a campaigning organization driven in a direction largely determined by its casework. Getting the balance right between casework and campaigning has been a source of tension within INQUEST over the years. However, and not entirely unrelated to this tension, it is also worth noting that INQUEST is unusual, although by no means unique, among pressure groups for its involvement across a whole range of what political scientists and policy analysts call policy communities and/or policy networks.[1] That is to say, while many groups will confine their activities to networking their own well defined lobbies, housing for example, INQUEST on the other hand is likely to network across several lobbies on a routine basis. To start with the example we have already touched on, it will be working in the penal lobby with groups like the Prison Reform Trust on suicides in prisons while at the same time networking with civil liberties groups over deaths in police custody and/or with MIND on issues around psychiatric care.

The story of how this networking first got started and how it has sustained INQUEST over the years is something I shall develop in subsequent chapters. We will also return to discuss the distinction that is sometimes drawn between policy networks and policy communities later. More immediately, however, it is important that we begin with a brief description of how inquests work; exploring, for example, the role of the coroner and his relationship with officials and public, and reviewing the procedures that govern the conduct of the inquest itself. What I am doing at this point is simply sketching in INQUEST's site of operations for the uninitiated, so to speak. A more detailed picture will emerge as the story of the group unfolds.

Inquests and coroners

The first point to make is that coroners are not involved in every death that is registered in any given year. What mostly happens when a death occurs is that a death certificate is signed by the general practitioner or hospital doctor involved and sent to the Registrar of Births, Marriages and Deaths. The matter rests there unless the death falls into one of the following categories, in which case the Registrar is obliged to pass it on to the coroner who is an independent judicial officer:

- a sudden or unexplained death,
- a death occurring in suspicious circumstances,
- a death caused by industrial injury or a death contracted at work,
- a death that may have been due to neglect, poisoning, drug abuse or abortion,
- a death caused by injury received while on military service,
- a death in prison custody,
- a death where the body has not been seen for fourteen days,
- and a death unattended by a doctor.

In 1994, the last year for which figures are available, the proportion of all registered deaths reported to the coroner was 34 per cent.[2] Some of these cases, for example, where the physical cause of a sudden death can readily be explained, are easily resolved, sometimes at the instigation of a telephone call to a doctor or a hospital physician by one of the coroner's officers. However, postmortems to establish the physical cause of death were still required in 68 per cent of all those cases reported to the coroner in 1994.[3]

The power to order a postmortem in order to establish the physical cause of death is vested solely in the coroner and is carried out on his behalf by a pathologist who is selected from a list provided by the Home Office. Interested persons, relatives, for example, are entitled to be represented at the postmortem, and if they are dissatisfied with the first postmortem they may finance a second one.[4] If having received the pathologist's report and any other information relating to the death the coroner is still uncertain about the cause of death or about the circumstances immediately surrounding it, he can order an inquest. In certain cases, for example prison deaths, inquests are mandatory.

In 1994 just under 21,000 deaths resulted in an inquest, 11 per cent of all deaths reported to the coroner.[5]

Exceptionally, inquests have to be held with juries:
- where the death has occurred in prison,
- where the death was caused by industrial accident or disease,
- where death occurred in circumstances that if continued would be prejudicial to the health and safety of the public,
- or where the death occurred while the deceased was in police custody or resulted from an injury inflicted by a police officer in the purported execution of his/her duty.

In 1994 only around 4 per cent of all deaths reported to the coroner required an inquest with a jury.[6] The verdicts available to a jury include unlawful killing, justifiable homicide, accident or misadventure, suicide or, where the evidence is inconclusive, an open verdict can be returned. These verdicts are drawn from a standard list that is usually employed, although coroners and/or juries can (and occasionally do) phrase their own verdicts. In Chapter 5, for example, I refer to the verdict of "suicide due to official indifference and lack of care" that was returned at an inquest into the death of an immigration detainee. Normally, however, more standard verdicts are returned under the coroner's direction. In 1994, deaths by accident or misadventure accounted for 47 per cent of all inquest verdicts and suicides for 18 per cent.[7]

On the face of it these procedures seem sensible, even desirable. In a free society it is surely important that in the absence of evidence that leads to an immediate criminal prosecution, all deaths, especially those that are sudden, unexplained or violent, should be subject to an investigation – usually in public – by an independent judicial officer. Furthermore, it is comforting to believe that while free societies regrettably have to use instruments and institutions of coercion, police and prisons for example, those who run them are especially accountable in this and other ways. We do not operate Gulags in the West where those detained are beaten to the point of death, driven to suicide, or simply neglected to rot away through lack of care, or if such things do occur, those responsible are held accountable for their actions.

True, our confident sketch about the role of coroners and inquests in these matters suggests some obvious omissions. For example, there is no statutory requirement to hold inquests – with or without juries – on those who die while in secure hospitals for the criminally insane like Ashworth, nor are they required on those who die having been "sectioned" to ordinary psychiatric hospitals under mental health legislation. Nor, for that matter, is it strictly necessary for a coroner to hold an inquest into a death in police custody; the only requirement here is that if he or she does hold an inquest it must be with a jury. But these omissions aside, some of which could easily be put right by simply amending the Coroners' Rules, surely these safeguards are adequate? And if they are not, what is going wrong?

Causes for concern

Perhaps the first thing to point out is that INQUEST does not believe, as some of its members once did, that the inquest system is so entirely worthless that it should be abandoned. Nor, for that matter, does it deny that in many routine cases inquests satisfy – even reassure – family and friends of the deceased. Its case is rather that in a relatively small but important number of instances often, although by no means always, involving institutional care and/or police arrests, the rules governing inquests, and the way coroners interpret these rules, work against discovering the truth. The effect of this is often to protect the interests of the powerful against the interest of the powerless. According to INQUEST this comes about in several ways.

In the first place, families and friends of the deceased cannot claim legal aid to pay for a solicitor or barrister to represent them at an inquest. True, under what is known as the green form scheme they are entitled to legal advice about inquest procedures and their rights within those procedures, but in controversial cases this is hardly sufficient and puts already distressed families or friends at a great disadvantage. An inquest into the death of someone in prison, for example, could take place – and sometimes has – with the unrepresented family and friends of the deceased having to confront a lawyer representing the Home Office, one representing the Prison Medical Service and yet another one representing the Prison Officers' Association. This is hardly a level playing field, and INQUEST has criticized successive Lords Chancellor for failing to explain why the public purse can run to funding Home Office barristers to protect civil servants and politicians, but not the bereaved.

However, even if a solicitor or a barrister is at hand – and some families go to great lengths to ensure this even if it means getting into debt – this is no guarantee of equal treatment. To take the example I referred to above, a death in prison custody. In a case like this the coroner would first contact a pathologist to undertake a postmortem. He or she might instruct one of his or her officers to attend the examination and/or speak to the pathologist about any suspicious or incriminating marks that are on the body. In the meantime other officers – sometimes retired or seconded police personnel – would be interviewing people and collecting statements from witnesses or anyone else at the prison with relevant information. In due course these statements would be passed on to the coroner, as would the results of the prison's

5

own internal inquiry or any police investigation. In other words, and unlike the procedure in a criminal court where the judge (and jury) wait to be convinced by the evidence unfolding before them in an adversarial setting as presented either by the defence or the prosecution who are at liberty within well defined rules to bring who they like before the court, the coroner arrives at court often – or so it seems – having already been through the available evidence and reached a conclusion. A conclusion, by the way, that will almost certainly dictate who should be called to give evidence, a prerogative that at inquests lies wholly with the coroner.

Furthermore, while in such a case any police report might be given to the barrister or solicitor representing the Home Office, it would not be handed over to the lawyers acting for the family and friends of the bereaved, nor would their lawyer be permitted to address the court on the facts, in other words, to sum up putting forward their version of events. These criticisms have led a long-time critic of inquests and a member of INQUEST to observe that:

> The fundamental defect of coroners' courts is that the coroner has too much power over the conduct and the outcome of the inquest, and the parties and the jury have too little. This imbalance can be redressed by giving the parties as nearly as possible the same opportunities to present an effective case to the jury as they would in a criminal or civil trial; to obtain legal aid, to see the statements of witnesses and other relevant documents before the hearing, to call witnesses (in addition to those selected by the coroner), and to address the coroner or the jury on the facts.[8]

While it is true that these several disadvantages are not insurmountable, and skilful lawyers with the help of flexible and fair-minded coroners can get at most or all of the evidence that is on record and technically available during the inquisition, INQUEST's experience is that those representing the deceased often face an uphill struggle, a struggle that is sometimes made all the more arduous when key witnesses exercise their legal right not to give evidence in case they put themselves at a disadvantage in any subsequent criminal hearing or civil action. This is not because coroners or juries can explicitly name them as guilty – this practice was outlawed after the inquest into the death of Lord Lucan's nanny in 1975 – but because their guilt or complicity might be inferred under cross-examination. A recent example of a key witness exercising this right to silence was at the inquest into the sinking of the *Marchioness* on the River Thames (*Independent* 8 April 1995).

Having introduced INQUEST and sketched in some of the difficulties that it confronts when advising families and friends, it is worth mentioning that mounting any sensible critique of coroners or inquest procedures would have been difficult a few years ago. There was, it is true, the authoritative Broderick Report (1971), but that had well and truly gathered dust by the early 1980s. With some early help from the prisoners' union, Preservation of the Rights of Prisoners (PROP) and Radical Alternatives to Prison (RAP), INQUEST claims to have transformed and politicized this debate, making very public what were hitherto mainly private concerns.

In this process, however, it has earned very few accolades from those whose behaviour it most seeks to influence and change, namely coroners. Indeed, one coroner has described INQUEST's former Parliamentary convener as being "anti-police", "anti-prison" and "anti-establishment", sentiments that have been echoed by Home Office civil servants and Conservative politicians.[9] How did this radical image come about? Indeed, why did INQUEST come about when it did? Must we accept the perplexed opinion of the organization JUSTICE, that while there have been changes in the coroners' system in recent years, "there is no obvious reason why they should have been such as to spark controversy"?[10] It is to these critical questions we first turn.

Chapter 2

Origins

Context and background

Perhaps the most important point to make about INQUEST is that it came into being when the long post-war consensus in British politics had well and truly come to an end. The Keynesian revolution that had created full employment, relatively high wages and modest but sustained economic growth since 1945 was already faltering by the late 1960s. The following decade, ushered in by the election of an avowedly right-of-centre Conservative government in 1970, saw a series of industrial and social conflicts that threatened to destabilize what looked like an increasingly fragile political order reeling under the impact of a quadrupling of oil prices and resurgent nationalism in Ireland and Scotland. The struggle to secure this order took various forms. The so-called Social Contract under the Labour Government of 1974–9 to buy industrial peace and secure wage restraint; draconian legislation to combat both internal and external terrorism; the tightening of immigration controls and the revamping of the race relations industry in an attempt to combat racism and the newly emerging National Front.

One of the indelible features of this period was the growing distrust of police by large sections of the public, particularly in large metropolitan areas. The sources of this distrust were many. The Metropolitan Police, for example, was seriously damaged by allegations of widespread financial corruption and the planting of evidence on innocent suspects, while in Liverpool the heavy-handed policing by some divisions led to serious concern.[1] Allegations of racism, especially around the operation of the "sus" laws, turned black youth in particular against police. This led to the mobilization of black communities around individual cases and their participation in the monitoring of local police practice and in the wider, national campaign to secure greater police accountability.

As important as all these concerns were, it is arguable that it was the general direction of public-order policing, and in particular the role of special patrol groups (SPGs) that caused most concern, particularly to organizations like the National Council for Civil Liberties (NCCL). SPGs were first introduced into London in 1965 and their original purpose was to combat crime. One hundred officers, answering to headquarters through their own command structure, were distributed around the capital as mobile units to respond to defined high crime areas and to provide, if required, saturation policing. This function was adjusted in 1974 by the then Metropolitan Commissioner Sir Robert Mark to emphasize instead public-order situations and combating terrorism – guarding embassies, for example.[2]

The violent potential of this policy was soon realized in Red Lion Square. This was the scene of an anti-fascist demonstration in opposition to the National Front, which had secured permission to hold a meeting in Conway Hall on the north side of the square. After some demonstrators broke through a cordon designed to isolate the hall a decision was made to clear the square using two SPG units and mounted police. In the course of this operation – in which one SPG officer boasted that his unit went through the demonstration like a knife going through butter – a young student, Kevin Gately, was killed.[3] This fatality, and the role of the SPG, caused public alarm and a full public inquiry was ordered by the then Labour Home Secretary Merlyn Rees and carried out by Lord Scarman. A similar fatality, which was to be significant for the origins of INQUEST, occurred in Southall in 1979.

During the General Election campaign of that year the National Front organized an election rally at Southall town hall. The location was deliberately chosen to be provocative. Southall has a large, well established immigrant community, mostly Asian although with a modest number of Afro-Caribbeans. Fearing unrest the police cordoned off the town hall across from the Broadway. Two rival demonstrations were permitted, a sit-down demonstration outside the town hall and a picket on the pavement opposite. Violence flared up between the police and the public and in the confusion that followed, one of the demonstrators, Blair Peach, was killed.

The immediate circumstances surrounding his death were contested. However, it was agreed that Blair Peach was leaving the Broadway and making his way from the main site of the demonstration along Beechcroft Avenue, which became the scene of an SPG charge. Caught up in the charge, Blair Peach received a fatal blow to his head as a result of a skirmish at the junction between Beechcroft and Northcote Avenues.[4] No-one now seriously doubts that a member of the SPG killed Blair Peach. As the Metropolitan Commissioner at the time was to put it a few years later:

> when all the evidence was assembled it showed that Blair Peach had died from a blow to his skull. The evidence pointed to the fact that the blow had been struck by a police officer. It is unlikely, however, that a police truncheon would have been heavy enough to inflict the injury. It is more probable that some other implement was used.[5]

A search in the lockers of those SPG officers on duty on that fateful day in Southall revealed a frightening array of illegal weapons from a sledgehammer to a crowbar, although it was thought unlikely that any of these weapons had been the one that had killed Blair Peach, who had an unusually thin skull. This was the original opinion of the second pathologist; the family and friends of Blair Peach having exercised their right to a second postmortem.[6]

The (by then) Conservative Home Secretary William Whitelaw decided against holding a public inquiry into the disturbances at Southall. He felt that such an inquiry would only rake over the embers of the affair and inflame passions still further and, arguably more disingenuously, that finding senior judges willing to take on such inquiries was becoming increasingly difficult. He also expressed the opinion that he thought it unlikely that any such inquiry would find out who had delivered the blow that killed Blair Peach. This refusal meant that the family and friends of Blair Peach – the Friends of Blair Peach as they later came to be known – could only rely on the findings of an unofficial committee of inquiry set up by the National Council for Civil Liberties, to which the police refused to give evidence, and on the subsequent inquest to discuss exactly what had happened at the junction between Beechcroft and Northcote Avenues. It was the conduct of this inquest that rekindled public interest in the powers of coroners and inquest procedures.

The start of the inquest was delayed by several factors, one of which was a legal wrangle over the refusal of the coroner to summon a jury. On this controversial question the coroner was on slightly firmer ground than he would be today, because the requirement for a jury in cases where the reported death resulted in "an injury inflicted by a police officer in the purported execution of his duty", a possibility never seriously ruled out even by the police, was not yet law. The coroner's decision was thus at first upheld by the Divisional Court, and only eventually overturned by the Court of Appeal.[7] But the Friends of Blair Peach – and indeed, other parties involved in the inquiry – soon found even greater obstacles placed in their way when it came to getting access to important documents.

I explained in Chapter 1 that when a sudden or controversial death takes place the police as well as the coroner's officers will make preliminary inquiries, and that this evidence is subsequently given to the coroner. This duly happened after Blair Peach was killed. Given the public concern surrounding the case, Commander Cass undertook a lengthy inquiry that entailed interviewing many witnesses and suspects. His 3,000 word report was given to the coroner and was also made available to the lawyers representing the Metropolitan Police, but expressly denied to those representing the Friends of Blair Peach and the Anti-Nazi League that had helped to organize the demonstration.

This decision was challenged in the higher courts, but the coroner's ruling was upheld.[8] What this meant, self-evidently, was that only the coroner and the counsel for the Metropolitan Police had full sight of all the available evidence and could, for example, match what witnesses said in court under cross-examination with their earlier statements, statements that would clearly have influenced the coroner. Yet, it has to be remembered that even if the Cass report had been made available to all the interested parties there is no guarantee that any of the witnesses favoured by the Friends of Blair Peach or the Anti-Nazi League would have been called. The decision to call witnesses rests entirely with the coroner. The dangers in this were not lost on the unofficial committee of inquiry, which observed:

> One of the most important elements is the coroner's discretion in the selection of witnesses. Dr Burton informed the inquest that he had drawn up a list of witnesses, based on his study of Commander Cass's report, which would include in particular,

everyone who claimed to be an eyewitness and all police officers present in Beechcroft Avenue at the relevant time. It was impossible, however, for the family or the ANL to judge whether the coroner's selection of witnesses was appropriate or to decide whether other witnesses – senior police officers for instance, not actually in Beechcroft Avenue, but in command on that day – should also be called. In our view it was quite wrong not to call the most senior SPG officer present . . . Despite arguments from counsel, Commander Cass was not called as a witness, nor was Commander David Helm the most senior officer with responsibility for police operation. Their absence, and the impossibility of determining whether relevant witnesses were not called, further damaged the credibility of the inquest.[9]

In the view of the unofficial committee these procedural faults were compounded by the coroner's lack of legal expertise. It acknowledged that Dr Burton had *acquired* legal qualifications, but that like so many other coroners coming from a medical background he had little experience in the *practice* of the law. This led him sometimes to make comments that no judge would dream of making; at times it was even alleged that he gave misleading information to the jury. For example, during the inquest – although thankfully not during his summing-up – he suggested that there were two extreme theories about Blair Peach's death. The first that the Anti-Nazi League needed a martyr and had killed him. The second was that Blair Peach had been murdered by a police officer using an unauthorized weapon. To bracket together these theories as "extreme" – not least because the second had previously been considered a serious possibility by Lord Justice Bridge in his decision to order a jury – was surely to suggest more to the jury than was proper.[10] The Friends of Blair Peach took strong exception to this particular intervention.[11] Finally, on the question of using "unreasonable force" in the execution of an arrest, the coroner suggested that there was ambiguity about whether or not recent legislation had changed the law; the unofficial committee could find no ambiguity and rebutted the coroner's muddled summing-up.[12]

After a case that attracted so much media attention – much of it hostile to Blair Peach and the demonstrators – the jury returned a verdict of death by misadventure, but added significant riders to their verdict. One of these was that frontline SPG officers should be more firmly controlled by their superiors and that there should be better liaison between the ordinary police and the SPG. Another was that there should be regular inspections of police lockers to prevent the build-up of illegal weapons or implements.

Although bitterly disappointed by the verdict, the Friends of Blair Peach did not give up. Financed largely from personal donations, although with some local trade union support, its campaign continued. Eventually it succeeded in gaining access to the Cass report and after a protracted rearguard action the Metropolitan Police eventually agreed to pay compensation to the family. It also began a campaign for reforms to the inquest procedure, some of which had been sketched out by the unofficial committee of inquiry towards the end of its work.

At about the same time, and in another metropolitan area characterized by deteriorating community–police relationships, the police were also under pressure at an inquest. This involved the death of Jimmy Kelly, who died on Merseyside just two months after Blair Peach. A 53-year-old unemployed working-class man, Mr Kelly had been out drinking with his brother who was visiting from Australia. He refused a lift home at the end of the evening, preferring instead to walk home. According to witnesses he was in a voluble mood and singing at the top of his voice when a police car mounted the pavement and drove after him across a piece of wasteland. A struggle followed in which it is alleged that Jimmy Kelly was beaten by police officers, bundled into the back of a police van and taken to Huyton police station where he died shortly afterwards.[13] The police later admitted that there had been a struggle, but claimed that only reasonable force had been used.

When the inquest first convened, the family were unhappy with the medical evidence, or to be more precise, about the answer they received about bruising and the possibility of internal injuries.[14] The family therefore raised the money for a second pathologist's report which concluded that:

It is evident that Kelly died with acute heart failure, due primarily to severe heart disease, brought about by a hardening of the arteries, and of high blood pressure. Although Mr Kelly may have died suddenly at any time, he was more likely to have died during a period of severe emotional strain, or exertion, or both. Immediately prior to his death Mr Kelly had sustained numerous injuries, the majority of them minor, the most serious being the fracture of the lower jaw. In view of the evidence submitted

14

to me, in the form of statements, I find Mr Kelly's injuries consistent with a severe beating. The only evidence of self-defence
or assault I have found were bruises on two of Mr Kelly's knuck-
les. It is my opinion that Mr Kelly was unlikely to have died
in that short period of time, despite his heart disease and his
high alcohol content, had the incident prior to his death not
occurred.[15]

The pathologist went on to criticize the police for failing to render
the most "elementary first aid" to the deceased and to suggest that the
family had every right to be concerned about the manner of his death.
This pathologist's report, a marked contrast with the first one ordered
by the coroner that appeared to have failed, among other omissions, to
have spotted the fractured jawbone, made the ongoing independent
police inquiry into the death of Jimmy Kelly even more important.
This inquiry – they are usually conducted by a senior member of
another force in such controversial cases – had been forced on the
Merseyside police because the family had lodged an official complaint. The inquiry was undertaken by the Assistant Chief Constable
of the West Midlands Police Force, David Gerty.

The family were later to question the thoroughness of this inquiry
when they learnt that in some instances Gerty had simply accepted as
given eyewitness statements already taken by Merseyside police
without bothering to contact the witnesses himself to verify their testi-
monies. Notwithstanding such faults, the Gerty report was naturally
seen as an important piece of evidence and the family were quite
taken aback when they heard that access to it would be denied to their
counsel at the inquest. Referring to the ruling that had suppressed the
Cass report into Blair Peach's death the coroner declared:

The judgement of the Lord Chief Justice fortifies the opinion
that I have already expressed in this case, namely, that so far
as any documents are concerned they are, in fact, the property of
the police and they are not in my disposition as such. What the
Chief Constable makes of these documents, they are at his disposal, they are not in my disposal, and they are still under his
jurisdiction.[16]

Similar reasoning was used to prevent the full disclosure of a third
postmortem that had been ordered by the Merseyside Chief Constable,

Kenneth Oxford. Other procedures also disadvantaged the family. For example, while coroners' courts are indeed inquisitorial and not adversarial, the order of cross-examination in contested cases remains of some significance, and in this instance the counsel for the Kelly family was consistently ordered to run first, allowing the Chief Constable's counsel the advantage of cross-examining last. The coroner refused to change this order.[17] The treatment of civilian witnesses also upset the family; it was felt that they were bullied and subjected to unsubstantiated allegations in order to damage the credibility of their evidence.[18]

After a long and acrimonious inquest in a heavily guarded courtroom, policed by members of K Division whose officers had arrested Mr Kelly, a unanimous verdict of death by misadventure was recorded. No further inquiry, official or otherwise, was held into this death. The Home Secretary was satisfied, having withstood earlier Parliamentary pressure for a public inquiry while he waited for the outcome of the Gerty inquiry and then the inquest. Nor did any prosecutions follow, although the Gerty report like the Cass report, was forwarded to the Director of Public Prosecutions (DPP). Given that the DPP is unwilling to proceed unless there is more than an even chance of success, and believing that it is extremely difficult to get convictions against serving police officers, even where inquest verdicts have manifestly gone against them, a prosecution in this case was always unlikely.

Beginnings

The inquest into the death of Jimmy Kelly attracted an avalanche of media attention and reinforced the interest that had been stimulated by the Blair Peach case into the role of coroners and their stewardship. During a period of political and social unrest when the activities of the police were being seriously scrutinized, and the issue of police accountability was moving up the political agenda, the suspicion that serious allegations of misconduct against the police were not being dealt with even-handedly in coroners' courts caused dismay. But the truth of the matter is that in the early 1980s few lay critics had any detailed, critical knowledge of inquests or their procedures, a point that the Merseyside academic Phil Scraton – he had been approached by the Kelly family for advice when he was living in Liverpool – is keen to stress.[19]

It was partly as a consequence of this ignorance that in 1980 Scraton applied to the Open University's Social Science Research Fund to finance a research assistant to look into the history and role of coroners. By then Scraton had taken up a short-term contract at Milton Keynes to work with Professor Stuart Hall who had served as a member of the unofficial NCCL inquiry into the policing of Southall and the death of Blair Peach. (Scraton appointed Melissa Bean who was then working part-time at NCCL to this post.[20])

This academic contact between the two groups was reinforced when the mainstay of the Jimmy Kelly Campaign, Tommy Banks, met Celia Stubbs at an NUS (National Union of Students) conference at Blackpool soon after the Merseyside inquest had ended.[21] As Blair Peach's partner, Celia Stubbs was active in the Friends of Blair Peach Campaign from the very beginning. This network was quickly extended to include the Liddle Towers' Campaign. Mrs Towers had written to Mrs Kelly urging her to "Shout loudly about your son's death. Never let it rest."[22]

Liddle Towers had been arrested at a nightclub in Gateshead. A number of witnesses claim he was badly beaten by eight arresting officers. He was released from police custody the following morning so badly injured that he could hardly walk. Three weeks later he died. In spite of a formal complaint from his family no prosecution ever followed, even although the first inquest into his death returned a verdict of "justifiable homicide". This was clearly an embarrassment to the police, and the Attorney-General successfully applied to have the verdict quashed as being inconsistent with the evidence. At the second inquest, and following a fairly explicit direction from the coroner, the jury returned a verdict of death by "misadventure".[23]

This case is significant for a number of reasons, but not least because it was brought to the attention of Michael Meacher MP who with his Labour colleague Stan Newens began to raise in Parliament the issue of deaths in police custody, trying to ascertain just how many deaths there had been in recent years.[24] This information was not readily available for the very simple reason that no central record of deaths in police custody had ever been kept. It had never been thought of as a problem. However, when the figures were eventually produced by the Home Office they were, *prima facie*, very disturbing, numbering 274 in all between 1970 and 1979.

There were several critical responses to these figures. These included one from Michael Meacher who tried – unconvincingly some later argued – to correlate these deaths with the number of complaints against the police alleging assault in certain, key metropolitan areas. The upshot of this and other pressures – the debate figured in *The Times* – was a Parliamentary inquiry into deaths in police custody undertaken by the Home Affairs Select Committee which began hearing evidence early in 1980. During this inquiry the cases of both Blair Peach and Jimmy Kelly figured prominently, although the families were not invited to give evidence. The role of coroners and inquests was examined and recommendations made.[25] What had previously appeared to be an arcane interest was by now almost front page news.

It was against this background of public concern and media interest, and building on networks already established, that a series of meetings was called of cases around deaths in custody to share experiences. These took place in the summer of 1980 and in February 1981. At one of the meetings attended by Michael Meacher, the participating campaigns were asked to consider forming themselves into a national organization and to consider what demands it might make. At a subsequent meeting in April 1981 the decision was taken to form INQUEST, United Campaigns for Justice.

According to Tommy Banks's account this series of meetings threw up a whole number of demands: an alternative to coroners' inquests to investigate deaths in custody; the right of families to have access to information and reports into deaths in custody; a more effective procedure for complaints against police; the abolition of SPGs; the right of political parties and trade unionists to demonstrate without harassment; and tougher controls on prescribed drugs in prison and restrictions on the use of solitary confinement.[26] Minutes from the Friends of Blair Peach prior to the April meeting confirm that this was roughly the shopping list.[27] With its interest in mental health the Matthew O'Hara Committee (see below) emphasized safeguards for the mentally ill and those in secure hospitals like Broadmoor. It also took to the April meeting some ideas about how the new national group might be organized and even suggested a name, the Campaign Against State Brutality. While we know that this name was not chosen, it has to be said that it reflected a good deal of the rhetoric at the time. There was much talk about state "repression" and being "against the state".

The presence of the Matthew O'Hara and Richard Campbell campaigns – Richard was a young black Rastafarian who died in Ashford remand prison – is important because they were concerned with deaths in or around *prison* custody and not *police* custody. In other words, while the final thrust to establish INQUEST came from those involved in police custody deaths, its focus on the site of inquests attracted others. This should come as no real surprise because while campaigns around deaths in prison custody had not concerned themselves centrally with inquest procedures *per se*, they too had been frustrated by coroners and had faced Home Office obfuscation.[28] Networking and sharing these frustrations was already a fact of life.

This sharing process is well illustrated by looking at the Matthew O'Hara Campaign. Mr O'Hara was involved in mental health projects in Hackney when in March 1980 he was committed to Pentonville prison for refusing to pay a fine. Shortly after his release he was found dead in his flat.[29] The Matthew O'Hara Committee was formed to find out whether his treatment in prison, or lack of it, had caused his sudden death. He told friends that he had been punched in the stomach by a prison officer and was refused treatment for diabetes, which eventually led to his emergency transfer to a local hospital. A press statement about a meeting sponsored by the Matthew O'Hara Committee in Hackney and introduced by an active member of the Blair Peach Campaign, Ken Worpole, reported that:

> Two members of the Hackney Workers' Educational Association (WEA) had recently died in disturbing circumstances. Blair Peach on an Anti-Nazi demonstration in April 1979 caused heated controversy about the conduct of police whilst the death of Matthew O'Hara earlier this year raised equally controversial questions about the medical treatment of prisoners.[30]

Introducing this meeting, which focused on the Prison Medical Service and Home Office secrecy, Ken Worpole spoke about how distressing it was that Hackney had lost "two singular and outstanding personalities". He had come to know them both through the WEA and he recalled the irony that his last conversation "with Matthew had been a discussion of the Blair Peach inquest" (press release November 1990).[31]

This closeness, based on the community centre known as Centreprise, and underpinned by active trade unionists working through the local WEA, helped to bond the London campaign together, particularly in the early days, giving it a strong community presence. There were also other advantages. MIND's legal advisor, Ed Fitzgerald, served on the Matthew O'Hara Committee as did two young barristers, Tony

Ward and Tim Owen, who were later to play a key role in INQUEST's future.

INQUEST's broadening remit was later confirmed by its 1982 constitution or charter of organization that defined it as being concerned with

(a) deaths in, resulting from, or connected with custody, police operations and related forms of state activity, and

(b) deaths, howsoever caused, which are subject to deception or concealment on the part of the state or of public officials or in which investigation and prosecution are deficient.

The purpose of INQUEST was to secure justice in these cases, to support the individual families in their struggle to discover the truth and to obtain where possible changes in the law (or procedures) to prevent such deaths in the future. A federal structure was adopted. The idea was that INQUEST should be driven by, and united through, its various campaigns, all of which were entitled to be affiliated and represented on its governing body or Executive Committee.

But this is to anticipate. What held INQUEST together for the best part of a year was not a formal constitution or charter, but the phenomenal energy of a group of loosely organized individuals campaigning around a specific set of demands. The fledgling organization was formally launched at a press conference in June 1981. The interest was substantial, and there was a trickle of support from local trade union branches, but INQUEST soon found that servicing it was difficult without full-time staff, without turning itself into a more formal organization. This particular and pressing difficulty was resolved by the Greater London Council (GLC).

Enter the GLC

The political changes at the GLC during this period were extremely important to INQUEST. When Labour regained control of the council in 1991, Ken Livingstone took over the leadership of the Labour group in a carefully planned coup promising a range of radical initiatives. One of these was the promise to establish a Police Committee for London which, alone among local authorities in England and Wales, was without one. Policing in the capital was the direct responsibility of the Home Secretary. This meant that although the people of London had to help finance the Metropolitan Police Force neither the GLC nor any of the individual London boroughs had any direct control over it; they could not, for example, call it to account over its policing of the demonstration in Southall in 1979, or question it about the use of "saturation policing" which arguably led to the Brixton uprisings early in 1981. It was against this background, the issue of police accountability, coupled with the growth of paramilitary policing and growing loss of confidence in the Met by Londoners in general, and by ethnic minorities in particular, that the Police Committee was introduced to deal with "Matters relating to the policing of Greater London law enforcement and public order therein, including links with other groups".[32]

This innovation was bitterly contested by the Conservatives on the council, whose leader argued that:

> The facts are that the Council has no powers of law enforcement in criminal matters, and very few powers in civil matters. In terms of public order our powers under the 1936 Public Order Act, again, are virtually non-existent, and as far as our links with other bodies, I presume [it is] to be linked with the National Council for Civil Liberties and other bodies of that ilk.[33]

He then went on to attack the Labour majority for its arrogance in assuming powers that Parliament had not given it and finished with a strong attack on the chair designate of the new proposed committee, the black barrister Paul Boateng, and his close colleagues:

> I see in Mr Boateng and Mr Livingstone and their colleagues a mirror image of Mr Knight of Lambeth who would even have us believe that he would like to have an amnesty for racist thugs in Brixton. So what we are seeing is not a willingness on the part of the Council to set up a proper Police Committee in the accepted sense . . . No, what we are seeing is a determination to have a political focus on the Police for attacks on their independence, for attacks upon the work they have to do, whether it be in Southall, in Brixton, or anywhere that is sensitive in the society in which we live.[34]

This perception of the GLC's Police Committee was to cause INQUEST some difficulties as we shall see. In the meantime, suffice to say that the Committee was established and it quickly set up what was called

21

the Police Committee Support Unit which was left, albeit within well defined guidelines, to oversee the allocation of grants totalling £400,000 that had been set aside for projects relating to its work.[35] It was to this source of funding that INQUEST turned in order to support its London activities. The first approach was an informal one. Phil Scraton, who was still very active in the group, but finding it difficult to fit in its activities around his work at the Open University, was particularly keen to appoint a full-time worker. He therefore approached Tony Bunyan, who had been appointed as deputy head of the Police Committee Support Unit, to see if INQUEST's activities would fit with the published guidelines. He was told that this was likely[36] and early in 1982 INQUEST applied for just under £13,000 for its first year. Ken Worpole, who lived and worked in London, successfully steered the application through a meeting with GLC officials. The officials reported back to the Police Committee that:

> Deaths in police custody in the Greater London area are a source of increasing concern and must be an area of special interest . . . Some deaths have given rise to questions about the use of custody in the case of drunks and mentally ill people; other cases have been the focus of campaigns alleging maltreatment or neglect. But even in relation to deaths where there are no disquieting circumstances . . . there remains the issue of the procedure in coroners' courts and the way they operate could be improved. After the Deptford fire in 1981 many people criticized what were alleged to be defects in inquest procedure; these include the lack of any adversarial system or legal aid, the extensive limits on representation rights of the deceased's relatives or friends . . . the process of selection of jury members.[37]

INQUEST was never entirely secure about this source of funding because of the political storm around the Police Committee. However, the Conservatives were arguably far less hostile to INQUEST than they were to the more mainstream police-monitoring groups that were operating, thanks to the Police Committee's financial support, in many London boroughs during this period and that quickly became a feature of the capital's increasingly radical landscape.

Summary

The fact that INQUEST managed to escape the full wrath of the Con-servatives on the Police Committee was partly explained by the simple truth that giving advice to distressed relatives or friends of the dead – often routine advice in non-controversial cases – is hardly an activity that can be complained about. However, this should not obscure another simple truth, namely, that INQUEST was the product of a par-ticular radical moment. It was born out of the struggle between police and certain communities that were in some senses very ordinary. The context was successive governments mobilizing the formal agencies of social control to counter what was perceived to be "the enemy within" in an attempt to reinforce social discipline in the wake of a series of political, social and economic shocks that threatened to destabilize the political order. In a phrase, INQUEST was the product of policing the crisis and its politics were correspondingly radical.

Chapter 3

Campaigns

Writing about the campaign around the death of Richard Campbell – its supporters were the founder members of INQUEST as we have already seen – Coggan & Walker have stressed the importance of families and local communities in the struggle to secure justice, arguing that all else – Parliamentary pressure, legal challenges, media coverage – is "peripheral and secondary".[1] While INQUEST's strategy was always more complex than this simple prescription suggests, its emphasis would have been widely endorsed by most INQUEST members, especially in the early days. The organization was to be driven from below with families and friends from widely different backgrounds coming together to exchange both material information and emotional support. Representatives drawn from these families and friends were to have a formal place on INQUEST's national Executive Committee, reinforcing its determination and authority. What people had learnt from their own campaigns would sustain and drive the national organization, energizing its commitment.

Given how important these constituent campaigns were to INQUEST in shaping its tactics we need to know something about how they worked. For example, how were they mobilized, financed and structured? And what was their actual relationship with INQUEST? There are no simple answers to any of these questions. Local campaigns feeding into a loose federal structure are likely, almost by definition, to be highly individual in their nature. It is possible, however, to get a flavour of how they operated if we look at some of the early campaigns that were particularly influential in defining INQUEST's ethos.

CAMPAIGNS

Lobbying from below

The first campaign I consider revolved around the death of James Davey in March 1983. Mr Davey was arrested on suspicion of murder and taken to Coventry's central police station. A squad of detectives from the Metropolitan Police Force arrived to take him to London for further questioning. He refused to go voluntarily and, following a visit from his solicitor, the police decided to lure him out of his cell and take him by force. In the process, which involved at least 12 police officers and the use of a headlock, Mr Davey was trussed up in handcuffs, ropes and a belt (*Sunday Times* 13 August 1983). Almost immediately one of the police officers noticed that Mr Davey was in serious physical distress, but by then it was already too late. By the time an ambulance was called and reached the nearest hospital he had suffered brain death from which he never recovered.

The manner of Mr Davey's death caused considerable public concern. The independent report of the Chief Constable of Manchester which concluded that no police officers were at fault did little to placate local opinion and 70 leading West Midlands figures, including at least one local Member of Parliament, demanded an immediate public inquiry. This was reinforced when the Director of Public Prosecutions considered the report and decided to take no further action (*Birmingham Post* 3 October 1983). Even more concern was generated by the coroner's failure to preserve the body in deep-freeze conditions. Surely this should have been done until the independent inquiry had been undertaken and the date of the inquest set? The family had exercised its right to a second, independent postmortem, but were anxious for a third opinion.[2] The inquest did not finally take place until March 1984 by which time the body had seriously decayed.

While the family was greatly upset by the delay in holding the inquest, the space it provided did at least allow it to mobilize an effective campaign that was to continue well beyond the inquest itself. Made up of close family members – they played leading roles throughout – friends and sympathizers mounted an informed, broadly based campaign. It was supported by several interested groups, including the Coventry branch of the National Council for Civil Liberties, students and staff from the nearby University of Warwick and, of course, INQUEST. Together these groups mobilized public meetings, issued press statements, and wrote letters to both the Home Secretary and the Prime Minister. The local Police Committee was also lobbied, as

26

were local trade union branches, councillors and leading churchmen. By the time a petition signed by 5,000 people (mostly local) demanding a full public inquiry was handed in to Downing Street early in 1985, few people in the West Midlands (and beyond) had not heard of the case.

Mobilizing very local support around the inquest had been the campaign's first priority. However, it slowly broadened its horizons. For example, it pointed out that the West Midlands Police Force had been the subject of a series of allegations in 1983. A woman peace campaigner who had written to a local newspaper was visited under a false pretext and questioned by the West Midlands CID, three pensioners were mistakenly held at gunpoint in a bungled drugs raid and three police officers were convicted of illegally assaulting a British Leyland worker.[3] Cases like these led the campaign to find out more about opposition to the Police Bill that was going through Parliament and to write to INQUEST asking for the addresses of other campaigns, in particular those around the Jimmy Kelly, Liddle Towers and Colin Roach cases that had also involved allegations of police mistreatment.[4]

By this time the James Davey Campaign was formally affiliated to INQUEST. One of INQUEST's two paid workers, Dave Leadbetter, had been very active in the campaign and had attended James Davey's funeral. It was largely through this contact that the campaign secured the services of the London solicitor Gareth Peirce – she had worked on many previous cases with INQUEST – and the high-profile barrister Michael Mansfield. (Kathryn Chadwick was also involved. She had taken over from Melissa Bean on the research project into coroners, which Phil Scraton had by then transferred from the Open University to Edge Hill College, Liverpool.)

This relationship, however, was far from being a one-way affair. In the process of the inquest, evidence was to emerge that reinforced INQUEST's case for reform. For example, Michael Mansfield was only allowed restricted access to police statements, the full text of which was only available to those barristers representing the police. The family felt particularly aggrieved about having to pay legal costs. The Metropolitan Police, the West Midlands Police Authority and the West Midlands Health Authority all had their costs paid from public funds; the Davey family on the other hand had to meet fees that were anticipated to be in the region of £8,000.[5] Finally on the learning curve, the overbearing power of the coroner was again well illustrated when coroner Kenderine refused to accept the jury's first verdict which accepted that the death was accidental but occasioned by unreasonable force. Kenderdine ruled that this was a contradiction in terms and the jury eventually felt obliged to return a verdict of accidental death with no qualifications. (The family were later given leave to have this direction judicially reviewed.)

All these – and other – unsatisfactory aspects of the Davey inquest were grist to INQUEST's mill and were repeatedly used to illustrate its case for reform. INQUEST reported to its wider membership that it had felt "privileged" to have worked with this "outstanding campaign".[6]

The fact that "outsiders" played a part in this campaign, or that national political figures like Tony Benn signed its petitions, cannot obscure the fact that it was largely driven by family, close friends and relatives drawing on a cross section of very local groups and interests. As a campaign document put it in the run-up to the inquest:

> The base amongst the community is essential to all this. But alone it cannot sustain the campaign. But the campaign must never become a rump controlled by a few political activists. Control must always rest with the family and friends.[7]

While there were tensions, it was also a campaign that united people and gave them strength. In the words of INQUEST's other paid worker, Tony Ward, "good came out of it", in spite of the tragedy that had inspired its being.[8]

A similar style and power can be found in the Jimmy Kelly Campaign. Tommy Banks, a former shop steward, gives the flavour of its essentially local, sometimes spontaneous activity:

> Two days after Jimmy Kelly was buried, a mass meeting was called outside the "Eagle and Child" pub in Huyton on a Sunday morning . . . I was elected chairman of the Jimmy Kelly Committee.
>
> When we first started off, James Jardine chairman of the Police Federation called us "ragbags". We were called left wingers, communists, criminal elements . . . police bashers – you name it, we were called it. But we ignored all that and just went our own steady way having marches and protests about the case.
>
> At one of our public meetings we had a representative who had come to tell us about a young lad who had been beaten up in Kirby – we were later to learn that his name was Michael

Cavanagh, who had lost his spleen and one kidney after being allegedly kicked by a policeman. We went to Kirby and helped the committee fighting the Cavanagh case to organize themselves. We went to their marches, they would come down to ours.

We had the support of the Liverpool Trades Council, the Sefton Trades Council. These bodies set up their own trade union inquiry into the question of police violence and then a conference was called at which we discussed how to take the campaign forward.

During the course of the campaign myself and Peter Cunningham, the secretary of the Action Committee went all over the country speaking . . . and raising funds. When we first formed the Jimmy Kelly Action Committee . . . we split into two sections, the Action Committee itself and a fund raising committee . . . because . . . when it came to the inquest there was no legal aid . . .

The Kelly family, like most Merseyside people live marginally above subsistence level and there was no way they could meet the considerable costs involved in the inquest . . . . At the time of writing, we have still not raised the £14,000 which we need. But we have most of it . . .

People were going each night from pub to pub, club to club, organizing dances, discos, fancy dress competitions – you name it, we did it. One night we raised a very large sum by holding a very successful cabaret evening; another time we had a river boat trip on the Mersey.

The Liverpool dockers gave us substantial financial support and so did members of the National Union of Seamen, which Kelly used to belong to. Even workers on one of the government's twelve month STEP (Special Temporary Employment Programmes) schemes donated money to our campaign.[9]

It is difficult to ignore the sense of pride in this passage. It is written as a tribute to the energy and spirit of ordinary working-class families and friends who have mobilized against what they see as an injustice. True, there is evidence of local, mainstream political and trade union support, but how could it be otherwise in such local communities where such activities are woven into the fabric of daily life? Likewise there is evidence, if you look hard enough, that fringe political parties were also involved, the WRP in particular played a useful part in publicizing Mr Kelly's death. But the energy behind the campaign, as with the Davey campaign, came from a small group of family, friends and sympathizers. It was this patterning, this largely non-sectarian practice, even where it existed among more articulate middle-class campaigners like those who mobilized around the death of Blair Peach, that was to inform INQUEST and that it sought to channel through its national federal structure.

Another campaign that was driven from below and to which INQUEST made some contribution was around the death of Colin Roach in Hackney in January 1983. Relations between the public and police had been poor in Hackney over a number of years and the local council had refused to set up a consultative police committee along the lines suggested by the Home Secretary following the Scarman report into the disturbances in Brixton.[10] The local black community felt particularly aggrieved, with Stoke Newington police station as the focus of its complaints, and it was here that Colin Roach died from shotgun wounds. The jury later decided by a majority verdict that he had taken his own life with a shotgun.

Given where the death had taken place, that the circumstances surrounding it were disturbing, and that Colin Roach's parents were insensitively treated by the police (something that was later singled out by the inquest jury), a campaign soon got under way following a spontaneous demonstration by black and white youths outside Stoke Newington police station. At this and subsequent demonstrations called by the Roach Family Support Group it is alleged that the police acted provocatively and both Gareth Peirce and the chair of the GLC's Police Committee, Paul Boateng, were called upon to intervene.[11] Public meetings were then arranged with the support of the Hackney Black People's Association which only a few months earlier had called for a more general public inquiry into policing in Hackney.

The first demand of the Roach Family Support Committee was to secure just such an inquiry into Colin Roach's death. Once this was refused – the Home Secretary quite wrongly informed the family that an inquest was a public inquiry – the family sought to have the inquest transferred from the small coroner's court at St Pancras to a larger venue. The coroner originally refused this request, and although his legal right to do this was subsequently upheld, he accepted the High Court's recommendation that he find a larger venue. The delayed inquest was finally opened at the Clerkenwell County Court in June 1983.[12]

As policing in Hackney already had such a high profile, and given the support offered to the family and friends of Colin Roach by the Hackney Black People's Association and police-monitoring groups like the Community Alliance for Police Accountability, INQUEST's involvement was modest. The campaign self-ignited, drawing in a number of other more overtly political groups and prominent local figures, including local MP Ernie Roberts who tabled a House of Common's Early Day Motion calling yet again for a full public inquiry.

Where INQUEST did play a role, however, was in the work of the independent committee of inquiry that came about after the inquest. This was an initiative proposed by the Roach Family Support Group. It wanted to see Colin Roach's death contextualized in a wider and more detailed study of police–black relations in Hackney. For this purpose it put forward a research project to the GLC's Police Committee that was eventually accepted. The report was formally published several years later with an introduction by Professor Stuart Hall who had been involved with the independent inquiry into the death of Blair Peach (see Ch. 2).

INQUEST was asked to nominate a member to sit on the Colin Roach inquiry in March 1984.[13] It was eventually decided that Melissa Benn should serve. By this time she was an active, voluntary member of INQUEST's Executive Committee and her presence on the inquiry enabled INQUEST's paid workers to give evidence without there being an obvious conflict of interest. As well as giving evidence to the inquiry on the conduct of the inquest, INQUEST also made available to the inquiry its own very detailed notes on the proceedings.[14]

INQUEST's public comments on this inquest, as well as its written submission to the inquiry, again reveal how valuable evidence for its reform agenda was being collected through its involvement with local campaigns. For example, INQUEST was again able to point out that the barrister representing the Roach family had only been given very limited access to the police report into the events surrounding their son's death, and that even this modest concession was entirely dependent on the goodwill of the barrister – paid out of the public purse – representing the police. But perhaps more telling was its critique of the coroner's direction of the jury as to its verdict.

In its evidence to the inquiry INQUEST reminded the committee that the coroner's summing-up is particularly important as effectively it is the only interpretation of the overall evidence that is put to the jury. Unlike in other courts, there are no closing speeches in which barristers pull the facts of the case together; this remains the prerogative of the coroner. In the Colin Roach case, argued INQUEST, this direction had been wrongly used to point the jury towards suicide. Quoting chapter and verse, its submission argued that suicide cannot be inferred or sur- mised, but can only be retained as a verdict when all other possibilities have been ruled out. If other possibilities cannot be ruled out then an open verdict is more appropriate. INQUEST's view was that in the Roach case an open verdict would have been more appropriate, and that the coroner was quite incorrect to have suggested that it would be "wrong" to return an open verdict after "the amount of work" that had been done.

This suggested to the jury that there was something wrong or unsat- isfactory with such a verdict, a suggestion directly at odds with the recent views of the Lord Chief Justice who, when quashing a suicide verdict on the Italian banker Roberto Calvi, had reminded coroners that to return an open verdict does not mean that they are "not doing their job properly or are insufficiently perceptive". He further directed them to bear in mind that, "There are many, many cases where there is real doubt as to the causes of death . . . and where anything else would be unjust to the family of the deceased."[15]

This criticism was all the more telling because INQUEST suggested that otherwise the coroner had handled a difficult and tense inquest very even-handedly. It was simply that he had misdirected the jury as to the law, a not uncommon occurrence.

Another death that caused strong feeling in the local black commu- nity was that of Richard Campbell. It was driven by his mother, Jean Campbell, and led to another, although less high profile, independent inquiry sponsored by the Battersea and Wandsworth Trades Council. A number of prominent figures gave evidence, including Alf Dubbs MP and Richard Geary, who had been researching and publishing on deaths in custody for the National Council for Civil Liberties.[16] MIND also attended, as did the national prisoners' movement (PROP) and Radical Alternatives to Prison (RAP).[17] (Active in RAP at this time was Tony Ward who was later to be appointed with Dave Leadbetter as one of INQUEST's two paid workers. It was Ward who had drafted INQUEST's skilful submission to the Colin Roach inquiry.)

All this evidence suggests, and there were several more local cam- paigns that made contact with INQUEST in the first few years of its existence, that the group was functioning very much as its founders had intended. Its organizing Executive Committee, composed mainly of volunteers drawn from its various constituent campaigns, appears to have been situated at the hub of a wider, national network of active campaigns, offering advice and support and collecting in return more evidence to support its case for reforming coroners' courts and inquest procedures.

The strategy of turning individual cases into broader campaigning issues was warmly endorsed by the director of the Institute of Race Relations and co-editor of *Race and Class*, A. Sivanandan, in 1983 when he addressed a GLC ethnic-monitoring committee. He said:

> cases are one off, local, disconnected; issues are national and anti-state. The trial of the Bradford 12, for instance, brought to national prominence the issues of self-defence and conspiracy law; the murder of Blair Peach brought into question the role of the Special Control Group and the validity of internal police investigations; the New Cross [fire] massacre and the Colin Roach case showed, among other things, the bias and inadequacies of the coroner's court.[18]

While this is not an entirely fanciful picture of INQUEST up to the mid-1980s, it could be argued that it was not as effective as it might have been, and in particular, that it was struggling to maintain a national presence. The source of this particular difficulty can be traced back to its funding.

The metropolitan bias

The GLC's Police Committee distributed grants through its support unit for activities to do with policing London; those were its formal terms of reference. True, the Police Committee Support Unit never pressed INQUEST on this issue by closely scrutinizing its books, and cases outside London could be taken on and justified by finding some London connection – for example, the presence of several Metropolitan Police officers in the James Davey case – but it soon became clear to the organizing committee that the bulk of INQUEST's work had to involve London cases. Certainly it could not ignore London cases for other cases in the regions, however important they might be.

In order to overcome what was very real restraint, an application for £13,000 to fund a northern worker to be based on Merseyside was submitted to several trusts in 1984. Among other things the worker was expected to work:

in conjunction with the London workers to establish an advisory panel of lawyers and provide informal support to campaigns and . . . in general to develop the identity and presence of INQUEST in the northern region in line with the policies of the Campaign.[19]

The choice of Merseyside is easy to explain. One of the unsuccessful candidates for the position as one of INQUEST's first paid workers was Mark Urbanowicz who had been active on Merseyside in the Jimmy Kelly Campaign. He had served on its committee and had first attended meetings at INQUEST in London with Tommy Banks and Peter Cunningham in that capacity. It was therefore logical to think of Merseyside as the northern base and of Mark Urbanowicz as the worker. This presumption was strongly reinforced by the simple fact that he was already working as INQUEST's unpaid northern worker and had submitted a formal report for 1982–3 to the organizing committee in London. A total of 31 northern cases had been monitored during 1982–3, seven inquests attended and legal representation obtained through INQUEST for two families. On one of these, involving Douglas Coverdale, Mark Urbanowicz had worked closely with INQUEST's London workers because although the Coverdale family lived in Manchester the suicide had taken place in a police cell in Hammersmith. The report also carried the announcement that the inaugural meeting of INQUEST North West was to take place at Edge Hill University College in September 1983 (where Phil Scraton had recently returned to teach).

Unfortunately none of INQUEST's trust applications were successful and, after struggling on with modest financial support from London, Mark Urbanowicz formally resigned late in 1984. In his letter of resignation he expressed concern that INQUEST was becoming "totally London centred" and added somewhat fatalistically, that perhaps this was "inevitable".[20] This concern about INQUEST's London bias has been elaborated on elsewhere by Phil Scraton who recalls that there was:

Terrible, constant awareness that officially INQUEST could not be seen to be involved with cases out of London . . . I never really believed that should happen, that there were ways around that . . . So I felt we could put more effort into the north, but INQUEST became very much based in London. I know Mark felt that he could or should have had more support . . . I also felt what was happening in London was very much a London struggle . . . To a lot of people [who get] involved in London politics

34

you go to national group meetings and maybe eighty per cent of the meeting is actually London based politics. To put it into its context there was a sort of GLC myopia that everything stopped at the boundaries of the GLC because this was the New Republic . . . something entirely different. You would go to meetings and there would be discussions about which councillor was doing what. We were out of it.[21]

This layers the critique. The implicit suggestion here is that it was a metropolitan bias that limited INQUEST's activities outside of London rather than any official restrictions on where its money could properly be spent. The evidence suggests that there is some truth in the charge of metropolitan bias.

There is no doubt that the GLC under Ken Livingstone saw itself in the vanguard of radical politics. What had been sleepy local government was turning itself into the local state, usurping central government powers according to the Conservatives on the GLC. But what was at issue here was not just the transformation and democratization of the institutions of local government, but rather an attempt to effect a broader cultural transformation for which the GLC engaged and funded a long list of groups organizing around a wide range of issues, although most notably around race and gender. INQUEST was very much a part of this dynamic, metropolitan process and its engagement with essentially local, London politics made those who were detached from this site – even very sympathetic supporters like Phil Scraton – feel like outsiders.

However, to accept that there was a metropolitan bias should not be taken to mean that this led to a conscious prejudice against financing activity outside London. Arguably more important than any notional prejudice of this kind was simply the time and energy that INQUEST had to put into responding to the various London police-monitoring groups, the constituent London boroughs and reporting formally to the Police Committee on its activities in and around the London courts.

In May 1983, for example, it was expected to participate in a large public meeting called by the Southwark Police Monitoring Project. This was about the conduct of inquests into several controversial cases, most notably the New Cross fire, in which 16 black youths died, and the death of Nicholas Ofusu. INQUEST had observed that in the former case the Southwark coroner had refused to take notes and "appeared to be totally out of his depth" while his conduct of the latter case showed a definite bias in favour of the police.[22] (Errol Reid, who was a member of the Southwark project, became an active member of INQUEST.) Also in 1983, Camden Council called on INQUEST's expertise to investigate into the death of an Irish labourer who had been arrested by the SPG. The inquest had several disturbing features, not least being the coroner's failure to call a key witness. As a result of INQUEST's involvement, a council sub-committee endorsed a list of reforms and agreed to give more attention to the issue of deaths in police custody.[23]

Servicing the constituent London boroughs in this way and then enlisting their support was to continue as a useful tactic. Perhaps the model here was INQUEST's report to Hammersmith Council's community and police committee. This began with a general discussion about the role of coroners and inquest procedures, but quickly moved to statistical analysis of deaths in the Western Coroners District and then went on to discuss the qualities of the existing coroner and his handling of two controversial deaths, those of Blair Peach and John Mikkelson, a black Hell's Angel who had died after a fight with police officers in Hounslow. These cases were sufficient to tease out most – if not all – of the defects in inquest procedures and the submission ended with a series of recommendations, one of which was that the council should lend its support as Hackney and Camden had done to a whole series of reforms that INQUEST (and other groups) had proposed.[24]

This London activity, sometimes it was frenetic, kept INQUEST not only busy, but busy in London. It was also expensive. As we shall see later, INQUEST was inadequately funded from the very beginning and money remained tight throughout the 1980s. This meant that even if it could find the time and was willing to step outside of London, the money to support such activity was either simply not available, or at best, strictly limited. The strong injunction that rounded off a financial report in late 1983 was to be repeated time and time again:

To repeat the obvious; there is absolutely no money for activities outside London (except the Davey case which involves the Metropolitan Police). If members, including the workers, are willing to spend their own money in this way, that is another matter.[25]

This is mainly why INQUEST fell well short of establishing itself as an effective national organization. There are satellite groups calling themselves variously, INQUEST North West, Canterbury INQUEST, but they were either very short lived or largely notional. The base remained stolidly London, and individual campaigns outside of the capital could not always be guaranteed much more help than legal advice over the telephone. INQUEST's sub-committee to link with and facilitate new campaigns, such as the one surrounding a series of deaths at Canterbury prison, and link them to the centre, was short lived.

But does this not suggest that INQUEST had become – shall we say by the mid-1980s – little more than a conventional, if specialized, legal advice centre staffed by two paid workers remote from its campaigning roots? While some were clearly worried by this potential – Ken Worpole mentioned this as early as 1983 and in 1985 there were renewed complaints that campaigns were out of touch – the evidence suggests something that is both more positive and more complex.[26]

To begin with, it is true that the appointment of paid workers in 1982 meant that those members active in the various campaigns were less and less required to keep the central organization going, to infuse it with their energy on a day-to-day basis. But the Executive Committee continued to attract new members like Shelia Heather-Hayes with campaign experience even when founding members like Ken Worpole and David Ransom from the Friends of Blair Peach Campaign had long since moved on.[27] Furthermore, when resources did permit, the networking of campaigns across the country continued to be vigorously pursued, especially by Dave Leadbetter who arguably neglected his routine administrative duties as a result. Finally, and this is an important point, the idea of INQUEST as a federation of active campaigning groups should not mask the fact that right from the very beginning it never succeeded – nor ever wanted to succeed – in turning every case into a campaign. Where families felt unable to cope with a public presence, or fell out among themselves under the stress as they sometimes did, INQUEST's role was simply to offer families and friends legal advice and emotional support; quiet, behind-the-scenes work that took up a lot of time, including the time of volunteers.

In short, INQUEST has never been just a campaigning organization, even although it was from the campaigns that it drew its energy, its expertise. Of course, the balance between INQUEST's various activities was (and is) subject to change and having sought to defend it against the simple charge that it had ossified into a wholly London-based legal advice centre, I admit that there is some evidence that its campaign activities languished in the second half of the 1980s. However, this was not in our view because of any conscious change in strategy or new constraints, financial or legal, but due to external factors. That is to say, INQUEST's early campaigns were a reflection of – and buoyed up by – the rapidly deteriorating relationships between police and local communities in several key urban areas. Once this tension was defused – contained or marginalized might be better terms – the broader community politics that had given a sense of urgency – centrality even – to INQUEST's early campaigns around policing diminished.

We will return to this wider context below. But again, it needs to be stressed that while vibrant, high profile campaigns gave INQUEST its original and defining characteristics, such activity never constituted all of its work, nor did it entirely disappear.

The Parliamentary road

If local campaigns did come first, INQUEST was always prepared to consider Parliamentary action in order to remedy the injustices these campaigns sought to make public. Indeed, it is fair to say that INQUEST tried to fuse both styles of campaigning right from the start. This initially took the form of setting up a group of MPs who were willing to sponsor its aims. A draft letter to likely MPs was considered in April 1981.[28] At this stage INQUEST goals were broadly defined in order to attract as many sponsors as possible. In the event, its letter attracted over 20 Parliamentary sponsors, mostly, although not exclusively, London MPs, plus a number of well known national figures on Labour's Left, including Neil Kinnock.

INQUEST sought to build on this support by holding a series of Parliamentary meetings scheduled to begin in late 1981. Two detailed briefing papers were prepared and circulated beforehand. The MP most involved at this stage – he booked the rooms and attended to other arrangements – was Michael Meacher. His interest was widely welcomed. This was not just because of his already well publicized interest in death in police custody, but also because he had drifted away from his Fabian background and was firmly associated with the radical wing of the Parliamentary Labour Party which was at that time in the ascendency under the leadership of Michael Foot. To put the same thing another way, INQUEST had secured the services of a powerful ally who within two years was tipped to become Labour's deputy leader (*Sunday Times* 14 August 1983).

The briefing papers were very different in style and content. The first claimed to be a background paper, the second a position paper. Separating out matters in this way may have seemed logical, but the background paper, while informative about some of the early cases I have discussed, was arguably far too long for the attention span of most MPs.[29] Also, while legitimately focusing on wider issues like police accountability, it contained the suggestion for an alternative to inquests that the position paper did not. Indeed, the position paper was reformist in tone and concentrated more narrowly on the question of improving existing inquest procedures.[30]

This confusion reflects the fact that INQUEST was still working out its detailed shopping list throughout 1981–2 in its legal sub-committee. In other words, it went to Parliament without a fully formed agenda on coroners and inquests. However, our concern with this narrower agenda here should not obscure the fact that the wider issues surrounding police accountability, police complaints procedures and so forth, were (and remain) fairly central to INQUEST's concerns. It regards campaigning on such issues as part of its *raison d'être*.

Apart from being succinct, the position paper had the advantage of focusing on a document that most of the interested MPs would have already seen, namely, the Home Affairs Select Committee on Deaths in Police Custody. This paper listed the recommendations of the committee that were consistent with the Broderick report (1971) and some of the committee's additional recommendations, including the need to disclose the content of police investigations. It then prioritized, arguing that:

> Without legal aid "interested parties" are not in a position to be represented at inquests, even where the police and other official bodies have such representation. Without access to investigators such representation is, in any event, of little value. Both illustrate the present unbalanced nature of inquest procedures, heavily favouring official bodies that may have been at fault.[31]

The paper argued that these two issues – plus some other minor issues on which some movement had been promised – should be taken up with the Home Secretary. It concluded by acknowledging that even the implementation of all the Select Committee's recommendations would still leave wider issues – those raised in INQUEST's background paper – unanswered.

Issues raised in both briefing papers were discussed by INQUEST's Parliamentary Group at various meetings throughout 1982. Interestingly, however, they featured only very briefly at the very first Parliamentary meeting organized by INQUEST because most of the time was given over to the families and friends representing its constituent campaigns. They had been invited to speak about their experiences and to report on the progress of their struggles. This took up so much of the time that there was little chance to discuss Parliamentary strategies. However, it did at least bring the families together and link the local and Parliamentary campaigns and, arguably more important, it conveyed to Members of Parliament through personal testimony the strength and raw power that was spiralling up to support them from the communities that these families represented. Celia Stubbs remembers this as being a particularly vibrant meeting.[32] The tactic of involving the families in this way was used on several occasions and was strongly endorsed by Ken Worpole in a note to INQUEST's paid workers in November 1982.

Throughout 1982 the Home Secretary was faced with a number of awkward questions about deaths in custody by INQUEST's Parliamentary Group and some gains were secured. For example, in previous chapters I have referred to cases where coroners have refused to hold inquests with a jury in controversial cases involving deaths in police custody. The change to make a jury mandatory in such cases was secured in an amendment to the Administration of Justice Bill.[33] This was tabled by the London MP Chris Price, a member of INQUEST's Parliamentary Group who had become involved with INQUEST following the death of three of his black constituents in the New Cross fire in 1981.

The amendment was drafted by Tony Ward who had just taken up his appointment with INQUEST at this time, and Terry Munyard, a barrister who had previously been involved in several cases involving controversial deaths in custody. Unfortunately, the amendment had to be hastily drafted over the telephone and while it does now mean that when a coroner decides to hold an inquest into a death in police custody he must summon a jury, the coroner is still under no statutory obligation to hold an inquest into such deaths. This is unlike the law governing deaths in prison, which requires (a) that an inquest must be held, and (b) that it is held with a jury. A chance to put inquest procedures into death in police custody on a par with deaths in prison

custody – which was one of the demands in the Parliamentary position paper – had thus been lost, a failing that INQUEST has acknowledged.[34]

Progress was also made – a little later it is true – in April 1983 on the
way in which juries were selected for inquests. Previously this process
had been open to abuse, and there were stories of coroners simply
sending someone out into the streets to collect the first available volunteers or leaving it to their officer, often an ex-policeman to contact
his friends and/or acquaintances. This potential for serious abuse was
put right in the Coroners' Juries Bill which put inquest jury selection
on the same random footing as the selection of other juries.[35] While
this was formally Chris Price's Bill it had full government support and
had, in effect, been drafted by the government, although not without a
series of delays which had so frustrated the government that it invited
INQUEST to draw up its own Bill in order to speed up Parliamentary
counsel, a tactic that seemed to work.[36]

In the context of what was a purely technical question Chris Price
managed to widen the debate on the Bill to cover a number of issues
and cases and, *en passant*, praising INQUEST for its role in getting the
Bill before Parliament. His mention of the Select Committee report on
deaths in police custody earned him further cross-bench support and
he drew from the minister an assurance that "within the Home Office
there is a willingness to embark upon a dialogue with all those concerned about the future of the coroners' jurisdiction".[37] In fact, this
dialogue was already under way. A few weeks before, Chris Price had
led a delegation to the Home Secretary who was flanked by four senior civil servants. Apart from Price, the delegation included lawyers
Gareth Peirce and Terry Munyard, INQUEST's paid workers and representatives from two campaigns, Jean Campbell and Celia Stubbs.

The discussion was structured around a list of demands submitted
by INQUEST, in effect an amalgam of its by now refined briefing papers.
It was wide ranging, covering inquest procedures, police accountability, including complaints procedures, and even touching on the Prison
Medical Service. Apart from encouragement to bring forward its proposal to reform jury selection (see above), just about all that INQUEST
got out of this dialogue was an explanation of how the Home Office
had come up with its figure of £3 million as the estimated annual cost
of extending legal aid to inquests. This was based on the unlikely
assumption that out of the 23,000 inquests each year some 15,000
would qualify for legal aid and that the average cost of each case

would be in the region of £200. INQUEST disputed these figures, but even its arguments for a limited extension of legal aid to cover inquests involving deaths in prison or police custody, inquests into tragedies like the New Cross fire, were turned down. The Home Secretary argued that:

> The particularly sensitive character of such inquests is recognized but the Lord Chancellor is of the opinion that this is not sufficient to justify distinguishing these from other inquests for the purposes of legal aid . . . When further resources become available to permit some extension of legal aid, the claims of coroners' inquests will certainly be considered, although it is not possible to say what weight would be given to them.[38]

The Home Secretary then went on to reject the disclosure of police reports, arguing that they might reveal information about an individual's previous connections and "much other information which would be prejudicial".[39] The suggestion that counsel should have the right to address the jury at the end of an inquest was also rejected, as was the suggestion that they might have more control over which witnesses might be called. The re-introduction of riders – they had been abolished following the Blair Peach inquest – in which juries had been able to make recommendations was also turned down. Where comment was required along these lines the Home Secretary thought it should be left to the coroner. As for other, wider issues, the independence of the police complaints procedure, the local accountability of police, the operation of the revamped SPG, the efficiency of the Prison Medical Service, all these were said to be giving no cause for concern or were being improved.

In his reply to the Home Secretary Christopher Price could not conceal his disappointment. On the other hand, a reply in detail to such an obvious rebuff was fairly pointless and he confined himself to chiding Whitelaw not so much for failing to hold a public inquiry into the death of Colin Roach, but rather for his failure to distinguish in that case between an inquest and a public inquiry.[40]

While INQUEST and its Parliamentary Group continued to push the Home Office on many of these matters over the ensuing months, the rest of 1983 was dominated by the passage of the Police Bill, or to be more precise, the two Police Bills, as the first was to fall as the result of the General Election in July. INQUEST had its own agenda here, although it was partly driven by its links with the GLC's Police Committee.

The GLC strongly opposed both Bills and the Police Committee set aside funds to campaign against them. The Police Committee Support Unit and INQUEST thus became not only involved, with organizations like the Campaign for the Right of Assembly and Dissent (CROWD), but also in drafting new clauses, and amendments to existing clauses, as the legislation passed through Parliament. Louise Christian, an energetic young lawyer who was the support unit's link worker with INQUEST, was actively involved in networking with groups like the NCCL and INQUEST over clauses relating to the "reasonable use of force". Obviously this was of crucial interest to INQUEST. The unreasonable use of force, or at least the suspicion of it, had been an issue in many of INQUEST's cases. The difficulty, however, is to determine what constitutes "reasonable force". Clearly, what might be regarded as reasonable force in arresting an armed assailant would not be regarded as reasonable when arresting an unarmed burglar. But translating such common sense notions into law is far from easy, and there was an anxiety that in being too specific the government's Police Bill would lead the law in this area to be interpreted less strictly than it had been.[41]

The technicalities, however, need not detain us. All we need to register is that when Alf Dubbs – one of INQUEST's sponsors – introduced amendments to those clauses dealing with the "reasonable use of force", the briefing paper from which he spoke, or at least where it dealt with individual cases, had been provided by INQUEST. This had quite an impact on the debate in committee. Another of INQUEST's sponsors, Robert Kilroy-Silk, observed:

> I am sure that every member of the committee has been provided with a copy of an amazing briefing paper from INQUEST . . . I remembered every case . . . but had forgotten the number of occasions where our police officers, in the last decade or so, have been involved in shootings and killings in public places . . . When they are herded together they add up to a formidable and surprising list . . . We know of the substantial concerns expressed by friends and relations of individuals such as Liddle Towers and Jimmy Kelly. Then there was the James Davey case that occurred recently in Coventry. Perhaps police officers acted over zealously in the use of force on these occasions. There is a whole catalogue of evidence that a small minority, but never-

theless a significant minority, of police officers in the Metropolitan Force use excessive force in imposing their authority.[42]

Kilroy-Silk also spoke of his own involvement in the Jimmy Kelly case. (He had been interested in this by Phil Scraton.)

While this was all good publicity for INQUEST, the amendments in question were easily defeated. Furthermore, INQUEST's activities were implicitly challenged during the passage of the Bills by Eldon Griffith who, representing the Police Federation, claimed that:

> During the past two or three years many police officers and I have been deeply disturbed by the near vendetta that has been waged in the press and on television over deaths in custody. It is true that many people ... die in police custody ... But the implication is that they have all been brutally beaten up by the police ... The scar of that vendetta, which was waged irresponsibly, remains in the service.[43]

Griffith went on to single out – again by implication – Michael Meacher for criticism when the debate moved on to the question of intimate body searches, which the GLC and INQUEST had also opposed.[44]

The first onslaught from Eldon Griffith, ironically, came when the debate had moved on to a clause about deaths in police custody that had nothing to do with police beatings, but that resulted from faulty police procedures, or when the police fail to follow their own procedures when looking after people in their care, say a drunk or someone who is under the influence of drugs. The use of force is not the issue here. In such cases the code of practice required that police custody officers should make a judgement about whether or not medical treatment was required. INQUEST strongly opposed this, arguing in its brief that the Association of Police Surgeons of Great Britain had pointed out that police officers "cannot and should not" be expected to assume the responsibility of "knowing the presence or absence of injury" for a number of reasons, not least because many infirmities are "known to mimic alcohol and/or drug addiction". It was therefore quite inappropriate that the draft code of practice attached to the Police Bill should contain a paragraph which recommended that "incoherent or somnolent" prisoners should be the subject of a medical check only if "the custody officer is in any doubt as to the circumstances of his condition". This was simply not a judgement that custody officers were qualified to make. Prisoners in this condition should be auto-matically examined by a doctor. INQUEST also felt that the failure of a custody officer to order such an examination should be a disciplinary offence.[45]

This was an impressive, many-layered briefing that drew directly on INQUEST's detailed casework and sought to expose the shoddy, dangerous and uneven procedures followed in many police stations, not only in London, but also in areas like Kent. Kilroy-Silk's praise notwithstanding, this briefing was INQUEST's main contribution to the debate on the Police Bills. In other areas it was mostly in support of the GLC and NCCL. At one point during the complicated passage of these Bills it looked as if INQUEST's arguments about the treatment of incoherent and somnolent prisoners had been accepted and a more acceptable code of practice was drafted. This was the work of the Metropolitan Police. However, a third and final draft from inside the Home Office itself turned out to be almost as objectionable to INQUEST as the first.[46]

On a rather different issue, although in some senses uncomfortably close to home, INQUEST was asked by the Police Committee to brief it on the position of coroners as set out in the Local Government Bill (1984–5) that provided for the abolition of the metropolitan counties, including the GLC. The situation was fairly straightforward. As things then stood coroners were appointed, funded and supported by the GLC. After abolition of the council it was proposed that where the coro-ners' jurisdiction spread across more than one borough, a lead bor-ough – designated by central government – would be responsible for the appointment of the coroner in consultation with the boroughs who would jointly share in the cost of running and administering the service.

These practical arrangements were reasonably sensible and INQUEST (in my view) strained hard to find serious fault with them. However, it took strong and arguably justifiable exception to a new power, namely that in future the appointment of coroners was to be subject to the approval of the Home Secretary. It was argued that this centralizing tendency not only compromised the position of coroners as independ-ent judicial officers – if anyone in central government should interfere with their appointment then it should be the Lord Chancellor – it also compromised their impartiality when investigating deaths in prisons and in police stations, or as a result of police action. Such deaths were especially sensitive, that is why they require inquests with juries.

That in future such inquests would be conducted by officials whose appointment had been vetted by the government minister responsible for prisons and police was seen as unacceptable.[47] The fact that this change was being proposed at this particular time was not lost on the Opposition spokesman – he had been sent INQUEST's brief – who during the passage of the Bill argued that:

> One of the most important points . . . is that concern has been expressed in the press and the population about deaths in custody – that is, in prisons and police cells . . . the last government department that should be put in charge of reorganizing the coroners' courts when such anxiety exists is the Home Office, because that department has responsibility for the prisons and the police. It is a bad policy . . . whether in constitutional theory or in practical politics . . . [to] alter the arrangements for coroners' courts.[48]

This criticism was endorsed by the Liberal spokesman Simon Hughes – he singled out INQUEST for special mention[49] – but the government easily forced its proposals through.

If INQUEST's Parliamentary successes were modest, they were not entirely without significance, and its efforts on the Police Bill especially had at least helped to sustain its Parliamentary profile. But after this its Parliamentary Group declined. Attempts to revive it were called for early in 1984 and again in 1987,[50] but these came to nothing and during the second half of the 1980s the Parliamentary Group was effectively moribund. The viability of the group had been undermined when Christopher Price lost his seat in the 1983 General Election and when Michael Meacher was promoted to the frontbenches with a different portfolio in 1984.

The demise of the Parliamentary Group did not mean INQUEST then absented itself from Parliament entirely. Far from it. New initiatives were sponsored through Opposition spokesmen, first Clive Soley, and then towards the end of the 1980s, Barry Sheerman. Interested backbenchers, in association with other lobby groups, were also mobilized. This was to bear fruit with the introduction into Parliament of a Ten Minute Rule Bill to incorporate the Prison Medical Service into the NHS. INQUEST jointly sponsored this with the National Association of Probation Officers. The Association did most of the detailed work on the preparation of the Bill and INQUEST provided some of the case histories that accompanied the briefing.[51] Both groups were involved in extensive Parliamentary lobbying. The need for incorporation had been one of the issues INQUEST had raised with the Home Office at its meeting with the Home Secretary some years earlier. Having been firmly rebuffed then, and by now a little more attuned to the limits of Parliamentary action, INQUEST was not surprised by the government's unhelpful response. But the Bill did receive a good deal of publicity at a time when prison suicides were increasing; it also reinforced the group's presence in the penal lobby.

All in all, INQUEST did not secure many Parliamentary victories during its first ten years, even although it managed to sustain a presence among a sympathetic group of radical MPs. Several explanations for this failure can be canvassed. It could be argued, for example, that the best opportunities came early on when it presented unfinished, even contradictory, policies that failed to convince. There is some truth in this. Not only was a chance to secure mandatory inquests into all deaths in police custody lost, but the original Bill drafted for Christopher Price to pressure Parliamentary counsel had to be sharply amended because it contained some clauses that were either thought to be unnecessary or were at odds with INQUEST's stated policy. One such clause provided for High Court judges to conduct controversial inquests which was certainly not what INQUEST wanted.

But even if such confusions were damaging, it is difficult to see how it could have been otherwise in a fledgling, federal organization which was itself on a steep learning (and sharing) curve. And on the other side of any such equation, it cannot be denied that the "unfinished" organization brought the raw energy of its campaigns right into the heart of Parliament itself and gave the issues that concerned it a passionate resonance.

But were the issues it sought to campaign on far too diverse, dissipating its focus? Again, this is not an entirely implausible line of argument. The shopping list it eventually presented to the Home Secretary as we have seen covered everything from police accountability, inquest procedures to prison medicine. There appears to have been little attempt to prioritize between these broad areas, which arguably at least gave Whitelaw ample scope for an unusually bland response. But defining priorities is easier said than done, not least in a federal organization that emphasized the centrality of its constituent campaigns that often came from very different directions. What was a priority in terms of reform for one campaign was not for others.

But what of the criticism that INQUEST was far too partisan from the start? This charge has been laid in a public, although unattributed attack on Michael Meacher which claimed that in order to advance his own political career Michael Meacher had taken up a whole sheaf of radical causes – including deaths in custody – but had proved "ineffective" in securing reform even in those areas where normally backbenchers, even Opposition backbench MPs, can make progress. The reason given for this failure was that "Meacher never seemed to want to master the consensus" (*Observer Profile* September 1983).

Prima facie there is some evidence to support this view. For example, Meacher found nothing to disagree with in this letter from INQUEST's David Ransom about the involvement of Conservative MPs in its Parliamentary Group:

> I raised some points about the "courtesies" between MPs and had to explain why the group is constituted as it is. Would it be possible to invite the MPs with cases in their own constituencies (Prosser's is a Conservative) to attend specific meetings if they wished without degenerating into an "all party" group of the kind we have already decided we do not want? Where local MPs are involved, we shall of course advise people to tell their MPs that they want to be involved with INQUEST. The really crucial thing is, of course, to establish as far as possible a group of Labour MPs for whom INQUEST is a priority – I'm sure you will understand that this is a cause of some anxiety for us![52]

This shows a degree of naïvety about Parliamentary arithmetic and procedures that is probably more excusable in INQUEST's case than Michael Meacher's. On the other hand, it is highly unlikely that INQUEST's limited Parliamentary success was due to this partisan approach. The simple truth is that it was difficult to master a Parliamentary consensus on issues when the basis on which it might be built was rapidly falling away, which was the position in the first part of the 1980s. In reality, the Home Affairs Select Committee report on deaths in police custody was the high-water mark of any consensus. During Mrs Thatcher's first and second administrations the Conservatives dug in under the banner of law and order, supported unabashed paramilitary policing and tougher prison regimes and were only willing to make concessions on these fronts when they had to. In a word, they were far more inclined to listen to the Police Federation and the Coroners' Society than they were to INQUEST.

Recent and detailed studies by political scientists and policy analysts into the effectiveness of liberal pressure groups generally during the Thatcher years lend support to this interpretation.[53] Their argument is that in spite of New Right rhetoric about pressure groups being a danger to democracy, inhibiting government from taking bold and decisive action in the public interest, and that too close a relationship between groups and government departments undermines governmental authority and constrains innovation, Thatcher governments were more than willing to listen closely to pressure groups, but only to those whose groups that shared their ideological predispositions.

It was this more than any tactical or organizational failures – although there were plenty of these – which explains why INQUEST had so few Parliamentary successes, and why its Parliamentary activities significantly declined, although without disappearing altogether, as the 1980s progressed. The same pessimism about what might be achieved by campaigning from below around individual cases also helped to reduce INQUEST's activities on this front too, something we touched on earlier. It is just as difficult to mobilize on the streets as it is in Parliament when it is manifestly clear that nobody is listening. While it is true that the hegemony of law and order was never as complete as some radical critics would like us to believe, it did strengthen its grip throughout the 1980s and plenty of civil liberties groups, the NCCL to give one obvious example, suffered a loss of momentum. INQUEST was not alone.

Summary

Should this sound too pessimistic, it is important to keep in mind that by the second half of the 1980s INQUEST's reform agenda had won the support of other, potentially important allies. For example, its proposals on coroners' procedures and inquests were taken up by JUSTICE, the all-party association of jurists. It is true that the JUSTICE report in 1986 was not entirely all square with INQUEST's position. It was against the re-introduction of riders and suggested that controversial inquests should be undertaken by a senior coroner assisted by a lawyer appointed by the Treasury Solicitor. On the other hand, it agreed with INQUEST on the central issues that: legal aid should be available for inquests; families or friends or their lawyers should be free to call whatever witnesses they chose and be permitted to see any reports submitted to the coroner before the inquest and be entitled to address the jury.[54] Furthermore, the fact that JUSTICE was discussing the issue at all was largely due to the activities of INQUEST, something that seemed to have eluded JUSTICE which struggled to understand why coroners' procedures had suddenly appeared on the political agenda.[55] Leaving this aside, INQUEST's written evidence, and its informal contacts with JUSTICE members over the issue of legal aid, helped to secure a favourable result. This support, combined with that of the NCCL and the Liberals had started to broaden INQUEST's appeal and, by the end of the 1980s, move its once arcane agenda more centre stage, a very real achievement.[56]

Finally, and arguably more important, we support those theorists who suggest that the state is composed of many different agencies operating on a variety of sites and at a variety of levels. The fact that evidence so far suggests that INQUEST did not win many battles with the DPP, persuade ministers, their senior civil servants or Parliament, does not mean that its influence was negligible. To believe otherwise would be to give in to one of the prejudices of political science and policy analysis, namely, their overconcern with the central apparatus of state which is their narrow vision of where power lies.

Chapter 4

Defining issues

I pointed out in Chapter 1 that INQUEST operates across a number of lobbies. In any given week it might be working with groups in the penal lobby on youth deaths in custody, investigating with MIND an alleged suicide in a psychiatric hospital, while at the same time helping rank and file trade unionists over what they believe to have been an avoidable death at work. This suggests that there are no boundaries to its concerns, to the sites on which it operates. To some extent this is true. The fact that it was originally established to deal with deaths in state custody has not prevented it, for example, from extending its brief to include deaths at work and/or the investigation of transport disasters such as the sinking of the *Marchioness* pleasure boat in the Thames in 1987.

Nonetheless, a bulk of its work has kept faith with its original, defining brief, and it is to a more detailed study of its involvement with deaths involving the state, its institutions and its personnel, that we now turn in order to assess its contribution to understanding these issues and securing change. As this chapter progresses we will be looking less at inquest procedures *per se*, or for that matter the dynamics of individual campaigns, and more at the issues that are raised during inquests about the treatment of people in a range of state institutions and how those charged with their care are held accountable.

Deaths in police care, custody and during arrest

I have already dealt with deaths in police care, custody and during arrest in some detail as they were so important in defining INQUEST's

51

early identity, but these regrettably continued to be a cause for concern in the second half of the 1980s and beyond. Such deaths happened in a number of very different circumstances, some were drink related and occurred in police cells, some were recorded at inquests as suicides. Others involved those who died during the course of violent arrest or questioning, while still others involved police shootings.

Drink-related deaths

INQUEST's involvement in these cases has already been touched upon. The John Mikkelson inquest, for example, had revolved around the treatment of a suspect who was allegedly drunk when arrested (Ch. 2). More generally INQUEST had done its best to change the police code of practice for dealing with incoherent or somnolent detainees during the committee stage of the Police and Criminal Evidence Bill (Ch. 3).

The John Mikkelson case continued to run. At the original inquest a verdict of unlawful killing had been returned and as a consequence seven officers, including a Chief Inspector, were immediately suspended.[1] This verdict was judicially reviewed in the Divisional Court and a new inquest ordered. This time, a year later in 1986, the jury returned a verdict of death by misadventure. This was not entirely unexpected given the Divisional Court's ruling on what the standard of proof needs to be in such cases, and the disappearance of one of the key witnesses and the refusal of another one to testify.[2] However, what mostly interests us here is that the case caught the attention of the Labour dominated Association of London Authorities (ALA).

The ALA had been set up to carry on – as best it could – some of the strategic thinking of the GLC that had been abolished in 1985, and it was the ALA's police committee that approached INQUEST for two reports. One specifically on the John Mikkelson case, another on preventing deaths in police custody more generally where suspects are not fully conscious, through the effects of either alcohol or injury.[3]

It is true that neither the ALA nor INQUEST got little change out of the Met on the John Mikkelson case, but their collective pressure to provide alternative treatment facilities for drunken offenders was echoed in the Chief Commissioner's next annual report which noted with some concern that of the 15 deaths recorded in London during 1985, ten involved suspects who had been arrested for drunkenness. The report then went on to highlight the need for "approved centres" for this "category of prisoner". INQUEST continued to press the point with the Met by pointing out that whereas 42 per cent of all deaths in police custody since 1982 had been of alleged drunken offenders, the figure for the Met was 65 per cent.[4]

The suspension of senior police officers and the ensuing legal struggle made the John Mikkelson case a very high-profile affair, but it was the death of Wilma Lucas at about much the same time that brought home to INQUEST the full scale of the neglect it had unearthed. Mrs Lucas was a 40-year-old alcoholic. She was on probation having committed minor offences associated with attempts to obtain alcohol. She was arrested early one morning for breaking the conditions of her probation order. Remanded to Holloway prison by Chertsey magistrates later in the same day, she was returned to police cells when the duty officer found that she could not be admitted to prison until the following morning. In the early evening she was certified by her local GP as being "fit to be detained", in spite of the fact that after 12 hours in police custody her speech was still slurred and she was incontinent.[5] In the early hours of the following morning when she was unable to stand, this diagnosis was effectively overruled by a police surgeon who recommended that she be transferred to Holloway's prison hospital.

After some delay this transfer took place, but it was hardly a comfortable one. Mrs Lucas was unceremoniously bundled onto the floor of a police transit van and handcuffed. At the prison she was carried in face downwards and Holloway staff noticed severe bruising on her hands and face. One prison officer said, "Her face was dark black . . . I have never seen anything like it before." In the absence of a medical report – one had not been provided by the police as it should have been – the prison authorities decided to move her to a local hospital. There she was examined by a newly qualified doctor who, finding no fractures, judged her fit enough to return to Holloway. A few hours later she fell into a coma and was admitted to the Royal Free Hospital for an emergency operation from which she unfortunately failed to survive.[6] One newspaper commented about her treatment:

Few of those responsible for her emerge with any credit. People involved in caring for the adult flotsam and jetsam of society say the case epitomizes how alcoholics are dealt with; if she had been a child who had died while social workers dithered there would have been a public outcry. Seen as unhygienic and the worse for drink, Wilma was treated more like a body than a person. (*Sunday Times* 17 June 1984)

This appalling neglect raised a number of detailed questions about Lucas's treatment in both police and prison custody, and these were later taken up by Women in Prison (WIP).[7] INQUEST, on the other hand, used the jury's open verdict and its recommendations that local authorities should provide alternative care for the treatment of alcoholics, to further its ongoing campaign in this area which it had begun with its lobby of the Police and Criminal Evidence Bill. Thus, its public statements on the Wilma Lucas case drew attention to the new draft code of practice accompanying the Bill that, had it been in operation, might have prevented her death. However, it sounded a note of caution.

First, it pointed out that the police had failed to obey even their own existing and inadequate regulations in the case of Mrs Lucas, so there was no guarantee that they would follow the new ones. Secondly, the government's intentions for the treatment of alcoholics were, it felt, far from clear. Its policy objective, the decriminalization of drunkenness, was acceptable in itself, but that this might simply lead to routine cautions with drunken offenders then being dumped back on the streets was wholly unacceptable. If the government was serious then it should take heed of the Metropolitan Police and others – like the jury in the Wilma Lucas case – and provide alternative care for such an obviously disadvantaged and neglected group. In the context of London in particular it observed:

> It is not every day that INQUEST rallies to the support of the Metropolitan Police Commission, but in the matter of drink related deaths in police custody, we believe that Sir Kenneth Newman is broadly right and the Home Secretary [Leon Brittan] is wrong. Only when provision is made for detoxification centres – or some other kind of designated centre under the Criminal Justice Act (1982) – to be established in London will this problem be substantially alleviated.[8]

In the following year INQUEST joined Out of Court in pursuing these arguments on a national basis, reporting back to its membership that:

> The Association of Chief Police Officers in a letter to Out of Court, the group campaigning for alternatives for drunken offenders, states that "cautions should not be seen as an alternative to proper treatment in detoxification centres". The secretary to the Association of Chief Probation Officers makes the same

point. Clearly, both bodies are worried by the signs that the Home Office does see cautioning in precisely this way. The Police Federation has also reiterated that it supports wholeheartedly the establishment of "drying out" centres on a permanent basis.[9]

In spite of this strong lobby, little has been done, and the treatment of drunken detainees continues to be a serious problem. The ethics committee of the British Medical Association (BMA) has issued a pamphlet *Health care of detainees in police stations*, that, while sympathetic to the unreasonable demands placed on police, nonetheless concludes that police cells are "dangerous places" for alcoholics.[10] The latest annual report of the Police Complaints Authority (PCA) (1994–5) endorses the concerns of the BMA, questions whether police are qualified to deal with drunken offenders, and urges the Home Office to conduct more research into the problem and how it might be resolved.[11] INQUEST is far from convinced that this will happen, not least because arguably what is needed is not more research – the essentials of the problem are known – but the allocation of more resources, something that in the present climate the government is unlikely to commit.

Suicides in police cells

INQUEST became involved with investigating several suicides in London police stations in the early 1980s. The first of these involved Douglas Coverdale, a 34-year-old heroin addict who took his own life at Uxbridge police station in 1982. He hanged himself using his shoelaces, having tied them to the open hatch of his cell door, known as the wicket-gate. In most forces it was (and is) against police rules to leave the wicket-gate open, but police justified their action on this occasion because it was exceptionally hot and cell ventilation was poor.[12]

Despite the controversy surrounding this case the same abuse of police rules occurred at Leman Street police station about a year later when Matthew Paul took his own life by tying his jumper around the outside of the wicket-gate. On this occasion the police could find no excuse and the jury returned a unanimous verdict of lack of care and took the unusual step of adding that, "We the jury as members of the public must obey and conform to all the law and regulations enforced by the police . . . We do not believe that police should be exempt from obeying their own regulations."[13] INQUEST had worked closely with both families, but the Matthew Paul case was particularly distressing.

This was because it was only after listening to a member of the James Davey Campaign speaking about the failure of coroner Kenerdine to preserve the body of James Davey that Matthew's father decided to check that this had not happened to his son's body, only to find that it had. INQUEST pursued this case with some vigour and Tony Banks MP took up some of the issues with the Home Office.

Despite assurances from the Home Office and the posting of notices in police stations this particular negligence continued. In 1992 INQUEST reported on two more suicides involving the use of the wicket-gate, those of Len Corley and Gary Grace at Dartford and Holloway police stations respectively. In the case of Gary Grace the jury returned a verdict of lack of care. During the inquests it became clear that some of the station staff had little idea about why it was thought necessary to close the wicket-gate, some even thought it was for their own protection.[14] The wicket-gate was again an issue at the inquest at Walthamstow coroner's court into the death of Christopher Marchant in 1994.

How little progress has been made since INQUEST first raised this issue is perhaps best illustrated by this quotation from the latest annual report of the PCA, which starkly observes that:

> Although most force orders require hatches to be closed, our inquiries suggested that the ventilation in some cells was totally inadequate unless hatches were open. In a number of forces this decision was left to the discretion of the custody officer.
>
> The seriousness of the problem was confirmed by the figures for the 12 months ending on 21 March 1995. During that period the Authority supervised inquiries into 25 deaths in police stations, of which 15 were by hanging.
>
> These figures show no improvement on the position over the preceding years.[15]

INQUEST continues to be involved with such cases, many of which involve young offenders. While the police continue to ignore their own orders then this caseload is likely to continue.

Deaths during arrest and/or questioning

It is useful to remind ourselves here that the radical mantle of the GLC did not just rest with the ALA. Equally important were those groups funded by various London boroughs to research and monitor policing after the GLC's own police-monitoring groups petered out. INQUEST

56

continued to network with these. A fairly typical example was its on-going relationship with the Haringey Police Research Unit, which in the second half of the 1980s was led by Tony Bunyan who had first encouraged INQUEST to apply for funding when he was at the GLC's Police Committee Support Unit (see Ch. 2). INQUEST's experience was called upon by Haringey on several occasions, but most notably after the disturbances at Broadwater Farm in 1985, which had been sparked off by the death of Cynthia Jarrett, and had led to the equally tragic death of PC Keith Blakelock.

Cynthia Jarrett died when police searched her home and questioned her following the arrest of her son. The Met claimed that Mrs Jarrett had died from a diseased heart and flatly denied that she had been pushed by any of the police officers present. The jury's verdict of accidental death was taken by INQUEST to be an indication that while the death had indeed been an unfortunate accident and not deliberately intentioned, it had nonetheless resulted from the physical contact that the police had so vigorously denied in open court. In other words, the jury chose to believe those members of the Jarrett family who had been present during the search and questioning and not the police.[16]

INQUEST gave oral evidence on the inquest into Cynthia Jarrett's death (and the subsequent disturbances) to an independent committee of inquiry carried out by the Labour barrister, Lord Gifford. It also provided a transcript of the inquest.[17] Lord Gifford's final report was extremely critical of inquest procedures generally, particularly over the lack of legal aid and the inability of lawyers to address the jurors on the verdicts they might consider.[18] Given strong local support, including that of MP Bernie Grant, INQUEST's involvement in the public campaign as such was modest. However, it did have a tangible benefit in the form of Caroline Rickets who came onto INQUEST's Executive Committee. She worked closely with the Broadwater Farm inquiry as member of the Haringey Police Research Unit.

INQUEST's involvement with the case of Oliver Pryce, who died during arrest by police in Middlesborough, was far more decisive. Mr Pryce was a security guard. After visiting friends and family in the city he was reported to the police for behaving strangely on a housing estate. It is likely that he was in the process of suffering a nervous breakdown. The police were called, as was an ambulance. Behaving warily at first (the police were cautious because of Mr Pryce's strong physique), several officers eventually moved in and overpowered him. He was then bundled into the back of a transit van and taken back to the local police station. He was dead on arrival having been asphyxiated. Stunned by the manner of his sudden death, Mr Pryce's family eventually contacted INQUEST, which was able to take up his case as his sister lived in London.[19]

Working in conjunction with a Midland solicitor appointed by Mr Pryce's employer, INQUEST advised on what preparatory legal work was necessary and secured the services of a sympathetic barrister to take on the inquest which returned a verdict of unlawful killing. No judicial review of this verdict was ever sought, even although the police were as usual well represented at the inquest. But perhaps this is not too surprising. A named police officer had grabbed hold of Mr Pryce without having first tried to speak to him; the same officer had applied a headlock that was kept in position both during his arrest and in the transit van and, most telling, had applied that headlock with such force that a photograph of the officer's arm revealed the indentation caused by a neck chain Mr Pryce was wearing at the time of the arrest.

The use of a headlock can lead to death very quickly and INQUEST has continued to voice its concern over the use of this form of restraint. It caused the death of Shiji Lapite who was arrested by the police for "acting suspiciously" in Stoke Newington in 1994. As in the Oliver Pryce case, the police officers involved flatly denied that they had ever been warned of the dangers of using headlocks. INQUEST was actively involved in this high-profile case and helped the family to explain its concerns to the media when the inquest was finally held in the early months of 1996. The jury returned a verdict of unlawful killing that has forced the Crown Prosecution Service (CPS) to reconsider its previous decision not to prosecute.[20]

The CPS had also refused to act on the coroner's report in the case of Oliver Pryce, again in spite of an unlawful killing verdict. In an unprecedented move, and following contacts with INQUEST, the Bar Council demanded that the DPP reverse this decision in 1992, a demand that was supported by the Society of Black Lawyers.[21] In spite of securing through INQUEST the services of the London-based lawyer, Raju Bhatt, and a third and supportive report from an independent pathologist, no prosecution was forthcoming, although financial compensation to the family has now been paid.

As in the case of Winston Rose (1981), who was also found to have been unlawfully killed during a physical confrontation with police, it continues to be almost impossible to persuade the DPP that the police may have indeed acted unlawfully and should therefore be prosecuted.[22] Such reluctance might be understandable in some of the cases I have touched upon, say where who struck the blow is in doubt, where a verdict is contested as in the case of Leon Patterson (1992), or where the situation facing the police has been unduly violent or takes an unpredictable turn and where the inquest jury reasonably returned a less certain verdict, but it is wholly incomprehensible to friends and families of the deceased where the jury has arrived at more pointed verdicts.

The fact that the Home Secretary of the day invariably decides against instituting a public inquiry on the basis that the DPP is not pressing charges only makes matters worse since what is at issue here is not the narrow legal one of whether a conviction will be secured, but rather demonstrating to family, friends and the public at large that where *prima facie* breaches of the "reasonable use of force" occur they will be fully investigated. This is a political issue about safeguarding civil liberties and one that cannot be brushed aside by simply arguing that it would be wrong to prosecute any individual to placate public opinion. Nor for that matter is it sufficient for politicians to argue – as William Whitelaw did in the case of Blair Peach – that a public inquiry would simply rake over the embers of an unfortunate affair. The other side of this complacent and dangerous argument is that such affairs are left to fester, leaving the impression, among minority communities especially, that the police are largely unaccountable.

This is not to suggest, of course, that securing verdicts against police who kill – or even seriously injure – in the execution of their duties is easy. Those charged with the manslaughter of Joy Gardner, who died resisting arrest and deportation in 1994, were acquitted at the Old Bailey. It is perhaps this that invariably persuades the DPP in such cases to lay the charge of manslaughter rather than murder.

For all these reasons INQUEST has only secured modest gains in this area. But as we have seen, in some instances damages have been paid out to the families of the deceased and the issue is clearly moving up the political agenda as more unlawful killing verdicts are returned. The PCA has been forced to give more attention to these cases and, through the media has actively sought to assure the public that where the use of unreasonable force is proved, disciplinary action will be taken. (See, for example, its contribution to the BBC television programme, *Public Eye*, 13 February 1996.[23])

Police shootings

While INQUEST was keen to join with others in reminding the public that the Metropolitan Police Force has never been entirely unarmed, the number of armed officers patrolling London's streets during the 1970s and 1980s grew alarmingly in tandem with the rise of the SPG and fire brigade policing. This increase was stunningly out of proportion to the increase in other forces,[24] and unfortunately made police shootings all too common. They occurred in a variety of situations, including sieges, but perhaps the most sensational involved the totally innocent Stephen Wardorf who was almost fatally wounded in a hail of gunfire in west London in 1983. On this occasion two police officers were charged, one with attempted murder, but both were acquitted by the jury, leaving yet again what constitutes "reasonable force" when effecting an arrest a very vexed question.

This case was dealt with in some detail in a book sponsored by the GLC's Police Committee Support Unit and written by two INQUEST members, Melissa Benn and Ken Worpole, *Death in the city*.[25] Other controversial shootings involving the Met – this time during ambush situations – occurred first in Tottenham and then later at Woolwich.[26]

But the problem of police shootings was hardly confined to London. Indeed, INQUEST's detailed involvement in such cases began when it took up the controversial deaths of two young men, Ian Bennett and Ian Gordon, both of whom were in possession of replica firearms when they were shot dead by police in Brighouse and Telford respectively. Barrister Terry Munyard spoke at INQUEST's 1992 AGM on the latter case, telling his audience how he had been refused access to the police manual that sets out guidelines on the use of firearms, and how Ian Gordon's mother had been the subject of an attempted "character assassination" by the barrister representing the police. This is apparently quite common. The Kelly family had to confront similar tactics.

INQUEST became so concerned about the number of police shootings in the late 1980s and early 1990s that it published a special bulletin on the issue. This revealed that between March 1979 and April 1993 19 people had died in police shootings – 16 of these between February 1987 and April 1993.[27]

More recently the shooting in southwest London during 1995 of unarmed David Ewin, a suspected car thief, led to a series of public demonstrations and relations between the police and the Afro-Caribbean community became tense. Exceptionally, the CPS charged PC Patrick Hodgson with murder in a case that has yet to be heard

(*Independent* 18 October 1995). However, anger over this case led to disturbances in Brixton shortly afterwards when it was coupled with the death during arrest of another black suspect, Wayne Douglas (*Guardian* 14 December 1995).

The PCA

Finally in this section, it is important to remember that public concern over police accountability generally during the 1980s led to the setting up of the PCA in 1984. Since then it has been open to members of the public to register with the Authority any complaints they have over police conduct involving the death of a friend or relative in any of the circumstances I have outlined – if the police themselves have not already done so under Section 88 of the Police and Criminal Evidence Act – and the matter is then investigated.[28] Where wrongdoing is found, disciplinary action may be recommended or matters referred to the CPS to consider criminal charges. To give two examples, the cases of Cynthia Jarrett and Oliver Pryce were both investigated by the Authority and the appropriate papers then made available to the DPP alongside the coroner's report and the jury's verdict.

The difficulty for the PCA is that many people do not believe it to be impartial. This is because the detailed investigations of the complaints submitted to it are conducted by police themselves, albeit in controversial cases, by police from another force. The Authority's own research has recently confirmed this majority perception among the public at large, and among ethnic minorities in particular.[29] This gives rise, to put the case at its least damaging, to a feeling that the Authority is not determined enough in its pursuit of misconduct. Lord Gifford, for example, was scathing in his comments on the Authority's investigation into the death of Cynthia Jarret that exonerated the police, arguing that there were at least 13 examples of police wrongdoing. He came to the conclusion that the then members of the Authority "have no idea what standards of conduct are expected by reasonable members of the public".[30]

INQUEST's experience since 1986 has reinforced this judgment, even although one drawback to going through the Authority, namely that the evidence (including statements) obtained during its investigations could not be used in later civil proceedings, has recently been removed.[31] It seems unlikely that this change on its own will influence the prevailing preference of complainants and their lawyers to bypass the Authority and go direct to the civil courts. As a mechanism for securing greater police accountability the PCA therefore remains a seriously flawed institution.

Prison suicides

Our opening emphasis on deaths in police custody has been justified on the basis that it was mainly around such cases that INQUEST came into being and that helped to mark it out from other groups in the criminal justice lobby, to define its unique presence. However, it should already be clear that from the very beginning INQUEST was very much concerned with deaths in other forms of custody, most notably those occurring in prisons. Indeed, the family and friends of Richard Campbell had been among its founding members, as was Dorothy Prosser whose husband was unlawfully killed in Winson Green prison. It is to prison deaths I now turn, but first I add an important word of refinement.

When INQUEST was formally founded in 1981 there were other groups active in the penal lobby and elsewhere who were taking a critical interest in deaths in custody, most notably the prisoners' union, PROP, RAP and the NCCL. The 1970s had seen a number of serious disturbances in British prisons and successive governments devised control strategies involving harsher forms of segregation, the use of powerful psychotropic drugs, and the further militarization of the prison service as a whole through the introduction of such things as riot squads.[32] These strategies arguably made prison tensions worse, and radical groups in the lobby campaigned vigorously against them, sometimes using the deaths of individual prisoners to focus their protest. However, it is fairly clear from the individual cases taken up that the concerns of these groups were significantly different from those of INQUEST, at least in terms of their emphasis.

First and most obviously, perhaps, there were the issues around inquest procedures and the role of coroners. While these other groups had something critical to say on these issues in publications like *Frightened for my life* (PROP) and *Deaths in custody* (NCCL), they were nonetheless secondary concerns. For INQUEST on the other hand they were central, even paramount. For example, PROP was active in support of the Prosser family, but had little complaint in this case about the inquest in which the jury took just 15 minutes to decide that Barry

Prosser had been unlawfully killed and the coroner was highly critical of medical routines.[33]

Secondly, groups like the NCCL and PROP were concerned with a wide range of prison deaths whereas INQUEST came to concentrate more and more on self-inflicted deaths. It is not entirely clear why INQUEST took this turn. It was obviously to some extent client led in that INQUEST simply responded to the families and friends who came to it for help, but this itself was the reflection of the growing number of suicides recorded in British prisons in the 1980s as conditions worsened, especially for remand prisoners, and regimes became deliberately more repressive. It is to these deaths, and an assessment of INQUEST's role in forcing the government to answer for its neglect – sometimes sheer incompetence – in this area, that we now turn.

Ashford

Public concern over the running of Ashford Remand Centre which had contributed to the death by "self-neglect" of Richard Campbell in 1980 obviously had little impact. Within two years there was another tragic death, that of Jim Heather-Hayes. On this occasion the jury returned a verdict of suicide aggravated by lack of care, making it plain that in its view the governor and his staff had failed to follow the government's Standing Orders on suicide prevention.

This was a crucial case for INQUEST for at least two reasons. To begin with, this was the first time – following a legal judgment by the Divisional Court arising out of the Richard Campbell case – that a lack of care verdict had been accepted at an inquest on a self-inflicted death. Previously such a judgment had been thought impossible since under the Coroners' Rules (1953), "no verdict shall be framed in such a way as to appear to determine . . . civil liability". The Divisional Court's ruling that lack of care could be used since all it did was to suggest a general liability rather than a specific one – it did not point the finger at any individual – opened the door for similar verdicts in prison (and police) custody cases.[34] Secondly, in as much that such verdicts openly arrived at suggest some degree of fault or neglect on the part of prison (and police) authorities it is much easier for families and friends to campaign for action.

This is precisely what happened in the case of Jim Heather-Hayes. Those concerned to discover the truth about his death became convinced that staff at Ashford were at fault. For example, it became clear during the inquest that prison censors had failed to act on evidence of

Jim Heather-Hayes's distress in letters home, while crucial evidence about his state of mind was not communicated to the governor who sentenced him to solitary confinement for causing a disturbance in the prison canteen.[35] Spurred on by knowledge of these failures, the campaign – which was in touch with INQUEST throughout – used Michael Meacher to table a written question to the Home Secretary asking him to set up an inquiry.[36] This was followed up a month later when the Home Office was ambushed – this time by Michael Meacher and Chris Price – during oral questions.[37] Eventually the Home Office conceded, although it avoided holding an inquiry into the death of Jim Heather-Hayes *per se*; instead the Home Secretary announced that:

> Her Majesty's Inspector of Prisons is currently engaged in a routine inspection of Ashford and his team will in any event return to the prison for that purpose. I have asked him to pay particular attention to the establishment's observance of central instructions and guidance in arrangements for the prevention of suicides, and to cover these topics in his inspection report which will be published . . . in the normal way.[38]

In the same reply it was also announced that a more wide-ranging, thematic inquiry into suicide prevention arrangements was to take place during 1983.

By any standard the inspector's report was a sharp indictment of Ashford. The inspector acknowledged that relevant medical information about an inmate's suicide potential did not always arrive at Ashford from elsewhere on time, but even when it did arrive, he "did not consider that it was picked out, acted upon and presented to the Medical Officer in any systematic way". Furthermore, "staff took the view that if the CIs [Circular Instructions] were strictly interpreted most, if not all, the inmates would have to have been designated potential suicides . . . reception staff . . . faced with the sheer weight of numbers, tended to disregard the instructions".[39] More particularly, the report concluded that the F-marking system, where those displaying clear suicidal tendencies have their files marked with a distinctive red F, was taken to be discretionary when in fact it was compulsory. Given this sort of evidence the report was naturally critical of managers at Ashford, and by clear implication, the governor, arguing that, "no priority had been given to the prevention of suicides in the local training programmes . . . [and] that the governor should review his training plans at the first opportunity".[40]

Although the report said little about self-injuries or attempted suicides, it was generally welcomed by INQUEST, not least because of its
emphasis on poor communication both within Ashford itself and
between Ashford and those courts that sent prisoners to it. However,
hopes that things might improve were soon dashed when Paul Ducatt
committed suicide there in March 1986. Like Jim Heather-Hayes, Paul
Ducatt had been worried about his ability to cope, but again this was
not picked up by the prison censor. The jury concluded that there had
again been a lack of communication between the discipline and the
medical staff.[41]

In an attempt to exert further pressure on the Ashford governor
INQUEST had earlier written to the House of Commons Home Affairs
Select Committee urging that the Ducatt case was pertinent to its current inquiry into the Prison Medical Service. It suggested that attendance at the inquest would be a "first rate opportunity for members
of the Committee to see what changes had actually taken place at
Ashford since the Inspector's report".[42] The Select Committee did not
respond to this invitation directly – INQUEST could hardly have
believed that it would – but its final report did at least acknowledge
"there is some evidence, such as that given to the jury at the inquest
into the death of Jim Heather-Hayes at Ashford Remand Centre, that
the 'fitting' of prisoners for punishment is sometimes perfunctory and
the medical examination is not sufficiently thorough to be certain that,
for example, mental disturbances or suicidal tendencies on the part of
the prisoner are noticed".[43]

Home Office report on prison suicides (1984)
INQUEST also submitted evidence to the more general or thematic
inquiry into prison suicides that had been announced alongside the
Ashford inquiry in 1984. Like other groups submitting evidence,
INQUEST stressed that the general pressures on the prison system,
especially those brought about by overcrowding, would have to be
relieved before suicide prevention measures were likely to have any
measurable effect. Indeed, reducing prison numbers, ending the isolation of prisoners from society, breaking down barriers between staff
and prisoners, were likely to be the "most effective" ways of reducing
suicide rates. More particularly it wanted the government to put more
pressure on governors to implement Standing Orders and Circular
Instructions on suicide prevention and to insist that they must put in
writing to headquarters any reasons why they are not being followed.
And equally important, Standing Orders and Circular Instructions

should be made available to the coroner, juries and friends and families of the deceased so that they can make a reasoned judgement about whether they have been followed in the case before them – whether care has been duly and properly exercised.[44]

In his summary of the evidence submitted to him the Chief Inspector's report noted INQUEST's misgivings about the extent to which Circular Instructions and Standing Orders were being obeyed.[45] The report also picked out the view – attributed on this occasion to the Prison Reform Trust rather than to INQUEST – that the present procedures for examining unexplained deaths in custody did not always allay public fears and that the Home Secretary ought to use more public inquiries.[46] Apart from airing these more controversial opinions, the report's recommendations were fairly anodyne. It was noted that little was known about prison suicides and called for more research. It also concluded that the F-marking system had broken down and that in its place there should be procedures that referred potentially suicidal prisoners to the prison medical officer who should then decide what treatment was required. Discussions about suicide should be arranged for all staff, not least because the inquiry had discovered that few officers were aware of the contents of the relevant Standing Orders and Circular Instructions.[47]

INQUEST wrote one of its more acerbic responses to this particular report. It pointed with sharpness to the apparent detachment of the report when referring to the breakdown of the F-marking system and how the 15-minute suicide Special Watch was often not complied with because landing officers were simply too busy. INQUEST wondered – perhaps on behalf of frontline staff – about the quality of the management that had allowed this state of affairs to develop and endure. But perhaps more significantly, INQUEST questioned the underlying assumption of the report, namely, that preventing prison suicides was something that could be safely left with the Prison Medical Service, that it was primarily a medical problem.[48] INQUEST refuted this, and was more inclined to the scepticism of those prison governors who had observed in written evidence to the Chief Inspector that:

> It appears to us that there is too much emphasis upon the role and decision of the Prison Service Medical Staff in this area. Not wishing to put too fine a point on it, the medical profession retains unto itself a form of "mystique" in diagnostic areas. It may well be that some lay people are equally adept at recognizing

signs of depression and in so doing may be unencumbered by the need to recognize and reduce malingering which, quite properly, influences medical officers.[49]

The virtue of this approach as far as INQUEST was concerned was that it was half way towards acknowledging that suicide is a form of behaviour that is encouraged by the experience of prison, say the fear of being bullied, and depression brought on by isolation from family and friends. It is such wider pressures, essentially non-medical pressures, that have to be addressed by all staff if prison suicides among otherwise normal, healthy prisoners are ever going to be reduced. Of course, the Prison Medical Service has a role to play in this process, and no doubt with certain types of prisoner a very central role, but the narrow medical concern must never define the problem, not least when so few of its members have any psychiatric training.

In spite of INQUEST's trenchant criticisms, the Home Office accepted the main thrust of the report, agreed to abolish the F-marking system, introduced a new system of documentation and improved medical and screening procedures.[50] No doubt the Home Office was thankful to have something positive to act on as it continued under pressure, although the focus of INQUEST's attention had now shifted from Ashford to Brixton, a potentially more embarrassing site. In fact it was while the suicide report was still being put together that INQUEST joined in a picket of Brixton prison – in March 1984 – to protest at the ten deaths that had been recorded there in just over a 12-month period. In a highly critical press handout, INQUEST drew attention to the death of Arthur Neale whose "suicidal predilections" had been well known. Mr Neale had allegedly been transferred from Special Watch A in the prison hospital to Special Watch B in an ordinary cell in another wing which required that he only be visited every 15 minutes, an arrangement that allowed him to commit suicide by hanging. INQUEST observed that it hoped the forthcoming Home Office report on suicide prevention would suggest something "more intelligent than putting the potentially suicidal prisoner on his own in a cell with a minimum of furniture – a sheet to tear into strips for a noose, a bed and a chair to stand on, and bars conveniently placed."[51]

Responding to criticism

Inquests that invited this sort of comment were clearly very damaging to the Home Office, and it is perhaps no surprise that in 1984 it amended and re-issued its Circular Instruction (33) on *Deaths in custody; follow up action*. Staff were reminded that any death had to be immediately reported to the Home Office by telephone through the appropriate regional director. A more detailed written report on the death and the circumstances surrounding it then had to be filed with headquarters well in advance of the inquest "so that the department can consider whether legal representation is necessary and so brief Counsel". Where a suicide was suspected, details of any special measures taken must be listed. Was the F-marking system in operation, for example? Was the prisoner on Special Watch? The department's policy was to consider in every case of a death in custody, "but particularly cases of suicide", whether legal representation was necessary. Even more revealing, this decision would be based on issues revolving around:

> the extent and nature of public and media reaction to the death; whether the inmate's family appear critical of the Department; whether the family (or any other party) are to be legally represented, and if so by whom and whether there are any aspects of the case on which the Department would be open to criticism (whether or not such criticism appears to be well founded).[52]

These considerations might seem prudent viewed from the Home Office. An alternative view – the one taken by INQUEST – was to label them as defensive and cynical, an indication that the government was on the run over deaths in prison, increasingly sensitive to public concern, but prepared if necessary to use its very considerable resources to protect itself where families and/or friends of the deceased had the temerity to call it to account. The fact that the Home Office wished to know exactly who was representing the family and friends is perhaps an indication that the small band of lawyers INQUEST had recruited to its cause was beginning to make its mark.

To be fair to the government, action was taken on the thematic report of 1984 and two years later the Home Office set up a Working Party on Suicide Prevention. Long-term research into deaths in custody was also commissioned from the Cambridge Institute of Criminology. The labours of the Working Party led to revision of the government's Standing Order on Suicide Prevention in 1987 – which set up local suicide management committees – and again in 1989. Yet none of these measures were sufficient to halt the rising spiral of suicides.

Risley and Brixton

By 1987 Risley had become the focus of attention. Built in 1965 Risley was a remand centre holding both male and female prisoners. Its suicide rate had not been exceptional before 1987, but in the summer of that year three suicides took place in close succession. The Chief Inspector was asked to bring forward his routine inspection as a direct consequence. What the Inspector found at Risley clearly appalled him, particularly on the male wings where "the squalor in which men lived for over twenty hours a day . . . contributed to a profoundly depressing atmosphere".[53] More particularly he expressed grave concern at the almost total disrespect shown for Circular 3/1983 on suicide prevention. Procedures at reception were flawed, communications between the censor and the medical officer poor and astonishingly there was no suicide management committee in place at all. "Grisly Risley", as it came to be known, did not improve, and in an 18-month period between 1988 and 1989 eight more suicides were recorded.[54] In May 1989 prisoners took matters into their own hands, destroying a complete wing and holding a dramatic rooftop demonstration.

INQUEST kept up its pressure on the government, not just by working prison inquests, which were regrettably becoming all too frequent, but through Parliament and the media. For example, working directly through the Opposition spokesperson Barry Sheerman – he had by this time replaced Clive Solely – INQUEST tabled a series of questions asking the Home Secretary to list all deaths in prison service establishments in England and Wales for the years 1987 and 1988, and to indicate the causes of death.[55] Using this material Sheerman called a press conference in April 1989.

The briefing paper prepared by INQUEST for this meeting noted, among other things, that the number of prison suicides had risen sharply in 1987 and 1989 and linked this directly to a rise in the remand population where most suicides happened. The plight of mentally ill prisoners was also singled out as being particularly distressing.[56] More narrowly, and given its growing notoriety, INQUEST focused on Brixton prison and a subsequent Parliamentary question tabled by Sheerman confirmed that no less than 11 prisoners had died there (or after transfer to a local hospital) in 1989.[57]

INQUEST's campaign around Brixton was well supported by the Southwark coroner Sir Montague Levine. Before his appointment in the mid-1980s INQUEST had to deal with a coroner and his deputy who it believed were less than even-handed; the police and prison authorities it seemed were rarely at fault. One of the pair was also thought to be peremptory and inconsiderate, a view partly endorsed at least by comments made by a judge in the Divisional Court (*ex parte* Hicks). By contrast, Sir Montague Levine was not only more considerate towards those families who appeared before him, but also far more critical of the authorities when he thought it justified and in the late 1980s voiced his concern, often in open court, about conditions and procedures in Brixton.

These concerns – they were shared not just by INQUEST but by most of the mainstream penal reform groups by this time – stemmed largely from the fact that Brixton was being swamped by remand prisoners, many of whom had psychiatric problems, sometimes quite severe problems, which the prison was ill equipped to cope with. So under Rule 43 of the Coroners' Rules Sir Montague made a series of recommendations – sometimes repeating them – relating to this issue. For example, in 1988 and 1989 he called for an urgent review to speed the psychiatric assessment of prisoners, something that could be achieved by establishing a local panel of psychiatrists rather than having to wait under existing procedures for one to be called from the prisoner's catchment area. In 1988 he declared in open court that there was a need to explore and explain the range of alternatives to remands in custody that were available to all courts under the Mental Health Act (1983). There was also a stream of recommendations relating more generally to medical care in Brixton, about how it was administered within the prison and about how medical information was passed between the prison, police and the courts.

In an important respect, what was happening at Brixton, and there was little doubt that it fuelled the suicide statistics, was a reflection of the far wider problem, the emptying onto our streets under the banner of community care, psychiatric patients who often lacked support, who were (and are) quite unable to cope. They then find themselves being arrested, often for quite trivial offences, and later imprisoned, a traumatic experience for most people, let alone the mentally ill. Sir Montague's stream of recommendations reflected this state of affairs, but also, and this is an important point, the pressure that it put on the routine medical services provided at Brixton and the level of care it could offer to those other patients who had no previous history of mental illness arguably tempted some of them to suicide or attempted suicide.[58]

The combination of public, Parliamentary and judicial pressure led to the announcement of an inquiry into suicides at Brixton by the Chief Inspector of Prisons in 1990. The subsequent report acknowledged that if all Brixton had to do as the principal remand prison for unconvicted prisoners in the southeast was to deliver short stay prisoners to and from the courts it might function reasonably well. However, it was being asked to do much more, to both take on board a number of seriously ill prisoners and to house a population of convicted prisoners who were banged up for 24 hours a day – some of them three to a cell – with little constructive activity to occupy their time. Overall, the regime was judged to be "destructive and depressing".[59]

On the specific question of suicide prevention the report found that the pressure on medical officers at reception was "too great for anything more than a cursory examination".[60] Still, the Chief Inspector felt that they coped reasonably well on this front, notwithstanding the shortage of time and the almost complete lack of privacy. The main hospital, where potential suicides were sometimes housed in open wards, left much to be desired, especially in staffing terms, but it was at least passable when compared with the overspill wards on F-wing, known to staff and inmates alike as Fraggle Rock after a television puppet show. The Chief Inspector was clearly appalled by what he found here – dirty mattresses, faecal traces on some of the walls, tiles ripped up and not replaced and a heating system that could not be regulated.[61] It was here that many potential suicides were placed, sometimes with cells with bars conveniently placed from which they could (and did) hang themselves. The report recommended that F-wing be completely refurbished. The Chief Inspector was clearly suspicious that cell sharing was not being sufficiently encouraged as an antidote to suicide and was critical about how medical officers communicated from reception to staff on the landings at F-wing.[62]

On the question of severely mentally ill prisoners the Chief Inspector encouraged Prison Medical Health Officers to make greater use of Section 48 of the Mental Health Act (1983) to transfer these "patients" elsewhere. He felt obliged to acknowledge, however, that in spite of pressure from the Home Office and the Department of Health many psychiatric hospitals were unwilling to take such prisoners.[63]

The language of the Chief Inspector's report – strong by any standards – came as no surprise to those groups like INQUEST who had campaigned against conditions in Brixton for so long. Having worked closely with the *Guardian's* John Carvel to bring to light what was happening there, INQUEST particularly welcomed that newspaper's withering leader which commented that:

> Bedlam lives on. Those who doubt it should read Judge Tumim's report on Brixton prison. Some of the Chief Inspector's report is all too depressingly familiar; a story of overcrowded cells, degrading conditions, long hours locked away from other inmates and inadequate exercise. Remember 888 of the 1,000 people in the prison had not been convicted or were still awaiting sentence. Yet their conditions were far worse than they would suffer in a long term prison. In Judge Tumim's words a "grim" prison was imposing an austere, miserable and wholly negative experience.
>
> But Brixton is not just a prison. It is a major psychiatric facility. Most of the 300 beds – 82 in the prison hospital and 239 in F-wing – are reserved for the mentally disturbed. The prison houses more psychiatric patients than any other prison in the UK, and possibly in Europe. Several hundred are on remand for reports. The uninitiated may well ask why a criminal justice system intent on assessing the mental state of a suspect should have defendants remanded in a prison to determine their mental state. The same question has been asked for three decades, yet they continue to be remanded ... One glimpse of our Home Affairs Editor's Report on the prison today prompts the obvious conclusion that anyone who was not unstable before being remanded would quickly become so under Brixton's conditions.
>
> Consider being sent to F-wing. Down one side all the cells have been stripped of all the furniture except a mattress. The luxurious cells are opposite; cells with cardboard furniture. Every cell door has a hatch. Most hatches on some nights are being banged, the inmates are screaming or else babbling incoherently. Add to that medical officers with inadequate qualifications, and prison nurses who are really prison officers who have only taken a rudimentary training course and it is no wonder that the suicide rate at Brixton in the last three years has been one, eight and five so far. Over 10 per cent of the total number of suicides in a system with 120 prisons. (*Guardian* 14 December 1990)

The government's response to the report – conveniently it was not released until just before Christmas in the run-up to the Parliamentary recess – was an exercise in damage limitation. It stressed that new remand places were coming on stream to relieve the overcrowding; that more staff had already been allocated to the prison hospital; that a consultant psychiatrist had been drafted in to help decide which seriously mentally ill patients should be transferred to other hospitals, and that a booklet – echoing a suggestion made by Sir Montague Levine in 1988 – had been prepared for the courts on alternatives to prison sentences for the mentally ill. A working group to plan the comprehensive redevelopment of Brixton was also announced.[64]

Another inquiry: suicide and self-harm in prison service establishments in England and Wales (1990)

As if to repeat the sequence of events that surrounded the inquiry into Ashford the government paralleled its inquiry into Brixton with a more general management inquiry into prison suicides.[65] But this was to be more extensive than the 1984 inquiry with more prisons visited and more interested groups canvassed for their views, including INQUEST. In its letter to INQUEST in February 1990 – the same letter was sent to all groups – the inquiry group wrote that it hoped to produce some "pragmatic recommendations" on suicide and self-injury prevention in prisons and asked for guidance on what "modest improvements" might be introduced. Apart from this initial general request for guidance, the remaining eight topics inviting comment raised issues about facilities and procedures around mentally ill offenders, for example, about the use of powers to transfer such offenders to outside psychiatric hospitals.[66]

This sent alarm bells ringing at INQUEST. Here was the Chief Inspector of Prisons, straight from his inquiry into Brixton with its own very special problems, starting an inquiry into prison suicides in general with a psychiatric and procedural focus, the very failings of the 1984 report. What the Chief Inspector and his team must be made to realize was that while it was true that some mentally ill patients who are potentially suicidal are perhaps wrongly committed to prison and that screening (and transfer) procedures must be adequate to detect them, most people who enter prison do so in a perfectly reasonable state of mental health. It is the process of confinement itself, the reaction of ordinary healthy prisoners to overcrowded and unproductive regimes that drives them to take their lives. In a tactful submission INQUEST got straight to the point:

73

It is important to stress that suicide in prison should not be seen primarily as a psychiatric problem. Indeed, one recent study suggests that prisoners who kill themselves are less likely to suffer from mental illness – particularly depressive illness – than people who commit suicide while at liberty, although the proportion who have had previous psychiatric contact is somewhat higher than in the general prison population . . . Brixton prison, to which most of our evidence relates, is in some ways a special case, since it has a concentration of inmates with psychiatric problems and it is among these inmates that most suicides have occurred. Even in Brixton, it is notable that few if any of those have been diagnosed as suffering from depressive illness – the condition most commonly associated with suicide outside prisons; most have been diagnosed as suffering from schizophrenia, personality disorder or mental impairment . . . [para. 2: 1] While we understand the limits of the Inspectorate's role, and the reasons for adopting a "pragmatic approach", we hope that you will at least define the scope of your review somewhat more broadly than your predecessor did in his 1984 review of suicide prevention.

The Prison Service's own 1986 Working Party on Suicide Prevention criticized the 1984 report's narrow focus on procedural matters and acknowledged the importance for suicide prevention of the regime as a whole and staff/prisoner relationships in particular. INQUEST's submission went on to point out that because of the pressure on the penal system:

the scope for improving the response to suicide risk is most limited in those parts of the system where the risk is known to be particularly high, such as the remand system. Until the pressure from the over use of custody, and especially custodial remands, is reduced only limited improvements can be expected from "pragmatic" reforms. (2: 4)[67]

The drift of this message was reinforced in subsequent paragraphs. For example, it was agreed that medical officers are not especially good at identifying suicide risks during screening (2: 8) but felt it was hardly surprising. Few prisoners were likely to unburden themselves to someone they did not know. Much more significant was likely to be the developing relationship between prisoners and disciplinary staff as the sentence was being served; this is where vigilance (and common sense) had to be directed (2: 4). The need for improved communication between prisons, police and the courts was also stressed (2: 10–12) as were links between prisoners and the outside world, especially with their families and friends (3: 1). Throughout the submission there is little good said about the quality of existing psychiatric care (see 3: 17, for example).

The Chief Inspector's report began by tracing the evolution of the prison department's suicide and self-injury prevention policy, giving particular attention to the 1986 Working Party's report whose recommendations led to Circular Instruction 20/1989 and the setting up of suicide prevention management groups in most local prisons.[68] The report was reasonably happy with the content of the Circular Instruction *per se* but felt that it could be made more user friendly and that more effort was needed to implement it in the spirit in which it was intended (2: 2–3). It was more critical of the suicide prevention management groups that sometimes failed to meet at all, and that generally speaking had little impact on the overall culture of most establishments (2: 23). INQUEST had ample evidence to support such conclusions and its only criticism was perhaps that the language of the report was so restrained. However, it was more than satisfied with the apparent shift of the inquiry's focus and it found little to disagree with the report's argument that:

Despite its wide scope the main thrust of Circular Instruction 20/1989 was perceived as treating self-inflicted death as exclusively a medical problem, and the task for staff (medical and non-medical) is declared to be an attempt to identify inmates at risk, put them before the Medical Officer, and carry out the Medical Officer's instructions. Whilst we acknowledge the important part played by doctors in determining those who are at risk and in recommending appropriate treatment, self-inflicted deaths in custody is by no means an exclusively medical problem.

Current Prison Department policy fails to communicate the social dimension to self harm and self-inflicted death. It does not stress sufficiently the significance of the environment in which staff and prisoners are expected to live and work, or the importance of constructive activities in helping inmates cope with anxiety and stress. Above all, it fails to give weight to the need to sustain people during their time in custody, the importance of relationships between inmates and between staff and inmates in providing that support. The danger of targeting suicide prevention as primarily a medical problem is that the service may have become conditioned to the view that all the answers lie with the prison doctors. This is not the case. Prisoners, staff, families, visitors, the regime, the environment, all have parts to play and management must stress and encourage progress on all these fronts. (2: 7–8)

INQUEST endorsed this critique and welcomed the report's emphasis on general issues, such as the quality of living space for prisoners, their education and their leisure. Perhaps there was some disappointment that the issue of remand prisoners had not been treated more centrally, but even here there was much to support. For example, the Chief Inspector stressed the urgent need to stop remanding people to prison for psychiatric reports when remanding them to a bail hostel would do just as well. He was clearly impressed by the experiment at Bow Street and Marlborough Street courts that provided a psychiatrist to interview and mediate between police, the Crown Prosecution Service and magistrates in an attempt to secure diversion from custody, or even better in the case of the mentally ill, to prevent prosecution altogether (3: 74–5). Perhaps the one aspect of the report that pleased INQUEST most – and which it was to use against the Home Office time and time again – was its attention to the needs of families and friends. The inquiry, it was reported, had heard of the difficulties that families and friends had encountered getting information from prisons about the deceased and the circumstances surrounding his or her death. The report made it plain that this is wholly unacceptable, recommending that:

At the earliest possible opportunity the next of kin must be given details of what happened to the deceased. While we recognize potential problems in respect of the sub-judice rule, the air of secrecy and lack of cooperation which has surrounded some cases adds to the sense of loss. These circumstances often provide a point on which to focus anguish, desperation and all manner of prejudices if not handled carefully. When the next of kin feel that they are in need of outside help from solicitors then those acting on their behalf should be given access to, or copies of, papers and if necessary, allowed to visit the scene of the death. *It seems appropriate that the next of kin should enter the inquest procedure with the same amount of information as the Prison Service.* (5: 9; emphasis added)

It is difficult to judge how influential INQUEST was in persuading the inquiry to broaden its focus. Other organizations made their views known and perhaps not too much should be read into the fact that INQUEST was placed first in the otherwise alphabetical list of all those organizations who submitted written evidence. However, INQUEST itself has claimed that the concerns of families that it put to a member of the inquiry team who took the trouble to visit its cramped offices in Finsbury Park were fully addressed.[69] The fate of all official inquiries, of course, is that even when they are thought to get close to identifying the real problem, their recommendations may not be accepted in principle, or even when they are, they may fail to get translated into practice. INQUEST was to find this out to its cost, which is well if tragically illustrated by the suicide of Paddy O'Grady in Brixton prison just 18 months after the publication of the Chief Inspector's report.

Paddy O'Grady was a healthy 24-year-old labourer who was arrested in February 1991 for attempted burglary. He was already in trouble with the police and subject to a curfew order. Originally remanded to Wormwood Scrubs where his pregnant girlfriend could visit him fairly regularly he was then transferred to Brixton in March. In the meantime his girlfriend had given birth to their daughter. He was formally convicted in May, and as a convicted prisoner his visits were restricted to just one per month. He became increasingly depressed and his physical condition deteriorated rapidly. When he was visited on F-wing within two weeks of his death his wife and brother were quite shocked by his appearance. On 27 May he hanged himself by tying a sheet to the anti-suicide grille attached to the window of his single cell.[70]

INQUEST was first alerted to this case by Heather Mills, the Home Affairs correspondent of the *Independent* who, like John Carvel of the *Guardian*, had done much to bring the troubles at Brixton prison into the public arena. The O'Grady family were devastated by the manner of their son's death and were more than willing to accept support and advice from INQUEST when it was offered. The family simply wanted to know how such a thing could have happened. Finding out was far from easy.

To begin with, the Home Office refused full disclosure of all the relevant documents before the inquest, thus running counter to the Chief Inspector's recommendation that all the parties involved should "enter" the inquest on an equal footing. When this documentation was eventually prised out of the Home Office – the coroner made no objection whatsoever about such disclosure – a sorry tale of mismanagement and muddle was revealed. No attempt had been made to implement the provision under Circular Instruction 20/1989 to allow extra visits to potentially suicidal inmates, even although a visiting probation officer had gone so far as to say that she had never seen any one so at risk of killing themselves; and the eight prison doctors who saw Mr O'Grady no less than 25 times did not consider his condition worthy of a case conference, although one doctor, it is fair to say, accepted that mistakes had probably been made about where to place him within the prison. The jury took under half an hour to return a verdict of suicide aggravated by lack of care.

The coroner's critical remarks about how the case had been handled by the prison authorities, plus the fact that it turned out to be the fourteenth death to have occurred at Brixton in just two years drew harsh editorial comment and the governor felt obliged to defend his staff in public.[71] However, Brixton's disregard for procedures was far from being exceptional. The case of Delroy McKnight who also died in 1991, but in Wandsworth prison, was arguably even more worrying. Mr McKnight was a 29-year-old schizophrenic with suicidal thoughts, transferred to Wandsworth because Highpoint prison did not have adequate medical facilities to treat him. Unfortunately, information about his active medical condition was not communicated in writing to Wandsworth's medical staff and Mr McKnight was put into an ordinary cell. It was believed that he had been the subject of a disciplinary transfer. Within a few weeks he had taken his own life. During the inquest it was admitted that Circular Instruction 20/1989 had not been properly followed and one doctor even went so far to admit that he had never read it![72]

These examples well illustrate why INQUEST's welcome for the Chief Inspector's report was a qualified one. Nor did these problems go away. Self-inflicted deaths in prison custody continued to be at an unacceptably high level well into the 1990s and INQUEST's role in bringing such cases to public attention and pressing for procedures to be followed was clearly resented by Prison Department officials who were reported to have sharply criticized INQUEST for subjecting frontline officers to hostile cross-examination at inquests. Deborah Coles for INQUEST hit back, denying any vendetta against prison officers and pointing out that advance disclosure and more openness by the Home Office at inquests would make such searching examinations unnecessary.[73] (Converting the Prison Department into a semi-autonomous agency (1993) has so far done little to secure greater accountability.)

Young offender suicides

The tragedy of prison suicides was made worse by the fact that so many young people were taking their own lives, especially young men. While these were not confined to young offender institutions, as we shall see, Alison Liebling is correct to argue that the first hint of the tragedy that was unfolding came from Glenochil in Scotland.[74] The Glenochil complex comprised a detention centre for short-term offenders and a young offenders' institution for those serving over nine months. It was situated well away from Scotland's main urban areas and was consequently difficult for most families and friends to visit. Between 1980 and 1985 there were seven deaths at Glenochil.

Information about what was happening at Glenochil first reached INQUEST through Phil Scraton who had been alerted to the problems there by Jimmy Boyle who was then working with young people at the Gateway Exchange project in Glasgow.[75] In an important series of articles, one of which appeared in *The Abolitionist*, which also carried INQUEST bulletins, Scraton & Chadwick challenged the official conclusions of a working party that had been set up to investigate the deaths. The working party had concluded that the deaths were unconnected, other than being an "outbreak of suicidal behaviour" which happens in most closed institutions from time to time, as is "well known".[76]

The starting point of the Scraton & Chadwick critique was that the working party's terms of reference had been drawn far too tightly. It had been charged with "a review of procedures" that might, or should, have led to the identification of individual inmates with a "potential for suicide". This invited the working party to concentrate on individual offenders and draw up a set of "at risk" indicators rather than looking at wider, structural constraints. Yet it was precisely these wider constraints in terms of the regimes in place at Glenochil that needed to be investigated first.

According to Scraton & Chadwick these regimes were almost wholly negative. In the detention centre the emphasis was on physical training rather than on education. The inmate's day started at 5.45 a.m. with slopping out. From then on they were mostly marched everywhere, reacting at the double to shouted military-style commands. At the end of the day they were allowed just 30 minutes' association after already having spent a long period in isolation in their own cells. This routine might be broken twice a month if relatives and/or friends were able to visit. While the young offenders' institution had the advantage of offering more educational opportunities and a structured system of progression leading to more privileges, the regime there was impregnated with violence and intimidation where the weak, the unassertive, the sex offender and the mentally retarded were all subject to a "relentless barrage of physical torment and mental torture". For those others who were isolated for their own protection, or who were thought to be potential suicides, the cells provided were poorly heated and ventilated with grilles that could not be easily closed. The furniture was spartan and the blankets were made of coarse canvas. Apart from a dressing-gown no other clothing was provided or permitted.

It was in the context of such "flawed" regimes that the Glenochil suicides had to be understood. Of course, procedures were important, and Scraton & Chadwick acknowledged that the working party had been highly critical of some of these, and of the care of those who had been identified as at risk. But its report failed to situate these criticisms properly, to understand that the problems of suicide and self-injury had to be located in the interaction between young offenders – mostly quite normal human beings – and Glenochil's harsh, unbending regimes:

> research shows, and it is supported by extensive research on the effects of harsh regimes of incarceration on inmates, that people who resist such regimes or crack up within them are not necessarily suffering from "broken homes" or "personal disorders" . . . but are responding rationally to inhuman practices that are inherent in harsh regimes of detention. It is the emphasis on the individual . . . and the failure to either recognize or come to terms with the highly punitive forms of detention that severely flaws the analysis contained in the report.[77]

Not surprisingly this critique had much in common with that made by INQUEST on the official 1984 report into suicide prevention in England and Wales following the death of Jim Heather-Hayes, although admittedly that gave more attention to variables such as overcrowding. However, both critiques were given added resonance by the debate that surrounded the introduction of the "short, sharp shock" regime into detention centres in England and Wales. Neither, though, it has to be said, had any impact on William Whitelaw who carried on with the experiment until it was discreetly discarded some years later, apparently having achieved very little.

Young prisoner suicides in local prisons

As the 1980s progressed there were other suicide clusters among young prisoners. One of the most disturbing was that which occurred at Armley prison (Leeds) where, between May 1988 and February 1989, five young men aged between 17 and 19 died while on remand. Verdicts of suicide were returned in each case. The government minister in charge of prisons, Douglas Hogg, refused to hold an independent inquiry, but instead sanctioned an internal report that reached the perhaps predictable conclusion that the deaths "were in no way connected". The Howard League did its best to investigate what was happening in Armley in a more critical spirit, and its own independent report concluded that the prison's endemic overcrowding particularly affected remand prisoners, especially vulnerable young men.[78] There were also other young offender deaths, at Hull, Hindley and Swansea; that is, in busy often overcrowded local prisons that were not specifically designed for young, unsentenced prisoners.[79]

These deaths put an enormous strain on INQUEST, particularly around 1990. Apart from coping with what by this time had become an unusual run of adult custody deaths in prisons like Brixton, the workers' report for November of that year shows that five days were spent in Leeds at the Armley inquests; negotiations were going on to secure a barrister's services for the forthcoming Philip Knight inquest at Swansea, and attempts were being made to contact the family of Craig Walsh whose son had died in Glen Parva Young Offenders Institution. INQUEST was also supporting the families of two young men, Tony Hook and Iain Mckinlay, who had killed themselves in adjoining cells in Hindley, the latter after complaining of repeated sexual abuse.[80] He had been transferred to Hindley following the riot at Strangeways prison in April 1990.

Of all these tragic cases the one that perhaps received the most attention was that of Philip Knight who hanged himself in Swansea prison in July 1990. His behaviour in a local children's home had become disruptive and social workers had secured a certificate of unruliness against him. However, because there were no local authority secure accommodation places available, Philip had to be held temporarily in Swansea prison. As he had cut his wrists on at least one previous occasion while in care, and this was in any case his first time in prison, his social workers informed the prison that he was a potential suicide risk. Within a week Philip had slashed his wrists. He was then placed overnight in a hospital wing, not, as might have been better, in the observation ward with other prisoners, but in a single cell under hourly observation. Within a week – he was still waiting for secure accommodation to become available – he hanged himself. An open verdict was returned after a strong direction from the coroner that "lack of care" would be inappropriate. Deborah Coles for INQUEST, the only group to have supported the family and which had represented it throughout the hearing, made it fairly plain on national television that she believed the prison authorities were responsible for Philip's death.

The media attention given to the Philip Knight case encouraged the Howard League to launch a campaign to dissuade the government from its practice of remanding juveniles, however unruly or dangerous they might be, in prison. The government built its defence around the apparent shortage of places in secure accommodation provided by local authorities. As the high cost of providing such accommodation was a real bone of contention, the dilemma was not resolved until the government hit upon the idea of turning to the private sector to provide these places.

INQUEST was anxious that such a policy would simply expand the number of juveniles in custody and wondered whether there was evidence to support the taken-for-granted benefits of secure accommodation.[81] To be fair, the Howard League too was anxious about how juveniles were processed through the existing accommodation, pointing out for example, that in 1990 over 60 per cent of those in secure units had been admitted through non-criminal procedures which was "wholly inappropriate".[82]

Feltham

While the debate around juveniles in prison was gathering pace, there was a new cluster of deaths, this time in a young offender institution. Feltham was a large, sprawling institution, the product of an amalgamation between Ashford Remand Centre where Jim Heather-Hayes had died in 1982 and Feltham Youth Custody Centre. For several years the poor regime there had been the subject of criticism. In 1989 the Chief Inspector of Prisons had described the "largely barren" regime there as being "woefully short of expectations". A later report was hardly more reassuring; it was acknowledged that there had been some improvements, but commented that there was an over-reliance on the use of "control and restraint" techniques.[83] It was in such an environment that four young offenders took their own lives between August 1991 and March 1992. One was only 15 years old.

What the inquests into these deaths revealed about the regime at Feltham prompted the Howard League to set up its own independent inquiry, much as it had done into Armley two years before, but this time on a bigger scale. The League's interest in custodial deaths, belated although it might have been, had certain clear advantages for INQUEST. To start with, INQUEST's workers were simply overwhelmed by the sheer number of cases they were having to deal with at this time. Their best and most effective contribution was surely to work the various inquests, to tease out the key issues and let others run with them on the wider, political stage. Secondly, the League was a larger organization with the necessary resources to take on board such an inquiry without disrupting its other routines. INQUEST had the expertise it is true, but simply lacked the staff to carry on its other (and arguably more important) roles. In any case, INQUEST was to play its part. One of its workers provided the League with detailed case notes from the four inquests she had attended and gave extensive evidence to the inquiry on inquest procedures generally, while one of its founder members – he had recently (through INQUEST) represented the Knight, Cash, Hook and Mckinlay families at inquests – Tim Owen, served on the committee itself.[84]

When it was eventually published in 1993 the League's report revealed serious breaches of procedure. For example, form POL1 that identified Johnny Cash as an "exceptional risk" prisoner never reached Feltham, an error compounded by the failure of the medical officer to see him on his arrival, a clear breach of Circular Instruction 20/1989.[85] Johnny later hanged himself from the frame of an upturned bed in his cell in the segregation unit. Lee Waite took his own life in the same way. When admitted to Feltham he told the duty officer of previous attempts at self-harm. He also told them he was asthmatic. This information was not passed on to the probation officer who was supposed to share in the assessment of his needs. Also, when he returned from the courts he too was not seen by the medical officer, another clear breach of Circular Instruction 20/1989.[86]

Feltham's regime appeared to have changed very little since the Chief Inspector's report. Many of the prisoners had little work to do and most complained of boredom. Violence was acknowledged to be widespread. It was used – excessively according to the inquiry – by staff in the form of "restraint and control" techniques and between inmates. Bullying was endemic and attempts to restrain it unsuccessful, even during periods of supervised association. Lee Waite, for example, had suffered a brutal sexual assault just a few hours before his death which, according to the report, had taken place during association, even although both the officers on duty claimed that they were unaware of this.[87] Because the Home Office had forbidden prison officers at Feltham to speak about the four deaths under investigation, many of the report's details were either derived from the inquests or what families and friends had pieced together from other sources. This not only hampered the inquiry, it left families and friends feeling that they had been marginalized, as if the Home Office and officialdom were doing their best to keep them in the dark. This feeling was expressed very clearly by Mrs Waite who told the inquiry:

> I still don't feel as though I know the truth about what happened to Lee. Initially, I did not know there would be an inquest, and when I was told there would be, I didn't know what to expect or what to do . . . I thought the inquest would answer my questions about his death, but I was very disappointed . . . My son is dead. I know I can't bring him back, but why can't I be told the truth? The Home Office refused to let me see Lee's prison records . . . It's like some sort of cover up. The Home Office shouldn't be allowed to hold their own inquiries.[88]

The report observed that the only possible reason for withholding records was that they might reveal grounds for suing the Home Office.[89] It later took the opportunity to remind the Home Office of the Chief Inspector's recommendation that all parties in an inquest should enter it on an equal footing. Feltham's governor – he admitted faults that were later laid at his door – was not against such openness. It was he, for example, who had told Mrs Waite and other families about INQUEST and later publicly took the Home Secretary to task over his attitude towards the rights of families at inquests.

This exchange prompted the following leader from the *Guardian*:

If only there were more people like Joe Whitty – the prison governor who directly challenged the Home Secretary from the floor of a public meeting of the Prison Reform Trust . . . to make the penal system more open and accountable. Mr Whitty's complaint centred on the department's secretive approach to deaths in custody and the need to give grieving families more help and support in discovering what happened. The governor wants every family to have legal aid so they can get access to the various papers and reports on a death before the inquest. The Home Secretary replied that "the Lord Chancellor would have my guts for garters" if he tried to extend legal aid and anyway thought such aid inappropriate. Mr Whitty from Feltham stood his ground insisting that as a public servant he wanted to be publicly accountable when a death occurred in his prison. Four prisoners under his care have committed suicide. It was crucial there was no hint of a cover up. It is three years since the *Guardian*'s John Carvel began by drawing attention to the rise of suicides in prison. Much progress has been achieved since then. Judge Tumim produced a special report two years ago. A National Suicide Awareness Unit was set up [in the Home Office] in 1991 and now every prison has a suicide prevention group . . . The Woolf Report helped by improving prisoners' links with families. And yet the Home Office's instinct for secretness, as old as the cement in Dartmoor walls, remains . . . The most important message from Woolf was that justice must not stop at the prison gate. And justice demands that when a prisoner dies in custody, the next of kin should have access to his papers and files before the inquest. It should be a basic human right for the relatives to arrive at the inquest with the same information as the Prison Department. Judge Tumim insisted as much. Yet, two years on, it's still procrastinating. If Joe Whitty wants to be accountable, why is Kenneth Clarke resisting? (*Guardian* 26 March 1993)

While INQUEST obviously welcomed this public intervention, Whitty's support was not entirely disinterested. The more information he could release the more it would become apparent that his beleaguered staff could only muddle through, following suicide procedures as best they could, but, without more frontline staff, wholly unable to provide the positive regime that the Chief Inspector and others called for as long ago as 1989. He had earlier applied none too subtle pressure on the Home Office by pointing out that his legal duty to get prisoners to and from the courts had to be balanced against the need to give them more time out of their cells which was the agreed first step towards making life at Feltham more tolerable.[90]

These problems were compounded, as INQUEST and other lobby groups pointed out, by the vast size of Feltham's catchment area. Juveniles were remanded there from the whole of southern England and East Anglia. This meant that keeping in touch with family and friends was difficult. This arguably led directly to the death of 15-year-old Jeffrey Horler. Jeffrey had been arrested in Norfolk only to be sent 200 miles away to Feltham. Some time after he had been admitted he learnt that his grandmother had died. Greatly upset by this he requested compassionate leave through his probation officer to attend the funeral. This was duly given, but Norfolk Social Services decided that on balance the trouble and expense could not be justified. Soon afterwards Jeffrey committed suicide having confided to a friend that he was upset at not being allowed to attend the funeral.[91] He had also complained that he did not get many visits.

In October 1993 Feltham's catchment area was reduced to the Home Counties and East Anglia. But this is clearly still too large to sustain links with families and friends, especially at moments of crisis, the need for which is explicitly acknowledged in the government's own Standing Orders.

Given that the Chief Inspector's *Report on suicide prevention and self injury* (1990) devoted only six short paragraphs to juvenile and young offenders it is hardly surprising that this very practical restraint on Feltham went unnoticed. Perhaps it was felt that the problems facing juveniles and young offenders were much the same as those facing adult offenders. This judgement may turn out to be true in the longer term, but what reliable research we do have at this stage suggests that young offender suicides differ from other prison suicides in a number of ways. For example, they are likely to be serving shorter sentences and are significantly less likely to have received psychiatric treatment (while one third of all prison suicides had received psychiatric treatment, only about 13 per cent of young offenders had done so).[92]

Until the Home Office commissioned research in the mid-1980s, what was known about prison suicides in the UK was defined in fairly narrow academic terms. Alison Liebling, who later helped to carry out some of this research, has observed that prison suicide research had remained "isolated" from advances made in other areas of prison research, most notably the adoption of sociological perspectives that had significantly influenced applied research in the social sciences generally – and I would add, in academic criminology in particular. She went on to contrast the old with the new imperatives:

> the role of individual factors has been prominent; psychiatric explanations are assumed to play a major role in recent accounts of suicides both in and out of prison. Research in prison sociology [on the other hand] has indicated the importance of environmental variables in understanding issues such as absconding, riots and disturbances. The role of environmental variables and of interactive explanations for prison suicide have been slow to appear. Prison suicide research needs to be brought into the broader world of prison sociology.[93]

The evidence of this chapter suggests that INQUEST was a significant, although by no means the only, voice willing this transformation on the Home Office. Beyond its casework that came to annoy the Prison Department so much, and that arguably helped to persuade the Home Office to establish a Suicide Prevention Unit in 1990, beyond even its relentless public exposure of inadequate prison procedures at inquests, although significantly arising out of both, was this far more fundamental critique. It was perhaps not entirely inappropriate, therefore, that Alison Liebling and Tony Ward – he had drafted INQUEST's various submissions on suicide prevention – came together to edit a series of papers on "Deaths in custody" that were given at an international conference organized by the Institute for the Study and Treatment of Delinquency at Canterbury in 1991. Nor was it inappropriate, given the source of INQUEST's insights, for Deborah Coles to have insisted that this essentially academic conference should give over one of its sessions to hear the views of families who had lost friends or families in custody, although this was judged to be in "bad taste" in some quarters.[94]

Deaths in psychiatric and Special Hospitals

I pointed out earlier (Ch. 2) that INQUEST had always taken an interest in mentally ill patients, whether they were held in general psychiatric hospitals or what are known as Special Hospitals like Broadmoor. Key members of the Matthew O'Hara Committee, for example, had organized workshops on mental health issues around custody at Centreprise in 1981. At that time, however, there were few official worries expressed about the circumstances surrounding the deaths of mentally ill patients, whether these occurred in general psychiatric or Special Hospitals, or whether they were among those whose detention was voluntary or compulsory. Indeed, the Mental Health Act (1959) had abolished the requirement to report the deaths of all patients in psychiatric hospitals (whether compulsorily detained or not) to coroners. As a consequence, the number of reported deaths in psychiatric hospitals fell from around 10,000 to 1,000 in 1971.[95] True, the inquiry into Fairleigh Hospital in 1971 had recommended that reporting procedures should be reviewed, and it was a matter dealt with at some length in the Broderick report (1971) which recommended that there should be a duty to report, at least on those who had legally been detained. But neither of these recommendations was implemented.[96]

Even if they had been, however, they would not have been sufficient in themselves to guarantee that inquests were subsequently held. That discretion would have remained with the coroner, a discretion that was sometimes poorly exercised by any standard. For instance, MIND gave the example of a mentally ill patient who was said to have died from natural causes in a burns unit. The clinical cause of death was emphysema. This was uncritically accepted by the coroner and no inquest was at first contemplated, even although the circumstances surrounding the death were controversial. The patient had set himself on fire after being treated for depression. It was only after MIND's intervention that the coroner was persuaded to hold an inquest at which an "open verdict" was returned.[97] Such cases persuaded MIND and INQUEST to approach jointly the King's Fund for support of a project to investigate the whole issue of how deaths in all types of psychiatric hospitals were reported and processed.

Broadmoor

In fairness, not all coroners were quite so slack, and perhaps mindful of the Administration of Justice Act (1982) that encouraged coroners not only to hold inquests, but inquests with juries into all deaths in legal custody, the 1985 inquest into the death of Michael Martin, who had been detained in Broadmoor under the Mental Health Act (1983), became a very public affair. MIND, INQUEST and PROP involved themselves in the inquest in a joint effort to get at the truth, to prise open what until then had been a wall of secrecy surrounding Special Hospitals. As this case was to have important repercussions for patients being treated for schizophrenia, it is proper that we situate it and then follow it through in some detail.

Together with Ashford and Rampton, Broadmoor is one of the three Special Hospitals designated to treat those who need to be held "under conditions of special security on account of their dangerousness, violence or criminal propensities". Michael Martin was transferred to Broadmoor from Bexley Heath Hospital under Section 26 of the Mental Health Act (1959). At the time of the incident that led to his death he was held in the intensive care unit known as Norfolk House. This large Victorian block was organized around three wards. On the ground floor was ward one which received and looked after the most disturbed patients. As they progressed, patients moved up a floor to ward two and then finally to ward three on the top floor where supervision was less intense.

At the time of the incident that led to his death Michael Martin was in ward three. He had just returned from the canteen with other patients when he was involved in an argument with a student nurse. It was alleged that he was being threatening and abusive. This developed into a violent struggle during which a staff nurse gripped Mr Martin in a headlock to restrain him. An alarm was sounded, bringing several other nurses to the scene. Mr Martin was eventually overpowered and carried still struggling down several flights of steps to ward one. There he was forcibly injected and left sedated on his own in a side ward. He was periodically observed – an occasional glance to check that he was still breathing normally – and yet in spite of this he died just over an hour after being injected.[98] The jury at the subsequent inquest was told that Mr Martin had been the victim of a vicious headlock – there was extensive bruising – although it was the injection that was more likely to have been responsible for his death.

89

A "distinguished psychiatrist" expressed the view that it had been wholly inappropriate for the charge nurse to have administered the injection without first having consulted a doctor at the time.[99] Having heard the evidence the coroner expressed his preference for a verdict of accidental death, but was persuaded to allow the jury to add to their verdict "lack of care" by the family's counsel Ed Fitzgerald, one of INQUEST's regular advocates and an original member of the Matthew O'Hara Committee.[100]

This was an extremely important verdict for a number of reasons. First, recent changes to the Coroners' Rules had called into question whether lack of care verdicts such as that returned in the Jim Heather-Hayes case were still available. This made it clear that they were. Secondly, the publicity surrounding the case turned the spotlight on the general care of patients at Broadmoor. PROP, for example, latched on to the fact the senior medical officer in charge of Norfolk House at the time of Mr Martin's death was the same doctor it had criticized for carrying out unmodified electroconvulsive therapy – an issue taken up by MIND – and for the use of hormones as a treatment for sex offenders.[101] More particularly, the rules governing the use of "control and restraint" techniques, and the rules governing the use of powerful tranquillizers were raised, eventually leading the Secretary of State to order a special inquiry into the death of Michael Martin conducted by Shirley Ritchie QC.

The Ritchie report was critical of the general regime in Norfolk House; it was listless, building up a sense of frustration in both staff and inmates. It was also very critical of the use of neck holds and recommended that staff be given training in other methods of restraint and control. Finally, it recommended that the decision to administer a powerful tranquillizer should only be made by a doctor and not the nursing staff, and that observation of heavily sedated patients by staff should be constant and take place within the room where the patient was placed and not from without.[102] The Secretary of State accepted all the report's recommendations, except for arguably the most important one about the need for a doctor to be present at the scene to make the decision about whether or not to administer a tranquillizer after a violent incident. His argument was that the advance prescription to be administered in special circumstances was accepted medical practice.[103]

Shortly after the publication of the Ritchie report in April 1985 a series of articles appeared in *The Times* suggesting that the hospital was intent on shedding its oppressive image and that staff were now putting their "trust in therapy".[104] While no doubt some progress was made in this respect, serious flaws in Broadmoor's practice were revealed in two further sudden deaths, those of Joseph Watts in August 1988 and Orville Blackwood in August 1991.

Like Michael Martin, Joseph Watts died after he had been injected with a powerful tranquillizer. Whether he should have been injected at all became a central issue at the inquest. It was accepted that he was upset by a clinical decision that restricted his recreational opportunities, and that he had been involved in a serious altercation with another patient. But at the time of his seclusion and sedation the situation had apparently been resolved, at least to the extent that the patients were no longer fighting when the staff arrived. Yet no attempt was made to talk to either of them, or alternatives to seclusion seriously considered. Furthermore, it came to light that one of the key recommendations of the Ritchie report that patients who had been heavily sedated should be continuously observed by staff inside the room where they have been placed was not followed. Indeed, it was even claimed that an internal memorandum drawing attention to this recommendation was only circulated throughout the hospital in December 1988, three months after the death under investigation.[105] The jury returned a verdict of accidental death, which disappointed INQUEST and other groups supporting the family.

The debate about what was by then being labelled in the press as the "sudden death syndrome", was fuelled still further by the death of Orville Blackwood. Mr Blackwood had been sentenced to four years in prison for robbery, but later transferred to Broadmoor. He was very mentally disturbed and was moved at various times between different wards, eventually ending up in the Special Care Unit – the by then upgraded Norfolk House equivalent – where the highest grade of secure care was promised. On the day of his death Mr Blackwood refused to attend occupational therapy and urged other patients to do the same. He was persuaded to go to the seclusion room which he did voluntarily. There he refused his midday meal and his medicine. A decision was later taken to administer his medication by force if necessary. A doctor arrived accompanied by five – or perhaps even seven – attendants, but Mr Blackwood refused to co-operate, allegedly striking out at the doctor. He was quickly secured and the injection given. Within two or three minutes of the injection being given he was found dead by nurses re-entering the room.[106]

Given what had previously happened to Michael Martin and Joseph Watts, it was hardly surprising that some references would be made to these cases at the inquest into Orville Blackwood's death. However, these references were strenuously resisted by the coroner who also refused to consider even a verdict of "lack of care", the jury eventually returning another verdict of "accidental death". The coroner's judgment was challenged in the Divisional Court by Ed Fitzgerald and a fresh inquest ordered, although a different jury again returned the same verdict.

While the coroner might not have seen the relevance of the connection between these cases, the Special Hospitals Service Agency which took over the running of these Special Hospitals in England in 1991 wisely took a very different view, ordering not only an inquiry into how Mr Blackwood died, but also into any "significant common factors" between all three deaths.[107] The report of this inquiry was considerably delayed. This was partly because a second inquest had been ordered into Orville Blackwood's death, but also no doubt because the Prison Officers' Association had discouraged its members from co-operating with the inquiry "in any way".[108]

Whether or not this benefited the staff directly involved is an open question, not least because the inquiry found that some of the front-line staff had been at fault. For example, the report made it plain that it did believe that Mr Blackwood had been handled well on the day but agreed that there had been some "over reaction" among the staff, although it was less critical than the Ritchie report had been in similar circumstances about lack of observation in the seclusion room.[109] However, it was extremely critical of the way in which Orville Blackwood's mother – Mrs Buckley – had been treated, not least over the circumstances in which she was expected to view her son's body in the mortuary, something that the senior porter had at first said was impossible.[110] (Mrs Buckley later spoke about her son's death at INQUEST's 1992 AGM.)

But the report not only criticized frontline staff. Indeed, its criticisms of management were arguably more trenchant. In particular, it accused the hospital's management team of being blasé, of having failed to respond to earlier criticisms of its procedures surrounding the death of Joseph Watts:

> It is quite clear to us that the concerns raised in the Watts report have *not* been properly addressed. There remains a serious gulf between the official policies and beliefs of the Hospital Management Team and the actual practice at ward level [original emphasis].[111]

Yet as damning as such criticism was, perhaps the most worrying thing to come out of the inquiry was the evidence on the use of drugs. Simply put, serious questions were raised about neuroleptic drugs commonly used in the treatment of schizophrenia. Michael Martin, Joseph Watts and Orville Blackwood had all been diagnosed as suffering from schizophrenia in varying degrees, and all had been treated with neuroleptic drugs. The report acknowledged that there "appeared to be" a link between such drugs and death on "excited, aroused patients".[112] It therefore called for more research into neuroleptic medication, supporting a suggestion put forward at the Ashworth inquiry (see below) that a review of the link between such medication and sudden, unexpected deaths should be undertaken by the Committee on the Safety of Medicines and the Royal College of Psychiatrists.[113]

INQUEST obviously welcomed these recommendations. However, it was keen to point out that this was not a problem confined only to Special Hospitals:

> Department of Health and the psychiatric professions are hiding their heads in the sand if they think that deaths involving these drugs are rare. They are not collected nor publicized. This case [Orville Blackwood] received more public attention because it happened in Broadmoor; deaths are occurring in smaller hospitals up and down the country at a rate of at least one per month – and no one hears about them.
>
> Unless the Department of Health responds to the report's recommendations, and funds independent research into these drugs, it is self evident that a causal link with death will never be proven to scientific standards. And until a link is proven, psychiatrists will continue to prescribe them – inappropriately – and people will continue to die as a result.[114]

This was a timely reminder of just how widespread the problem was, although the media continued to focus on Special Hospitals, not so much because of Broadmoor, but because of Ashworth.

Inquiry into Ashworth

Ashworth Special Hospital had escaped serious controversy until 1991 when a television programme made what appeared to be serious allegations of cruelty against patients. A committee of inquiry chaired by

Louis Blom-Cooper was immediately appointed. The Prison Officers' Association at one point refused to co-operate with the committee but its attempts to block the inquiry in the High Court eventually failed.

The committee found a whole catalogue of appalling practices: improper placements; inadequate nursing and medical care; inadequate investigation of complaints about criminal violence and psychological harm; and, not perhaps surprisingly, a set of procedures in place that hindered families from finding out about how their relatives had died. It was on this last issue, which had implications for the whole of the Special Hospital system and not just Ashworth, that INQUEST was invited to submit evidence. This it did in open session during March 1992.

I should perhaps point out here that sudden deaths associated with the prescription of neuroleptic drugs did figure prominently in the Ashworth inquiry around the death of Sean Walton, but INQUEST had been invited to give evidence around access and secrecy rather than on medical issues *per se*.

In her opening remarks to the inquiry Deborah Coles began by emphasizing how families were treated:

> Families' experiences are characterized by lack of information, secrecy and often what they feel is indifference by the authorities and by the institution in which the deceased has died. They have a desperate desire to know the circumstances of the death and to find out what has actually happened. What they feel is that they face a wall of silence. The system of finding out what happened is totally inaccessible . . . the other key thing about deaths in custody is that because of the nature of custodial institutions families often have very limited access to people in Special Hospitals and are often kept at arms length throughout that person's detention. This causes tremendous distress and confusion, to find out that somebody has died and to be given no information. They find they have little information during the period of detention and this is made worse after the death when they are told absolutely nothing.[115]

This secrecy, this wall of silence had two separate but related dimensions. The first arose from the discretionary powers of coroners and inquest procedures. Would there be an inquest? Would there be a jury? Could the family afford to be legally represented, which most families felt was desirable in cases involving Special Hospitals? Secondly, there were the internal hospital procedures. Would all the medical records be made available? Would those responsible for the treatment be questioned?

It was to these issues – relevant of course to investigating deaths in most forms of custody – that INQUEST directed its attention. Not surprisingly it called for mandatory inquests – with juries – into the deaths of all those legally detained in psychiatric hospitals – and not just Special Hospitals. It also restated the demand for legal aid and for advance disclosure of all medical records relating to the deceased. It also suggested that families and friends might be allowed to visit the scene of the death and to talk informally to those most directly involved. The need to improve the quality and thoroughness of postmortems was raised, a longstanding concern with INQUEST that stretched back to the Jimmy Kelly case. Finally, the case for public inquiries to replace inquests in controversial cases was again floated.[116]

Deborah Coles and June Tweedie felt confident their open session had gone well. The retired coroner invited to the same session – he had been in charge of the controversial inquest into the deaths at Hillsborough stadium – had been less obstructive than they had anticipated. Indeed, in his written evidence he had even supported INQUEST's call for legal aid. This confidence was reflected in the committee's final report, not least its general approach, which argued that:

The mere occurrence of a patient death in a Special Hospital largely out of public mind and within the curtilage of a prison like institution, instinctively excites the notion that the death was unnatural . . . The only sensible public reaction . . . is for the relevant authorities to treat any death in a Special Hospital as suspicious, even if suspicion is proved mostly, if not always, unfounded. The approach by the authorities is not just a question of doing everything to avoid accusation and allegation afterwards, but because instances of death in closed institutions merit particular attention due to the perceived, if not real, heightened risk of assaults on patients by fellow patients, or unhappily on occasions, by staff. The index of suspicion of unnatural deaths is even higher where the death occurs when the patient is in seclusion. To start from a position of suspicion leads, therefore, to the need for special provision relating to the investigation of any death of a patient in a Special Hospital.[117]

More particularly, this special provision should include the summoning of inquests with juries. The coroner's power in this respect, although remaining discretionary, should be exercised in line with policy elsewhere. That is to say:

We would endorse the guidance given in Home Office Circular 33/1969 and 23/1981 that it is desirable for an inquest to be held with a jury in all cases of a death occurring in any form of legal custody, even though the death may have occurred in hospital or elsewhere, even though it may have been due to natural causes. Coroners we think should invariably exercise their discretion and organize an inquest with a jury whenever a person dies in a Special Hospital, irrespective of the perceived cause of death.[118]

The emphasis on juries was welcomed by INQUEST, not least because the Prison Officers' Association had predictably originally argued against their use, preferring to put their faith in the coroner sitting alone. On the question of legal aid the committee was plainly sympathetic, arguing that, "we recognize that the absence of the wherewithal to finance legal representation at coroners' inquests is a piece of social injustice". However, the committee did not wish to add its "puny voice" to the chorus clamouring for this particular injustice to be righted. Instead it took a more pragmatic approach, suggesting that INQUEST, "which holds itself out to assist – and does so remarkably well – the relations of those who die in legal custody, should be properly funded" in such cases, "even if the representation would inevitably have to be selective".[119]

INQUEST did not expect (or want) this recommendation to be acted upon – nor was it – but it was at least another public recognition of the problem and a reasoned attempt to resolve it. The report was similarly pragmatic, although arguably less convincing, in its response to the many deficiencies in inquest procedures and the suggestion by INQUEST that more use might be made of public inquiries, especially in controversial cases. The report's main line of argument here was that the wholesale reform of inquest procedures for such few cases had been made less pressing by the provisions of the recent Access to Health Records Act (1990) which gives the legal right of access to medical records – a right that extends to the legal representatives of the dead patients:

Armed with this prime documentary material relative to the case and treatment of patients before death, families will be in a position to probe at the inquest the reasons why their relative died. The present obstacles to the receipt of information will be removed and will materially assist the coroner and the coroner's jury to reach verdicts which are both objectively satisfactory and will often provide contentment to grieving families.[120]

INQUEST was probably less sanguine than the committee that this was sufficient to guarantee an acceptable level of accountability, even although it was recommended that hospitals should immediately inform the deceased relatives of their rights under the new Act and that the results of the hospital's own internal inquiries should be made available to them.[121]

Much more clear-cut were the report's recommendations on post-mortems. The committee was clearly appalled by the paucity of the one submitted on Sean Walton – taking the pathologist publicly to task – and suggested several changes aimed at highlighting the circumstances surrounding deaths, including possible contributory causes.[122]

It is important to report that the emphasis I have chosen to give to the high-profile deaths in Special Hospitals should not hide the fact that INQUEST was at the same time dealing with equally controversial deaths in other, ordinary psychiatric hospitals. For example, in 1990–1 it was concerned with the deaths of Lyndon Robertson and Gina Ditchman. The former had recently been released from the Derby Unit at Horton Hospital, while the latter had died there. At the inquest on both patients concerns were expressed about the use of certain neuroleptic drugs. In the case of Gina Ditchman the postmortem revealed that she had 17 times above the normal, therapeutic level of Largactil in her system.[123]

INQUEST's contribution to the debate on deaths in Special Hospitals was a significant one. In association with MIND it had highlighted such deaths long before the controversy over Ashworth was to bring the Specials to the forefront of public attention. True, it was arguably sometimes the junior partner in this, but this was never a problem as INQUEST's working relationship with MIND in the persons of Lydia Sinclair and Ian Bynoe was always a complementary one. MIND thoroughly understood the legal framework surrounding mental health. INQUEST lent its expertise to working inquests, drawing on a pool of lawyers whose relationship with both groups was close, even over-lapping.

To suggest that the various inquests I have referred to were "worked" by INQUEST could invite the suggestion that the families involved were being exploited, that the bereaved were being used for a wider agenda to "get at" the Specials whose dedicated staff were carrying out a thankless task. To the extent that individual cases exposed poor management, inadequate practices or plain incompetence then certainly the Specials were being "got at". But there is little or no evidence that such exposures were pursued at the expense of the bereaved. Indeed, reading the Ashworth report rather suggests that if the families portrayed there were typical, that is to say, "they perceive themselves to be powerless" in relation to the hospital authorities who view them at best as irritants, then it might simply be that groups like INQUEST are providing the bereaved with just the strength and support that the Specials so obviously fail to provide.[124]

Asylum seekers

The United Nations adopted its Convention Relating to the Status of Refugees at the outbreak of the Cold War in 1951. It was aimed at accommodating a relatively small number of individuals who were escaping political persecution, not least in the Soviet bloc. However, by the late 1980s and particularly after the fall of the Berlin Wall in 1989, this trickle had turned into something of a flood. In 1984, for example, in western Europe there were 100,000 applications for asylum; by 1992 there were well over 690,000.[125] This led to emergency measures in countries like Germany, France and Britain to restrict entry. This arguably fuelled xenophobia and encouraged the suspicion that every asylum seeker was an illegal immigrant in disguise, seeking the economic advantages the West had to offer rather than fleeing political persecution. While INQUEST's first contact with detained asylum seekers pre-dates these more restrictive policies, the stresses and strains they were to impose form the backdrop to its more recent involvement.

Article one of the United Nations Convention Relating to the Status of Refugees defines an asylum seeker as anyone who has a "well founded fear of persecution for reasons of race, religion, nationality, membership of a particular social group or opinion, is outside the country of his nationality, owing to such fear, is unwilling to avail himself of the protection of that country". On this definition Ahmed Katangole believed he would have no difficulty in securing political asylum in Britain. He claimed he was a member of a militant organization opposed to the central government of Uganda whose reputation for intolerance towards any form of opposition was well known. Although originally detained at Gatwick airport pending inquiries, Mr Katangole was soon able to provide the authorities with a permanent address in Britain and he was granted temporary permission to stay.[126]

Under this temporary arrangement Mr Katangole was obliged to report any change of address. When he sought to comply with this requirement by arranging what should have been a routine visit to the immigration authorities he was summarily arrested and taken immediately to Gatwick airport to be deported. Mr Katangole took an overdose in order to prevent this, collapsed and was rushed to a local hospital. The hospital administration sensibly informed the Ugandan Welfare Action Group (UWAG) who came to collect him, only to find that he had been spirited away by the authorities.

Over the next few days Mr Katangole was moved between various sites, eventually ending up in Pentonville prison rather than in one of the specialist detention facilities intended for detainees. The prison psychiatrist warned that if Mr Katangole continued to be imprisoned in Pentonville and threatened with deportation, suicide was the likely outcome of his reactive depression. Efforts to obtain his release through the intervention of a sympathetic MP were well under way, but UWAG found great difficulty in finding out exactly which prison was holding Mr Katangole. Unaware of the group's efforts, and fearing he would be deported, Mr Katangole hanged himself in Pentonville within a fortnight of his totally unexpected arrest in March 1977.[127]

This was the first of several asylum cases INQUEST was to become involved with. On this occasion it had worked closely with UWAG whose solicitor was Louise Balmain, a member of INQUEST's Executive Committee. With Ed Fitzgerald she worked the subsequent inquest to uncover an embarrassing level of official incompetence and neglect, so much so that the jury reached the unique and damning verdict of "suicide due to official indifference and lack of care".[128]

The death of Mr Katangole was to spotlight the plight of refugees and raise questions about how the government was responding to their special needs. For example, if short-term detention at the point of entry was prudent – as in the case of Mr Katangole – to check documents and trace UK contacts, was more prolonged detention in an immigration centre like Harmondsworth and Hasler really necessary, let alone in ordinary wings of mainstream local prisons like Pentonville and Wandsworth? Was detention – and Britain was increasingly more inclined to use it than most other EEC countries – simply not the government sending out a message to would-be asylum seekers that it was tough on refugees, and that even before a decision about their status was reached it was likely that applicants would have to spend a long time in detention, perhaps even in an overcrowded prison with convicted criminals?[129] Was the government unaware of the vulnerability of these detainees? That uncertainties about their future and those of their families and friends whom they have had to leave behind can lead to desperate measures? In the words of Tom Lando – for the Medical Foundation for the Victims of Torture – which were read out at INQUEST's 1989 AGM:

> Many of our patients, who have come here in the belief that the United Kingdom represents freedom, respect for human rights and their final hope for survival, find themselves again detained, in prison or a detention centre, sometimes for many months and for no apparent reason. The psychological effect of this is not hard to imagine, nor is it difficult to understand that a survivor of torture who, having escaped to "freedom", and being incarcerated with an apparent removal of his final hopes, will seriously consider suicide as the only possible alternative to deportation.[130]

In more coded language the Chief Inspector of Prisons was to comment on the sense of isolation and helplessness that detainees feel and voiced his strong reservations about their detention in prison, notably in Pentonville.[131]

The government's response to these anxieties was to suggest that the growing use of detention was simply a reaction to the pressure of numbers, including a growing number of bogus claimants. While the question of bogus claimants is a contentious one – it is often impossible for victims of large-scale ethnic or religious upheavals (in Bosnia, for example) to produce detailed evidence of their own individual persecution – there was unquestionably pressure on the asylum system. For example, in 1986 when Mr Katangole came to Britain there were just 5,700 applicants for asylum, whereas by 1991 they had peaked at 73,400.[132] This was why by the early 1990s the government was planning to expand the number of detention centres available for refugees by opening Campsfield near Oxford, why a number of prisons such as Rochester and Doncaster were being targeted and modified to accept overspill populations on a more permanent basis, and why new fast track procedures for processing asylum seekers were introduced in the Asylum and Immigration Appeals Act (1993).

The government was unrepentant that under this Act – in line with the original Immigration Act (1971) – its administrative procedures were not subject to the jurisdiction of the courts, nor was it defensive about the new measures to fingerprint applicants or the very short space of time – 48 hours – that the new Act allowed for appeals in those asylum applications that its own officials had judged to be "manifestly" unfounded. All these measures by the way were in line with proposals from the European Commission.[133] It is not necessary to go into further detail about the long drawn-out controversy surrounding this Act, or to evaluate the claim that it has led to a smaller percentage of permanent and exceptional leave (semi-permanent) applications being granted, but it is at this point that INQUEST re-entered this particular arena through the high profile case of Omasase Lumumba.[134]

Omasase Lumumba

Mr Lumumba was the nephew of Patrice Lumumba, the first democratically elected President of Zaire who, it is now accepted, was forced out of office by the United States (in collusion with the United Nations) and replaced by President Mabuto. Since then the Lumumba family has suffered persecution in Zaire and Omasase Lumumba had at first sought refuge in Switzerland where he lived for ten years before coming to London in 1991. He decided to come to England on a forged passport when his marriage to a Swiss woman ended. He came to the attention of the police in south London in connection with a stolen child's bicycle and an alleged assault, although neither of these accusations was ever proved. Suspecting his illegal status after an initial interview, the police called in the immigration service who were convinced that his claim to asylum was unjustified and he was ordered directly to Pentonville prison. It was there that he died a few weeks later in October 1991.[135]

The circumstances surrounding his death were in one sense straightforward. Early one morning he was being taken to the prison hospital from his cell in the segregation unit. On reaching the central area of the prison he refused to go any further. He did not struggle in any way, or become abusive or threatening. The two escorting guards then held the prisoner by the head and arms and led him back to a cell in the segregation unit. By this time there were six prison officers and one governor-grade officer in attendance. An attempt was then made to remove all Mr Lumumba's clothes using scissors. This was done because he was believed to be a suicide risk. Mr Lumumba resisted and a prolonged struggle ensued. The officers claimed to have used approved control and restraint techniques at all times, although this was contested by a prisoner in a nearby cell. The struggle lasted for between 10 and 15 minutes at which point the prisoner became limp. By the time the prison medical officer came Mr Lumumba was clearly unconscious and attempts to revive him failed.[136]

The pathologist's report indicated that there were no external injuries that could have caused death; nor was there any evidence that it was attributable to any significant natural disease. It was concluded, however, that there was a strong possibility that Mr Lumumba died as a result of a cardiac arrest following a long struggle, although this explanation could not entirely rule out the possibility that Mr Lumumba's breathing had been interfered with during the struggle, leading him to asphyxiate.

The fact that there was no precise medical cause of death was to present INQUEST, Mr Lumumba's solicitors and his counsel with an unexpected difficulty. They had intended to argue – on the basis of evidence heard in open court – for a number of possible verdicts to be put to the jury, including "unlawful killing" and "lack of care". However, during the course of the legal arguments towards the end of the hearing the coroner ruled that he had no intention of putting "lack of care" or "unlawful killing" verdicts forward for consideration by the jury as the pathologist could not give a precise cause of death. At this point Mr Lumumba's counsel and one of INQUEST's most experienced barristers, Tim Owen, politely pointed out to the coroner that neither the absence of a body nor a postmortem report establishing the cause of death would prevent a verdict of manslaughter being returned in criminal cases and that a similar logic – which distinguished between medical and legal evidence – should be applied in this case.

This opinion was flatly rejected. However, the coroner did agree to adjourn the case, even at so late a stage, in order that counsel might test this ruling in the Divisional Court. This was an extremely uncertain manoeuvre, as the Court of Appeal had recently made it quite clear (*R. v. HM Coroner for East Kent ex parte Spooner and others*) that it only expected to hear arguments when verdicts had been returned. On this occasion, however, an exception was made and the coroner's ruling thrown out. At a subsequent hearing the jury took just 25 minutes to decide by an eight to one majority that Mr Lumumba had been unlawfully killed as a result of "excessive force" being used by the application of "improper" methods of control and restraint.[137]

Given Mr Lumumba's family connections the case was extensively reported in the media. Attempts were made to link it to wider issues. One newspaper, for example, argued that:

> The Lumumba inquest comes at a time when the Asylum Bill has now reached the House of Lords and will therefore almost certainly become law in the near future. Among the furore and hysteria surrounding the question of refugees and asylum seekers, not only in Britain but throughout "Fortress Europe" the Lumumba tragedy is a sad but timely reminder of the fact that the overwhelming cause of the refugee problem is the imposition of pro-western, anti-popular regimes in the Third World and the repression, ethnic conflict, corruption, poverty and under-development that come in their wake.
>
> When the Asylum Bill becomes law, far more refugees can expect to be placed in detention and there will be no limit to the time for which such people may be detained, and in most cases no chance of bail or having the detention reviewed by the court. Furthermore, it is a proposal that all those seeking asylum should be subject to finger-printing, effectively criminalizing them. (*Caribbean Times* 16 February 1993)

It had taken more than two years to secure the verdict on Omasase Lumumba. His immediate family – a brother and a sister – were in Switzerland and therefore unable to play a major role in the legal processes I have outlined. The bulk of this was done by Mr Lumumba's solicitor, Matthew Davies, and INQUEST. As no legal aid was available counsel gave his services free. Predictably their task had not been made easier by the Home Office's refusal to give counsel sight of the internal Prison Department inquiry into Lumumba's death. This was later justified along the usual lines that, "it is our policy not to release such documents for publication as the information contained within the report was given on the basis of confidentiality".[138]

The secrecy surrounding this particular document, and the generally unhelpful attitude of the Treasury Solicitor who took an unusually close interest in this case, persuaded INQUEST and others that more investigation was required and the Crown Prosecution Service was again approached after the verdict had been returned. The CPS had already been involved, the coroner having sent off details of his own investigation at an earlier stage in the proceedings. On that occasion no action had been recommended, but it was now felt that the verdict might persuade the CPS to think again. Attention was drawn to the fact that the Divisional Court had itself agreed that there were grounds for an unlawful killing verdict to be considered; that the jury had been satisfied "beyond all reasonable doubt" that manslaughter had been committed; and that it had become apparent that the Prison Department's own internal inquiry had failed to interview a key witness, the prisoner who claimed to have witnessed the struggle. The CPS found none of these reasons compelling and again reiterated that having reviewed all the evidence they were still not convinced "that there were realistic prospects of a conviction".

With this second refusal to initiate criminal proceedings effort was redirected towards securing an independent public inquiry. It was intended that this should go beyond the circumstances immediately surrounding Mr Lumumba's death to look at the procedures under which he was arrested and detained. It was hoped that this would provide a wider platform to engage other groups. For example, evidence was put forward that suggested that Lumumba had been detained in Pentonville as a matter of administrative convenience and not because – as the Home Office claimed – his behaviour was disruptive, which is the usual justification for holding asylum seekers in prison rather than in detention centres. The immigration officer who had interviewed Lumumba in south London had found him calm. He had felt no reason to make any special recommendations about Mr Lumumba's detention and under questioning had agreed that he could have gone to any one of several destinations. In other words, there appeared to be no official policy of using prison for asylum seekers as a last resort. Indeed, during the inquest it was even implied that where detainees were placed could just as easily depend on who in the immigration service might be required to do the next interview rather than any more sensitive criteria that placed the needs of the asylum seeker first.

The call for a public inquiry came from Chris Smith MP whose constituency included Pentonville. An Early Day Motion on the case, initiated by Graham Allen, the Opposition spokesman on immigration affairs, attracted the support of 13 MPs. This linked Mr Lumumba's death to a list of reforms about procedures governing the detention of asylum seekers, including the right to be given written reasons for their detention and for these reasons to be challenged in the courts.[139] This initiative was supported by Amnesty International which not only vigorously contested this particular case, but also used the occasion to reiterate its concern:

> that the procedures to review the decision to detain an asylum seeker violate international standards, in most cases the detainee is not informed of the specific reasons for his or her detention; the review of the detention is internal, it is not conducted by a judicial or similar authority; and the detainee and his or her counsel have no opportunity to attend and participate in the review.[140]

Together with Matthew Davies INQUEST networked with a whole range of other lobby groups – some of them less well known than Amnesty – to secure publicity for the Lumumba verdict, and was instrumental with the Joint Council for the Welfare of Immigrants in drafting a Charter for Immigration Detainees that was eventually launched in May 1994. This was in many ways a hybrid document. The initial demands were for legal safeguards along the lines of those already referred to, focusing only later on INQUEST's special concerns, including the full disclosure of records, reports and assessments in cases where detainees have died in custody and that relatives and friends of the deceased should be entitled to legal aid. The Charter was eventually signed by 16 organizations, including Liberty, the Prison Reform Trust and the Church Commission for Racial Justice.[141]

INQUEST's involvement with these cases was fully justified. In almost no other area of public life do government officials – quite low-ranking officials in some cases – have such wide powers to deprive people of their liberty unhindered by the courts. In this respect immigration officials have greater powers than do the police. When vulnerable people die in these circumstances it is therefore doubly important that what little accountability there is should be exercised to the full. However, whether INQUEST should have devoted so much of its limited time and resources to drawing up and promoting the Charter is arguable. On the plus side, it helped to enlarge its network of supporters to include groups like the Catholic Bishops' Conference. It also helped to keep its activities before the public as the plight of asylum seekers continued high on the political agenda with the sustained campaign by local residents to close Campsfield Detention Centre following a hunger strike there in May 1994 by 144 out of 199 detainees, and a serious riot there sometime later when the police had to be called in to regain control. On the other hand, most of the demands enshrined in the Charter were already common currency in the immigration lobby, and given the pressures on its time it is at least arguable that it would have been more cost effective to have become a signatory to the Charter rather than one of its organizing sponsors.

Chapter 5

Other issues

I have pointed out that while INQUEST is primarily concerned with deaths in and around state custody, this has not prevented it from giving legal advice on deaths that have occurred in other circumstances, or from taking on board a limited number of non-custodial cases. It is to some of these circumstances and cases that we now turn, not least because they tell us still more about how inquests function and how some would argue that in very exceptional circumstances they might need to be superseded altogether.

Disasters

In recent years there have been a number of disasters, some of which are firmly engraved on the public psyche, the sinking of the ferry at Zeebrugge, the fire on the North Sea oil platform Piper Alpha, the deaths of spectators at Hillsborough football stadium and the fire in the tube station at King's Cross to name just four. When such tragedies occur the families involved will normally come together for mutual emotional support and to secure legal advice. Increasingly social service departments become involved as more is learnt about how to manage the trauma involved in the aftermath of such events. This collective action, which can lead to the creation of quite longstanding groups, e.g. the Herald Families Association, Disaster Action, reduces the need for groups like INQUEST which is mostly called upon to help individual families – sometimes their supporters – who feel isolated and powerless. However, given its considerable expertise INQUEST has played some part in many of these cases, albeit sometimes at a tangent. This was particularly so in the Hillsborough and *Marchioness* disasters.

107

Hillsborough

Hillsborough was the chosen venue for a Football Association semi-final cup tie between Liverpool and Manchester United in April 1989. The ground was owned by Sheffield Wednesday Football Club which had staged many semi-finals in the past. On the day in question there was a delay in getting Liverpool supporters into the ground in time for the kick-off. Who was responsible for this and the build-up of a large crowd at the Leppings Lane end remains a matter of bitter dispute between the police and supporters. What followed, however, now seems reasonably clear. Fearing that supporters would be crushed before they could pass through the turnstiles, the police – they were directly responsible for managing the crowd – decided to open a gate at the Leppings Lane end through which fans spilled, although in reasonably good order, onto an inner concourse. Once on the con-course the supporters had to choose one of several tunnels that would take them to a series of pens on the terraces surrounding the pitch. They had no means of knowing which tunnel to take. The entrance to each was unattended. Nor had they any means of knowing which of the pens at the ends of the tunnels were overcrowded as these were out of sight. Quite naturally – although tragically as it turned out – many took the tunnel directly ahead of them into pens 3 and 4 which were already overcrowded. The crush that this caused led to the deaths of 95 Liverpool supporters, many of them teenagers.

The scale of the disaster led to an immediate public inquiry directed by Lord Justice Taylor whose interim report identified overcrowding and poor crowd control as the principal causes of the disaster. The police were clearly responsible, accepting a "high proportion of liabil-ity" in many of the compensation cases that followed.[1] The role and legal responsibilities of the police were later clearly defined in a number of formal legal judgments delivered by Lord Keith:

> The South Yorkshire police force, which was responsible for crowd control at the match, allowed an excessively large number of intending spectators to enter the ground at the Leppings Lane end . . . they crammed into pens 3 and 4 . . . and in the resulting crush 95 people were killed and over 400 physically injured . . . The Chief Constable of Yorkshire has admitted liability and neg-ligence in respect of the deaths and physical injuries.[2]

INQUEST's involvement with the Hillsborough case came firstly (and mainly) through Phil Scraton who had been given financial support by Liverpool City Council to monitor and interpret legal, press and public reactions to the tragedy. The outcome of the Hillsborough project, as it came to be called, was finally published in 1995 and *No last rights* contains a unique assessment of how inquest procedures served, or arguably failed to serve, the bereaved in the aftermath of the disaster. Before we get to this assessment the legal stages following the tragedy need to be briefly sketched.

First and most obviously perhaps, we need to keep in mind that the formal inquests into the 95 deaths first opened but then adjourned almost immediately. This was because Lord Chief Justice Taylor – with the help of the West Midlands Police Force – was carrying out his own inquiry that might lead to criminal prosecutions. But this anticipated delay became more prolonged when the results of the inquiry – Lord Justice Taylor's interim report – were sent to the DPP whose officials decided that they needed even more information before they could decide whether any individual or body should be prosecuted. So for about a year there was no movement on the inquests and families were left not knowing how or when – except in very general terms – their relatives had died. This prompted several lawyers from the Hillsborough Steering Group which had been set up to represent the families to write to the coroner expressing their anxieties and asking if anything could be done.[3]

In an attempt to meet these anxieties coroner Popper approached the DPP for permission to hold a series of inquests into each of the 95 deaths that would take only very limited medical evidence, plus evidence to establish where the deceased had last been seen alive and where he or she was subsequently identified as being dead. The wider circumstances surrounding the deaths would not be addressed in order not to prejudice any possible, later legal proceedings. A generic inquest to look into these wider issues would be held later, depending again on the DPP's decision. Surprisingly, perhaps, the DPP agreed with this highly unusual procedure but insisted that the strict limits suggested by the coroner should not be breached.[4]

The mini inquests eventually took place in April 1990 at Sheffield town hall. Each lasted about 30 minutes, and the coroner was firm in not allowing questions that might "muddy the waters" of any future criminal action, although at the same time reassuring families that these questions could be legitimately raised at the generic inquest. As the coroner himself put it before the mini inquests, "I want people to leave here saying, 'I know I haven't heard all the answers but I know more than I did when I started.'"[5]

Whether the families felt like this after the inquests is doubtful. For all the coroner's good intentions, the formal and somewhat conveyer-belt nature of the process – eight inquests were heard each day – did little to put families at their ease or even answer some of the basic "medical" questions.[6] Some families and their lawyers had not supported the mini inquests on the basis that they were convinced that criminal proceedings would almost certainly be taken against the police, the council, their safety consultants, Eastwood & Partners, or Sheffield Wednesday, and that the coroner might subsequently then decide against an inquest on the basis that the circumstances surrounding the deaths had already been fully investigated, that all that was needed to be known about the deaths was known and a verdict handed down. In the event, this anxiety was unfounded. In the following September (1990) the DPP finally decided not to prosecute any body or individual.[7]

This left the way clear for the generic inquest – which opened in November 1990 – to get off to a very controversial start when on the basis of highly tendentious medical evidence, the coroner decided on a cut-off point of 3.15 p.m. This gave rise to the obvious complaint that while families would be allowed to address the central issue about how such a tragedy had happened, they would be denied the chance to probe the equally important question, namely, given that it did happen, was enough done to look after those who almost certainly still lay dying or were injured after 3.15 p.m.? June Tweedie from INQUEST had advised the steering group through one of its members immediately to challenge the coroner's ruling in the Divisional Court, but this advice was rejected and the inquest proceeded within the boundaries defined by the coroner.[8]

Other aspects of the proceedings were arguably also unsatisfactory. For example, counsel for the families – they had to raise £150,000 – was easily outmanoeuvred by a phalanx of legal expertise representing variously the police, local authorities and their safety consultants. Also, while the coroner was in possession of evidence given to the Taylor inquiry, this was mostly denied to these families, although that given by the South Yorkshire Police had been returned to the police following the DPP's decision not to prosecute. Finally, the coroner was serviced throughout by the same officers from the West Midlands Police Force who had serviced Lord Justice Taylor and who had liaised with the DPP. *No last rights* is highly critical of the conduct of the inquest:

The Coroner decided who to call as witnesses and he also decided on the order in which the evidence would be heard. In circumstances where there are hundreds, even thousands of witnesses, the selectivity of evidence imposed by the coroner is a major discretionary power. With no right of disclosure of the evidence in the coroner's possession and no capacity to call witnesses, legal representatives have no clear picture of why certain evidence is selected to be heard while other evidence is rejected. Because Lord Justice Taylor had carried out a public inquiry and because the witnesses had made known their evidence, some pressure was applied by families to persuade the coroner to call certain witnesses. In some cases he agreed, but there was no indication as to the criteria employed by him and the coroner's officers, the West Midlands Police, in making their selection.

Lord Justice Taylor's inquiry had produced a mass of evidence which had been rigorously cross examined by a range of lawyers . . . Much of this evidence, particularly the responses of police officers, constituted a "dry run" for the inquests. The coroner, however, ruled this evidence as inadmissible on the grounds that it was not given under oath . . .

The most significant limitation placed on evidence, however, was the Coroner's decision not to hear evidence concerning events occurring after 3.15 p.m. Thus it was crucial (impossible?) to consider the quality of emergency care and treatment received in specific cases in order to establish whether some of the fans who died might have been saved. The Hillsborough inquests were unique in not calling the representatives of the Emergency Services . . . to give evidence.

In taking the main body of evidence the coroner decided on the order of presentation . . . Effectively the first few weeks of the inquest were occupied by licensees, local residents and police officers making highly-charged and well publicized attacks on the behaviour of supporters in the lead up to the disaster. With fans not legally represented, it fell to the sole representative of the families to cross examine these various allegations. Yet because the police were so heavily represented, with six separate counsel, they were able to pursue this evidence with some force and enthusiasm . . .

Taken together the order of the evidence and the imbalance in the representation of interested parties constituted a serious flaw in the inquests. Given the controversy surrounding the disaster and the experience of the Taylor inquiry, it was inconceivable that the order of evidence was not given careful consideration by the Coroner and his officers. A fair conclusion is that the decision to hear the evidence in the sequence which left fans defensive after weeks of criticism, as they told stories of their survival, was purposeful.[9]

The report goes on to take issue with the coroner's direction of the jury as to its verdict which was accidental death by a nine to two majority.

Whether the inquest was purposely organized, as *No last rites* suggests, to give the police an advantageous platform from which to attack the clear and unambiguous criticisms of their conduct made by the Taylor report is not our concern. What is relevant, however, is that the report thoroughly demonstrates that inquests into disasters suffer from many of the same disadvantages as inquests into single deaths, say of a prisoner or a mental patient. It was therefore not entirely surprising that once they had reflected on its conclusions six families supported by the Hillsborough Disaster Working Party sought advice from INQUEST and its specialist barristers in London about the prospects of seeking leave to appeal.[10] They were encouraged to do so on a number of grounds, not least being the failure of the coroner to make out a better case for "lack of care" and his decision to insist on the 3.15 p.m. cut-off. Leave to appeal was granted in April 1993. But at the Divisional Court a few months later the request for a new inquest was turned down.[11]

The feeling seems to have been that there was little point in putting the families through the mill yet again. The essential facts were known, blame duly apportioned and compensation already secured. As Lord Justice McCowen put it:

What would be the purpose of a fresh inquest? To get a verdict criticizing the police? Such criticism has already been levelled by the Taylor Report. The police have admitted fault and paid compensation.[12]

To suggest that inquests into disasters share many of the deficiencies of inquests into more routine deaths is not to deny that they present special problems. Families of the deceased often have to wait on (and endure) the progress of a lengthy public inquiry before they get anywhere close to an inquest. The cost to the taxpayer too is enormous. In

Indeed, more people, 51 in all, died in this disaster than in the King's Cross or Clapham Junction disasters. The facts surrounding the sinking of the *Marchioness* now seem reasonably clear.

On the night in August 1990 a group of young people were on board a Thames pleasure boat, the *Marchioness*. They were celebrating a birthday. Following was a Thames sand dredger, the *Bowbelle*. Towards Southwark Bridge the *Bowbelle* collided with and sank the *Marchioness*. Some survivors were hauled aboard the *Marchioness*'s sister ship the *Hurlingham*, which had just passed the two vessels going in the opposite direction. An initial inquiry suggested that the *Marchioness* had altered course to port in front of the *Bowbelle* and that the collision took place above Cannon Street Railway Bridge.

This interpretation is now disputed, not least by passengers on board the *Hurlingham* who were arguably in the best position to see. However, what is not in dispute is that in order to see behind him, the skipper of the *Marchioness* had to leave the wheel, while the captain of the *Bowbelle* had his forward vision severely limited by the vessel's trim, the angle between the bow and the stern. As if these facts were not sufficient in themselves to invite a disaster, it turned out that there was no effective communication between the *Bowbelle*'s lookout and the engine room. Nor was there a loud hailer or fixed telephone and what "walkie-talkies" there were had not been in use for some time.[17] It did not help either that the lookout had been drinking heavily during the previous afternoon. The tragedy was further compounded when the Woolwich marine radio base misheard an emergency call from the *Hurlingham* to read Battersea Bridge as the location of the collision. When 20 minutes later, the emergency services were given the right location, they arrived to find no survivors.

Immediately following the tragedy the Department of the Environment launched an inquiry by its Marine Investigation Branch (MAIB). Its conclusions about the scene of the collision – the Cannon Street Railway Bridge – and the alleged change of course or drift of the *Marchioness* across the bow of the *Bowbelle* were not accepted by the families of the deceased who continued to press for a full public inquiry. This was resisted, although the government did agree to commission the Hayes inquiry in December 1991 that was asked:

> In the light of the Marchioness/Bowbelle disaster to examine the handling since 1980 by the Department of Transport of its responsibility for the safety of vessels on rivers and inland waters and to

report on the effectiveness of the present approach. The inquiry should take account of developments in the field of marine safety at the international level.

While the Marchioness Action Group was dedicated to improving safety on the Thames following the disaster, the Hayes inquiry, however critical it might turn out to be of government policy – and it was – was not asked to address the disputed facts of the accident itself which is what continued to trouble the families most. By July 1992 when the Hayes report was eventually published the Marchioness Action Group had little to show for its efforts. The inquest was still in abeyance having originally been suspended while the government followed up the MAIB's report with two prosecutions against the skipper of the *Bowbelle*, one of which was relatively minor, and both of which were not agreed to by separate juries. A private prosecution against the owners of the *Bowbelle* for corporate manslaughter had also been rejected at committal stage and the government clearly had no intentions of holding a public inquiry. The frustrations of the group were voiced in Parliament by Joan Ruddock who observed that:

The group has consistently called for a proper public inquiry, such as would be established – indeed, such as has been established – for other comparable transport disasters. However, as we heard those arguments have always been rejected by the government who first authorized the marine investigation branch to carry out an inquiry and then set up the broader inquiry into river safety conducted by Mr John Hayes . . .

I wish to put on record the continuing stress caused to survivors and to the families of victims of the disaster because of their great sense of injustice. The lack of a public inquiry has prevented public scrutiny. Many questions remain unanswered . . . Not least among those questions are those about possible negligence on the part of the operators, about lack of observation of the rules of navigation and the lack of enforcement by the Department of Transport, and – perhaps more significantly – about the lack of a proper analysis of the rescue operation . . .

The survivors and the families are still pressing for resumption of the inquest. Part one has been held for seven of the victims and the holding of part two is still a matter for debate. It is imperative that proceedings are resumed as quickly as possible.[18]

The continuing delay over resuming the inquest – it was not finally held until March 1995 – can be put down to two reasons. First, coroner Knapman – a senior coroner who had addressed the inaugural meeting of the Inquest Lawyers' Group – appeared to support the view of the government that all the facts had been established and that not much purpose would be served by continuing with the inquest, a position he was formally entitled to take. However, and secondly, in talking to journalists about the case four months earlier in March 1992 he had referred to a member of the Marchioness Action Group as "unhinged". This judgement was used as the basis for a judicial review by two of the bereaved families against his decision not to re-open the case. In June 1994 this was upheld. The Court of Appeal ruled that in view of his remarks there was a real danger that this decision had been unconsciously influenced by a prejudice irrelevant to the issue, and that the decision about whether or not to resume the inquest should be made by another coroner.

An article in *The Times* pointed to those parts of the court's judgment that praised aspects of coroner Knapman's handling of the case as being sensitive and sympathetic, but nonetheless thought the offending remarks "foolish" and "regrettable" and concluded that:

> There can be no dispute about the justice of a result that requires reconsideration of how and why so many people lost their lives. It is a continuing disgrace that the Marchioness disaster has not been the subject of a public inquiry, as demanded by many of the families and by the public interest.[19]

Such public pressure, and new evidence that called into question the official version of where the collision had taken place, eventually forced the west London coroner's hand. But Dr Burton was far from enthusiastic, telling a packed courtroom that he had great reservations about his decision to go ahead with the inquest and that he might "bitterly regret" it.[20] For the families there were still obstacles to overcome, not least the expense of what was likely to be a long and controversial inquest. The Action Group appealed for sponsors and eventually even secured a meeting with the Lord Chancellor to plead for legal aid, or more accurately funds from contingency reserves. June Tweedie of INQUEST was invited to join the delegation. Expectations were not high. The Lord Chancellor was in the middle of conducting a vigorous and very public campaign to cap legal aid in general, and like his predecessors had not responded positively to INQUEST's longstanding demand for it to be extended to inquests in certain cases. There was therefore some rejoicing – not to say astonishment – when the Lord Chancellor decided to provide funds, not by drawing on contingency reserves but by way of the legal aid budget itself.

The coroner's conduct of the inquest was again a bone of contention. One lawyer for the families complained that he failed to call a key witness – a maritime consultant to explain how and where the collision had taken place – and that some of his potentially prejudicial background comments would simply not be tolerated in other courts.[21] In spite of these impediments the jury returned a verdict of unlawful killing and attached 12 recommendations to their verdict, including the call for legislation to set maximum blood/alcohol levels for seamen on duty. The families took some satisfaction from this verdict but were angered when the CPS decided to take no further action against either the crew or the boat's owners (*Guardian* 27 July 1996).

The controversy surrounding the sinking of the *Marchioness* has led to calls for the introduction of statutory public inquiries into all disasters. The argument simply put is that they often occur in areas – most notably in transport – where the government itself is either directly or indirectly responsible for enforcing the industry's regulatory safety framework. To give governments the power to prevent wide-ranging inquiries in such cases, that is, where their own behaviour is called into question, is surely wrong. While I think there is much to be gained from this suggestion, the mechanism for triggering it remains unclear and it would do nothing to resolve the tensions identified in *No last rights* between public inquiries and inquests. Counsel for the families in the *Marchioness* disaster, for example, would still have been denied access to much of the evidence collected for a public inquiry even if there had been one.

The fact that INQUEST – as an organization – did not orchestrate the Marchioness Action Group or the Hillsborough project should not belittle its indirect influence. One of the key solicitors servicing families involved in the Marchioness Action Group was Louise Christian, one of INQUEST's founding members. Counsel during the long inquest was provided by members of the INQUEST Lawyers' Group, including Terry Munyard. Coroner Burton knew them well, and the exchanges were sometimes tense as counsel for the families stretched procedures to their limits. At one point, the coroner wearily remarked that he was not sure how he might stop Munyard from pressing an improper line of inquiry short of confining him to the Tower of London! Apart from this legal input, the arguments marshalled by the Hillsborough project, which prompted the appeal in that case, clearly drew on Phil Scraton's long involvement with INQUEST and his particular expertise in police accountability. INQUEST's full-time workers also got to know and supported the families campaigning around both disasters. These attended and contributed to annual meetings and INQUEST's decision to hold what was intended to be the first of several out of London meetings in Liverpool in 1993 was a reflection of such links. Finally, while these two disasters occupied INQUEST most, it has also given advice in other cases, most notably regarding the fire at King's Cross underground station in 1987.

Deaths at work

INQUEST is involved, again somewhat at a tangent, in deaths at work, whether they happen in either the public or the private sector. Inquests demonstrate the unequal relationship between individual workers and corporate interests, although they mostly fail to redress this imbalance. The issues in these cases particularly highlight the discretionary nature of the coroner's power. But first some necessary background about how such deaths are investigated by the police and then by the government's own Health and Safety Executive.

When a death at work occurs the police are almost invariably the first to be called. However, unless there is some risk to the public, for example, where poisonous fumes that were responsible for the death are still escaping into the surrounding atmosphere, they will rarely stay longer than is needed to take brief statements from those directly involved. Provided no "foul play" is suspected, say as a result of feuds and differences between workers, then the police will leave further investigation to the Health and Safety Executive (HSE). This significantly downgrades the seriousness of what has happened. That the police withdraw immediately suggests that "no crime has been committed here, just an accident".

The role of the Health and Safety Executive is to investigate how the accident took place and to see if any of the regulations governing health and safety at work have been ignored or circumvented, thus contributing to the cause of the injury or death. Sometimes the inspector will have visited the factory or site before and be known to the management. The Executive is not so much concerned with the extent of the injuries received – even if they result in death – but more with whether or not the regulations have been followed. It is the failure to adhere to these that is punishable in the courts under the appropriate legislation. The extent of the worker's injuries – or death – is only likely to be of interest to the other parties involved in the event of any subsequent civil litigation (or settlement). However, if the Executive believes that the management has ignored the regulations to the point of recklessness sufficient to warrant a criminal charge of manslaughter then it will pass on details of the case to the Crown Prosecution Service.

While this procedure seems reasonable in theory, it is rarely followed in practice. This point was well made in a 1991 pamphlet – which INQUEST jointly published – *Deaths at work*:

> If such a procedure does exist it is clearly both an ineffective and inadequate alternative to a proper police investigation from the outset. It is almost unheard of for a case to be referred by the HSE to the CPS for consideration of manslaughter liability. Since 1974 when the HSE was formed there have been over eight thousand deaths. Yet the HSE can't point to even a handful of cases where they have formally referred the case to the CPS. The one manslaughter prosecution against a director that has taken place in the last sixteen years, was referred to the CPS by the police, not by the HSE. The procedure may exist on paper, but that is exactly where it stays.[22]

In this situation it is easy to see why the inquest is seen as important. Families and friends who may believe that the death they mourn was anything but just an unfortunate accident, trust the coroner to uncover the truth and hope that, if appropriate, the jury might feel persuaded to reach a verdict of unlawful killing. But this rarely happens. Coroners do not often investigate beyond the immediate cause of death to consider how or what particular work practices are in place or whether those responsible for them might be culpable. Verdicts of "accidental death" are therefore invariably returned.

The case of Sidney Rouse well illustrates the stages and weaknesses of the process I have outlined. Mr Rouse was a pipefitter working in Gloucester Terrace in London during August 1988. He caught the full blast of a short circuit, receiving severe burns from which he eventually died in University College Hospital. His death was at first investigated by the police. This took under ten minutes, and consisted of a few sentences from the ganger and the workman who was actually drilling at the time. The case was then left to an inspector from the Health and Safety Executive. While he took more detailed statements from the ganger and spoke to an engineer from the London Electricity Board, no attempt was made to question the site agent or anyone more senior in the company involved, not least those managers and directors who had responsibility for safety. The inspector simply told the inquest that there were a lot of electricity cable strikes in London.

After what appears to have been a fairly routine inquest the jury were asked to choose between an open verdict or accidental death. They chose the latter. This in spite of the fact that instruments issued to workers to detect underground cables could only detect those drawing power at the time, and that the ganger had not been provided with a "mains" diagram that the principal engineer from the London Electricity Board implied was essential for such work. According to *Deaths at work*, these revelations were sufficient in themselves to have warranted a wider investigation, which if vigorously pursued might have led to a verdict of unlawful killing. But the coroner chose not to exercise his considerable discretion in this respect, instead settling on the limited approach taken by the police and the HSE.[23]

In fairness to the coroner, however, he was not the only one to have narrowed the focus. The lawyer acting for the deceased's family did likewise. This is apparently not at all unusual, even in those cases where the deceased's family is being represented by trade union lawyers. The situation seems to be that provided some question mark surrounds the death and compensation can be (or has been) agreed – usually out of court – then the inquest verdict is not thought to be important. This means that many managers and/or directors fail to be censored or punished, or if they are, they or their companies are only brought to book for relatively minor infringements of health and safety regulations, and even then mostly in magistrates courts where fines are modest. The fact that companies involved in the construction of the Channel Tunnel have exceptionally been fined large sums in recent years for repeatedly breaking health and safety regulations should not distort what routinely happens.

The failure of coroners and trade union appointed lawyers to secure accountability in these cases has led to rank and file agitation among a number of unions, although it was particularly strong in the construction industry in the 1980s where even the HSE had to admit the safety record was worrying. So, for example, whereas the HSE could boast in its 1989–90 annual report that fatal injury rates had fallen over the last 30 years in all industries, "fatal and major accident rates continued to cause concern in the construction industry".[24] Indeed, a senior member of the Executive went so far as to say in an interview with *Construction News* in 1989 that he regarded the accident toll in the industry as "appalling". The same article went on to claim that nearly 1,000 workers had been killed between 1981 and 1988 and, what is more telling perhaps, went on to quote from an official report that claimed that most of the 739 deaths that had occurred between 1981 and 1985 could have been avoided.[25]

The industry's appalling safety record in the 1980s was put down to a number of separate but related factors. First was the growing practice of subcontracting. Instead of a single construction company being responsible for all (or most) of the work on a given site, it came to be subcontracted out so that different firms were in charge of bricklayers, carpenters, plasterers and so forth. This made co-ordination awkward and getting together anything more than a purely nominal site safety committee became difficult. Secondly, there was "the lump". Some construction companies encouraged this form of tax evasion. But workers who failed to pay either their tax and/or national insurance were in no position to complain about the non-observance of safety standards. They too were breaking the law. Casualization also played its part. Contractors could take on workers, usually very young workers, with little knowledge of the industry or its safety requirements. This ignorance cost lives. Mobilizing opposition to these practices was difficult. In the second half of the 1980s there was a large surplus of unemployed labour, particularly in the construction industry. Workers who complained could be sacked and easily replaced. Those with a record of safety agitation could be blacklisted.

As for the HSE, some might claim that it did its best. For example, in 1987 it launched a safety blitz on construction sites that revealed that many site managers had only a very basic knowledge of health and safety regulations and that 14 per cent of the sites visited had no-one in overall charge of safety.[26] Critics of the HSE, however, would claim that little changed after these revelations, partly because the number of health and safety inspectors was (and is) so thin on the ground that no follow up was possible. In other words, the occasional blitz may bring serious deficiencies to light, but in the long term they do little to secure permanent improvements. It was partly this, perhaps, that persuaded the government to experiment with self-regulation in the industry during the 1980s. Not surprisingly this was simply seen by some as a means of undermining the effectiveness of the HSE still further.[27]

It was against this rising tide of concern that INQUEST was first approached by a local branch of the Allied Trades and Technicians Union (UCATT). In a letter that pointed to many of the changes (and dangers) in the construction industry outlined above, the secretary asked for a speaker, as:

> We are wondering how we can get the coroners to widen the inquiry into these areas, how to use the coroner's court as a platform to call for both more safety and a judicial inquiry into how coroners' courts can be used.
>
> The picketing of coroners' courts . . . is now official UCATT policy but it has not been taken up in a big way; we're wondering how this can be developed.[28]

INQUEST duly sent along a speaker who outlined inquest procedures, spoke about their limitations and suggested how they might be reformed to secure more thorough investigations. (Also in attendance at the meeting was Jeremy Corbyn MP.) Interestingly, however, while the local branch in question had itself been responsible for getting the policy of picketing coroners' courts onto UCATT's agenda, the secretary's letter (above) concedes that not much had been done by the official leadership on this front. This reinforces the suspicion that trade unions and employers were complicit in lowering the temperature in and around inquests in order to secure what both sides thought was an acceptable level of compensation for the bereaved families.

This was certainly the view taken by the more broadly based rank and file Construction Safety Campaign which asked pointedly:

> Where are the unions? Some of the blame for the toll of death and disease lies with the unions themselves. Companies have learnt to expect an easy ride from trade union officers . . . They are there to help with the compensation claims, but doing next to nothing at site level to stop accidents happening in the first place.[29]

The campaign's purpose was to raise the issue of construction safety within the labour movement and trade unions generally and, like UCATT, to picket inquests as one means of doing this. In the late 1980s this tactic was regularly employed by local activists. For example, Steve Reilly, a 26-year-old steel erector, fell to his death on a Bovis site at Canary Wharf in October 1989. The timber he was standing on collapsed and he fell 100 feet to his death. He was not wearing a safety harness. A picket was organized outside St Pancras coroner's court. Its dual purpose was clearly expressed. It was there both as "a mark of respect for Steve Reilly and to protest about the high number of deaths in the construction industry where HSE figures show that management negligence is responsible for seven out of ten deaths. Was it responsible for Steve Reilly's death?"[30] The issue of compensation was not mentioned; the campaign was concentrating on the broader issues.

Similar pickets were organized across London at this time, often supported by the campaign but not always organized by it. One of the earliest protested at the death of Lawrence Hoey. Mr Hoey was a 54-year-old widower and father of five. He died after being crushed when a forklift truck was being driven by an unauthorized person, although at the inquest it was claimed that this was common practice. Mr Hoey was from Louth and one of a number of Irishmen who died on London building sites during this time. The issue of construction safety was taken up by the Irish Embassy and the ideas behind the campaign's work were explained in the *Irish Times*.[31]

INQUEST had contact with the campaign during this period, offering legal advice and inviting its speakers to the INQUEST AGM to explain their strategy. However, and the same applied in the case of the local UCATT branch, INQUEST was by no means in agreement with all of the campaign's policies, not least its demand that, "in the event of death and serious injury a prison sentence on the employer should be mandatory".[32] In fact, INQUEST's most fruitful collaboration in this field was with the London Hazards Centre. This had been set up by the GLC to help occupational and community groups in London to improve public awareness of hazards at work and in the environment. INQUEST had worked with the centre on a number of cases/issues including the King's Cross disaster. However, it was mainly through its active involvement with the Construction Safety Campaign that the centre approached INQUEST to work on *Deaths at work* (1991).

This detailed pamphlet focused on three institutional failures – the lack of effective police scrutiny, inadequate investigation by the HSE and cursory inquests into deaths at work. While INQUEST obviously concentrated its attention on coroners it made detailed suggestions on early drafts to make the whole pamphlet more accessible. Regrettably this close intellectual collaboration was not in the end extended to financial collaboration. Having originally agreed to share the production costs of *Death at work*, INQUEST had to renege on its commitment due to a financial crisis. However, INQUEST did join the Hazards Centre in the successful search for another sponsor by writing supportive letters claiming that the pamphlet would provide "invaluable advice and information to bereaved families, lawyers and trade unions" and help those intent on "improving health and safety at work and seeking reforms in law and practice".[33] (The cost of producing the pamphlet was eventually met by the Workers' Educational Association.)

One of the complex issues that INQUEST had to confront in this area of its work – although it had already surfaced in the legal follow-up to the Zeebrugge ferry disaster – was how to pursue corporate manslaughter. It was one thing to persuade coroners to broaden their investigations and for jurors to return verdicts of unlawful killing that pointed suspicion at senior directors, or more generally, their companies, but how might this be translated into effective legal action? The DPP's prosecution against the ferry company had been thrown out at an early stage by a judge at the Old Bailey and a private prosecution against the owners of the *Bowbelle* did not even get through committal stage. What applied to these cases also applied to many deaths at work, namely, that there is – to paraphrase the Director General of the HSE – real difficulty in linking the boardroom to "the blood on the workshop floor".[34] In order to overcome this, *Deaths at work* suggested a number of strategies, including the creation of a completely new offence, intermediate between negligence and manslaughter, which would be applied specifically to companies rather than individuals.[35] (David Bergman was to follow up the complex legal framework surrounding corporate violence in a later pamphlet, *Disasters. Where the law fails*. A full-time employee at the Hazards Centre, he was briefly on INQUEST's Executive Committee in the early 1990s.)

While INQUEST has taken on individual workplace deaths, its main role has nevertheless been to service other groups whose main concern they are. In doing this it has enabled these groups to get the best out of the inquest system for their own purposes – which INQUEST broadly supports – while at the same time pushing its own somewhat narrower agenda of legal reform. This constructive and reciprocal relationship was particularly strong, as we have seen, in the second half of the 1980s and early 1990s when rank and file construction workers mobilized against deaths at work and when the Hazards Centre (and others) turned their attention towards making those corporately responsible more accountable for their actions. What has been achieved is an open question. For example, it is by no means clear that the undertaking given to UCATT by the police in 1991 that they would in future take a more active role in investigating deaths at work has been met, nor is there evidence that the introduction of EC health and safety standards has made corporate prosecutions more likely, as some campaigners had hoped.[36]

Race and gender

In 1991 the Institute of Race Relations (IRR) published a pamphlet on black deaths in police, prison and mental health custody; it drew on a number of sources, including the INQUEST archive. In the introduction A. Sivanandan complained that in such cases the inquest offers no relief:

> The coroner is there to tell you the facts of death, not who was responsible for it or why. But even the facts are loaded against you. For the coroner's court is not an adversarial court where you have an equal chance to challenge the authorized version of the facts. Instead, it is the coroner who, aided by the police, is both judge and advocate, and controls the proceedings of his court. He alone has access to vital information stemming from an internal inquiry, but he is not obliged to divulge it. He alone decides which witnesses to call and in what order the evidence should be presented. He alone sums up and directs the jury, leads them – and tells them to choose from a restricted range of four verdicts, only one of which, "unlawful killing" allows the relatives of the deceased a real chance to re-open the case with a view to prosecution and/or compensation. But such a direction to the jury is observed more in the breach.[37]

Apart from pointing out that the range of verdicts is not quite as restrictive as this suggests, or that all juries are quite so gullible, INQUEST would find little or nothing to quarrel with in Sivanandan's analysis. It reinforces most, if not all, of the problems surrounding inquests that the group has struggled to bring to light. However, it also suggests that inquest procedures *per se* pose much the same problems for black families as they do for white families. In our view there is much truth in this, even if some coroners are extremely patronizing to some black witnesses, and this helps to explain why INQUEST has not defined itself centrally around the issue of race. But as I have made clear throughout, inquests – even when poorly conducted – often call into question other policies, other practices that INQUEST is keen to contest, even if it is left to other campaigning groups to follow them through. In the context of black deaths in custody what is at issue is the practice of institutionalized racism. This can be illustrated on a number of fronts, not least in the areas of mental health and policing.

In the previous chapter I referred to the controversial deaths of three young Afro-Caribbean men who died in Broadmoor. All three had been diagnosed as suffering from schizophrenia. The issue of racism was raised in all three cases, but vigorously denied by the hospital authorities, and at first, even by those called in to investigate and report on the deaths to the Special Hospitals Authority. The Ritchie report into the death of Michael Martin, for example, found "no racial prejudice" among staff.[38] In the case of Joseph Watts the inquiry also detected "no sign of institutional racism"[39] and, in evidence to the committee of inquiry chaired by Hershel Prins into the death of Orville Blackwood, staff at first insisted, somewhat innocently I feel, that they treated all patients the same. Treating all patients the same, however, begs a number of questions, and these were later ruthlessly spelt out in the Prins report which concluded that the regime at Broadmoor reflected the institutional racism that was endemic in the mental health system as a whole. About this it observed:

> Over the last twenty years, studies have indicated that, if they come to the attention of the psychiatric services, black people are more likely to be removed by the police to a place of safety under Section 136 of the Mental Health Act 1983; they are more likely to be detained in hospital under sections 2, 3 and 4 of the Mental Health Act 1983; they are more likely to be diagnosed as suffering from schizophrenia or another form of psychotic illness; they are more likely to be detained in locked wards in psychiatric hospitals; they are more likely to receive higher doses of

medication; they are less likely to receive non controlling treatments such as psychotherapy or counselling. In addition black mentally disordered offenders are more likely than their white counterparts to be remanded in custody for psychiatric reports; they are more likely to be in higher levels of security and for longer, and they are more likely to be referred from prison to regional secure units or special hospitals.[40]

In the light of this evidence it was recommended that Broadmoor dealt "explicitly with the problem of racism in the forensic psychiatric system as a whole and its effects within the hospital".[41] More specifically it took up the diagnosis of schizophrenia and questioned Broadmoor's over-reliance on drugs for its treatment. It also, somewhat belatedly, called on Broadmoor to monitor the medication levels to include an "examination of how prescribing practices relate to the ethnic origins of patients".[42] It is important to note that the diagnosis of Orville Blackwood had been contested as it had been in the case of Richard Campbell who died in prison in 1980 and whose family were among INQUEST's founding members (see Ch. 2). Mr Campbell seems to have been diagnosed as schizophrenic on the basis of his over-relaxed manner and his Rastafarian religion. INQUEST is inclined to the view that what the Prins report defined as the "racism . . . in forensic psychiatry" applies in varying degrees to both Special Hospitals and prisons, although ironically in this context it was, according to INQUEST, the abject failure of Brixton's medical officers to detect Germain Alexander's mental illness that contributed to his subsequent death and the call for a full public inquiry.[43]

Before leaving Broadmoor a word in its defence. While there were unproven charges of name calling and other forms of individual racial abuse, it was never suggested in any of the inquiries that I have mentioned that this was as widespread or as offensive in Broadmoor as it was at Ashworth where a small number of staff were active supporters of the British National Party (BNP) whose racialist policies are well known. Stickers supporting the BNP were posted around the hospital and when a member of staff sought to have them removed she received a death threat. Links between the BNP supporters at the hospital and the Prison Officers' Association were strenuously denied by the union.[44] (The Ashworth inquiry and the Prins inquiry were conducted at the same time, although INQUEST only gave evidence to the former.)

127

Prising open the racial bias in forensic psychiatry and confronting its institutional expression in Special Hospitals and prisons has been a long and contested business involving many players, including government. It is therefore important not to overestimate INQUEST's role. Indeed it sometimes struck out rather crudely at examples of alleged individual racial abuse rather than looking more critically at the underlying causes of such behaviour. On the other hand, in tandem with families most closely involved, and other lobby groups, particularly MIND and, early on, PROP, it tenaciously pursued several controversial inquests that both sustained media interest and led to official investigations and reports. Significantly, it was also involved in all the cases around black deaths in Special Hospitals taken up in chapter 3 of the Institute of Race Relations' widely reported pamphlet, *Deadly silence* (1991).

The same pamphlet had also raised the issue of black deaths in and around police custody. As I have already noted, such deaths were frequently drawn to INQUEST's attention, but it was not until 1989 that it sought to quantify and analyze these in any detail, something it was pressed to do following the deaths of five black Londoners in police custody in the space of a few weeks in July and August 1989.

The death of Jamie Stewart in particular had led to a highly volatile situation. The Jamie Stewart Campaign, which INQUEST assisted, wanted to know why he had been stopped and arrested at all in the early hours of the morning, why he had been taken to the local police station and why he was searched – events that culminated in his tragic death at a local hospital. In order to head off "racial disorder", as they put it, the police announced long before the official inquest that a concentration of cocaine had been found in his stomach. This appeared to be an attempt in advance of any inquiry to justify a fairly random stop, search and arrest that ended in tragedy for no good reason.[45]

But what did the deaths of these young black men signify about police practice in general and about policing London in particular? Were they, for example, being picked on, and more to the point, were young blacks more likely to die in police custody than their white counterparts? INQUEST's *Report on black deaths in police custody (1970–1988)*, which was launched with the support of Labour's frontbench spokesman Barry Sheerman at a House of Commons press conference in November 1989, began cautiously.[46]

It pointed out that getting any sort of proper perspective was difficult as a record of deaths in police custody had only been kept following the 1980 *Report of the Home Affairs Select Committee* (see Ch. 2). This meant that figures for the 1970s – which were significantly lower than those for the 1980s – have been collected retrospectively through questionnaires and were therefore somewhat suspect. Further, the 43 per cent of all recorded deaths in police custody – 315 out of 733 – attributed to the Met might not be quite as alarming as it at first seemed because there is some evidence that provincial forces were not recording as deaths in police custody those deaths that took place where suspects were transferred to local hospitals – as in the case of Jamie Stewart. Also, of course, the report emphasized that police records did not include a breakdown of racial groups. Thus, if finding out just how many people had died in police custody was difficult, finding out just how many of these were black deaths was even more difficult – which by the way was one of the reasons that the Institute of Race Relations undertook the fact finding survey that culminated in *Deadly silence*.

Notwithstanding these limitations, and drawing on its own extensive archive material, INQUEST concluded that since 1980 it had been able to identify 20 black (Asian and Caribbean) people who had died in and around police custody since 1980. This figure included 10 of the 194 deaths in the Met during this period. The report concluded that this was a lower proportion than might be expected – just over 5 per cent – given that 17 per cent of those arrested in London were black, although this might be explained, in part at least, by black detainees being younger and healthier on average than their white counterparts. INQUEST also acknowledged that while its archive was extensive, it could not be certain that some black deaths had been overlooked.

While these figures must have brought some relief to the Met, INQUEST was quick to point out that its own concerns were not so much with the overall number of black deaths, but rather that a large proportion of such deaths involved controversial or suspicious circumstances, which was precisely why as a support and advice group it had so often become involved. INQUEST was again cautious – some might say judicious – when it went on in its report to argue that it was certainly *not* claiming that in all such cases – say that of Jamie Stewart – death had been directly caused by police violence, only that in a number of these cases a violent incident had allegedly taken place between the arrest and the death. And more to INQUEST's point, that the means of allaying the fears and suspicions surrounding these incidents was being denied to the families and the black community generally by the working practices of the Police Complaints Authority and the procedures adopted at inquests, both of which hinder rather than facilitate getting at the truth.

The report then goes on in some detail – it is a substantial proportion of the overall report – to outline how the police investigate themselves, and how too often inquests leave the bereaved feeling that all that needs to be known is still in fact, unknown. These well rehearsed procedural concerns, however, did not prevent INQUEST from situating its report within what it took to be the proven racism within the criminal justice system, any more than it evaded racism in the mental health system. While properly acknowledging that it was well beyond its brief to tackle this prejudice it concluded that:

> The cases we have mentioned have to be set in the context of studies such as the 1981 PSI [Policy Studies Institute] Report, the Islington Crime Survey and the Broadwater Farm Inquiry, and from numerous cases catalogued by the Institute of Race Relations and others, indicating that black people are more likely than white people to experience excessive force at the hands of the police. This in turn has to be set in context of police policies and practices such as the "targeting" of areas with large black populations for "heavy policing" and the over use of powers to "stop and search" (and of so-called "voluntary" searches) against black people, which reinforce the mutual hostility between many black people and the police and which make violent confrontations between them more likely. In short, black deaths in police custody are a small part of the pattern of institutional police racism.[47]

INQUEST's role in helping to discover the extent and circumstances surrounding black deaths in custody – right across the system – was publicly acknowledged by the IRR, which lent its support to many of INQUEST's proposals for reform. So, for example, *Deadly silence* supports the call for advance disclosure and the provision of legal aid for all deaths that have occurred in "any form" of state custody. INQUEST, however, has not given its public support to the Institute's call for an independent Standing Commission on Deaths in Custody. The thinking behind this proposal lies in the Institute's belief that however inquest procedures might (and must be) reformed they will never be sufficiently powerful successfully to take on cases where the "motive for a cover up by those in authority is so strong".[48] In these exceptional circumstances the Standing Committee would come into play, having been first approached by a pressure group, a prison Board of Visitors or even a coroner. It would make preliminary investigations and then if it felt it appropriate hold "full judicial and public hearings" and recommend disciplinary or criminal proceedings against those responsible where appropriate. The advantage of a Standing Committee over a conventional judicial or public inquiry is presumably that it would not be dependent upon the government of the day – which might itself be culpable – to set it up; it would already be in place and ready to investigate when and where it thought fit. However, as proposed it would dispense with the services of a jury, and it is not clear how the functions of a judicial or public inquiry could be combined with the suggestion that it could recommend disciplinary proceedings, a similar difficulty with the proposal put forward by Phil Scraton to investigate major disasters.

The issue of black deaths in police custody was to come to public attention again in 1995. In that year a young man died in a struggle with police, another was shot by police in his car, both in south London. Protests over these deaths, and that of Shiji Lapite (Ch. 4), were fuelled by the acquittal at the Old Bailey of three officers from the Met of the manslaughter of Joy Gardner who had been killed during a forcible attempt to deport her to Jamaica in 1994. INQUEST drew attention to the history of black deaths in custody in a letter to the national press (*Independent* 28 August 1995). This pointed out the legal difficulties of securing an effective investigation into such cases, an intervention that prompted a vitriolic reply, eliding racial and homophobic insults, from an unidentified right-wing group.[49] INQUEST also briefed Harry Cohen MP who forced a Parliamentary debate on black deaths in custody in July 1995 (*Caribbean Times* 22 July 1995).

Gender

INQUEST has been closely involved with several groups whose interests are primarily to protect the rights of women in prison, police or hospital custody. Co-operation with Women in Prison (WIP) was particularly close during the early 1980s. WIP was established as a referral, research and help group in London during the 1980s by the Women's Committee of the GLC. Its funding was formally voted in December 1983, shortly after INQUEST received it first grant from the GLC's Police Committee.[50]

One of WIP's early observations, made in INQUEST's 1982–3 annual report as it happens, was how little was known about the deaths of women in custody, about their numbers and the circumstances surrounding them. It noted, for example, that while *Frightened for my life* (see Chs 3 and 4) had many merits in bringing the issue of custodial deaths into the public arena, none of the cases it dealt with involved women. Even in death, or so it seemed, women were invisible.[51]

Putting this right was far from easy, but with the help of Parliamentary questions and archive material from INQUEST enough reliable information was collected for a series of short articles and reports. One of these was written by Chris Tchaikovsky (WIP) and Melissa Benn, who by this time was involved with INQUEST.[52] This pointed out that between 1975 and 1983 15 women had died in prison, some in very disturbing circumstances. This early co-operation between the two groups was reinforced by working together on a series of high profile cases in the first half of the 1980s.

The most important of these was perhaps that of Wilma Lucas in 1984, a case we have already considered in some detail (Ch. 4). There was also close co-operation over Sarah Brewer who died in Pucklechurch Remand Centre near Bristol. She had been remanded for stealing goods valued at 60 pence. After being prescribed antibiotics by the prison doctor Sarah told prison officers that these were "drying her out" and that she was having great difficulty in breathing. These problems were not alleviated when her antibiotics were changed. In spite of this she was twice stopped from seeing the duty doctor on the day of her death, even although a fellow prisoner testified that at the time she sounded dreadful, like "somebody dying". Instead of being taken seriously Sarah Brewer was told to go back upstairs and stop making that "stupid noise".[53] Shortly after this rebuke she was found dead. At the inquest key witnesses – including the Home Office pathologist – were not called and "crucial" gaps and disparities in the evidence were allegedly ignored by the coroner. INQUEST complained about these procedural inadequacies, about what it took to be an obvious case of medical neglect and worked with WIP to secure a judicial review.[54]

Another case involving both groups was that of Mark Sancto who died on Holloway's C1 psychiatric wing in 1985. Mark Sancto was a transsexual. On the morning of his death he was found with his trousers around his neck and one end loosely fastened to the cell window. Interpreting this as "attention seeking" the incident went unreported. Within an hour he was dead, having hanged himself by tying his cardigan around his neck and loosely fastening one of its sleeves to the window. The jury returned a verdict of "accidental death aggravated by lack of care". The implication of such a verdict was presumably that Mark Sancto's behaviour was indeed "attention seeking" and that he had not intended to take his own life, but that the danger or possibility he might should have been taken more seriously than it was. What particularly interested INQUEST in this case was that counsel Ed Fitzgerald had been successful in arguing for a "lack of care" verdict against the background of a recent argument by the *Times* law correspondent that had wrongly – in INQUEST's view – seriously called into question the availability of such verdicts.[55]

An earlier case in 1982 involving C1 concerned Christine Scott who had been sentenced to six months for breaking windows and committed to Holloway which was not only a long way from her home in Norfolk, but more particularly from Hillsdown Hospital where she was more or less a regular patient on the psychiatric ward. Unable to cope in C1 she regularly threatened suicide and eventually caused herself so much self-injury that she died of a subdural haemorrhage after transfer to a local hospital. In spite of being covered in bruises when she was eventually found, none of the prison staff supposedly watching her had noticed any signs of injury.[56] This raised serious doubts about the quality of supervision and medical care on C1 and WIP led a high profile campaign – actively supported by INQUEST and other groups in the penal lobby – to get it closed, or at least to secure major improvements. This lasted for several years, and some positive gains were secured, although so grudgingly that as late as 1986 WIP threatened to sue the Home Secretary for dragging his feet.[57] Recent deaths at Holloway to cause controversy were those of Donna Awadat (1994), a mentally ill prisoner on C1, and Claire Bosley (1995) who died in reception.

These cases suggest that those who investigate the deaths of women in custody face many of the same problems – and reveal similar short-comings – as those who investigate custodial death generally – inadequate inquests, poor institutional supervision, poor medical care and so forth. This is largely true. But what many of these cases also provide is evidence that women are treated differently from men, not only in prison and Special Hospitals, but in the criminal justice system generally.[58] To the extent that this disadvantages women – as it frequently does – INQUEST has been willing to support those who mobilize against it, just as it has been prepared to lend its voice to those who mobilize against racism in the criminal justice system. So, for example, WIP's campaign around C1 was seen as a struggle against the tendency of the authorities to "medicalize" the behaviour of women offenders as much as a struggle to protect them from self-injury or suicide. Scraton & Chadwick have traced and assessed the link between WIP and INQUEST in the following way:

> In the 1980s . . . with the publication of several articles and books, women's imprisonment emerged as a significant issue. That the issue had been taken seriously at all owes much to the organization Women in Prison, established to campaign solely for women prisoners. It has been the result of these developments together with the involvement of the organization INQUEST, concerned with the deaths of men and women in custody, that many of the problems faced by women in prison have come to light. These problems include repressive regimes and systems of punishment and discipline; the systematic neglect of women's health; the massive use of drugs and ultimately, deaths of women in prison.[59]

In our view, this probably overstates INQUEST's contribution. First, it contains no mention of Special Hospitals, or quite understandably, of the role of Women in Special Hospitals (WISH), the pressure group established in 1986 to protect the rights of female patients. Secondly, WIP always took the lead in the cases I have outlined. INQUEST has never defined itself narrowly in terms of gender any more than it defined itself narrowly in terms of race. This not only gives it a wider agenda, but also adds more to the demands that are placed upon it, demands that have necessarily limited the time it spends on gender and race issues. The extent, however, to which it networks across these issues is perhaps best illustrated by learning that one of its present co-directors previously worked for WIP and is currently on the management committee of WISH.

Chapter 6

Keeping afloat

Pressure groups like INQUEST have a precarious existence. They are always in danger of being confined to the margins, of being defined out. Unable to attract a high level of public support – their memberships are usually modest, in the case of INQUEST it has rarely been above 400 – their futures are always uncertain, their activities always circumscribed by a real shortage of resources. Financial constraints in particular have a debilitating effect. Instead of planning ahead in terms of managing and developing the organization, or developing new substantive policies their full-time workers all too often spend most of their time looking to secure next year's grant. This has an obvious impact on morale. Workers become frustrated that they cannot properly fulfil their other tasks – and they are all too often criticized for this by voluntary management committees – while the uncertainty that they face impacts on their private lives. They too have rents to pay, children to support.

INQUEST has had its fair share of these problems, and it might be argued that it is to the credit of those who have managed it over the years that it has survived at all, not least in the face of changes to its external environment over which it had little control. There is clearly some truth in this interpretation, although it is equally arguable that it has not always made the best of its admittedly slender resources, and that its unyielding radical culture has sometimes limited its ability to respond to wider pressures for change, pressures that at times threatened its very existence. It is in order to flesh out some of these arguments that we now turn to INQUEST as an organization, starting with funding and finance.

Funding and finance

In the early days the constituent campaigns were self-financing, while the central organization, such as it was, was funded by individual and campaign subscriptions. The sums involved were small and the nomination of Mark Urbanowicz (Jimmy Kelly Campaign) as treasurer on grant applications was more for presentational reasons than anything else.[1] Where costs were generated in London, the Blair Peach Campaign, which had more resources than most, seems to have willingly shouldered more than its fair share of the burden. Securing the promise of a grant from the GLC in mid-1982 and the appointment of two workers to job share significantly changed these informal arrangements. However, its immediate impact was to make INQUEST financially less, rather than more secure, and by November 1982 the workers were to inform the Executive Committee that the group's financial position was "impossible".[2] This early crisis arose for a number of reasons.

First and foremost, the workers were put in post a month before the GLC's grant was due to come on stream. Inevitably this was going to lead to a shortfall, particularly at the end of the first month. This particular difficulty was accentuated by the GLC's practice of paying its quarterly grants up to two or more weeks late, so in effect groups had to learn to budget for three and a half months rather than just three months, something that INQUEST had not anticipated. Secondly, the original budget projections to the GLC had omitted to cost certain key items. These included money to pay for a press cuttings service, essential to INQUEST before it had achieved a public profile, but nonetheless very expensive.[3] Finally, not enough had been allowed for travel expenses. The cost of subsidizing out of London trips, or paying for key committee members like Mark Urbanowicz to visit London for meetings, had simply not been thought through. (INQUEST's failure to secure funds for Urbanowicz as its northern worker intensified this strain.)

The immediate crisis that this generated was partly relieved by a loan of £1,500 from the Blair Peach Campaign and the willingness of one of INQUEST's workers to forgo part of his salary for the time being. This form of crisis management was hardly a good start, although it did at least force the Executive Committee to rethink the immediate (and likely future demands) on the organization, the result of which was a successful bid to the Police Committee for more resources, including the conversion of its existing job share into two full-time posts.[4] The extra income that this generated helped INQUEST to "muddle through", but it did not come on stream until well into 1983 and the minutes for the early months of that year are full of gloomy predictions about INQUEST's financial future. Furthermore, no sooner had these teething troubles been overcome than INQUEST ran foul of the GLC's accountants.

This was in the autumn of 1983. Discrepancies were noticed in INQUEST's accounts when they were matched with the detail of its formal grant allocation.[5] While no impropriety was ever remotely suggested, the delay that it led to in issuing INQUEST's quarterly grant caused considerable difficulties to the organization and at one stage it was even suggested that an approach to Paul Boateng might be needed to clear the log-jam.[6] Both the Executive Committee and the full-time workers must take their share of the blame for this perilous financial start. On balance though, more of the fault lies with the Executive that got the organization up and running far too early and then left the full-time workers to manage the accounts as best they could with little or no oversight. Whether INQUEST had the capacity to benefit from these mistakes, to tighten up its financial controls, seemed an academic question when in 1984–5 the government moved to abolish the GLC and at a stroke threaten INQUEST's main source of funding.

Abolition, of course, did not only affect INQUEST. The GLC's Police Committee alone supported over 37 projects across London employing some 50 workers. The demise of the GLC was thus a threat to a whole range of radical organizations, not least those involved in police monitoring and campaigning more generally around issues like race and gender. But INQUEST and some other groups were arguably particularly vulnerable because their activities were London-wide. That is to say, those groups with more of a local focus would (and did) survive abolition because their local boroughs had a Labour majority and would be willing to take over financing them, at least in the short term. INQUEST's position was altogether less secure and the possibility that it might fold was a real one. Discussions about how to keep it afloat after abolition, quite detailed discussions, were therefore held in mid-1985. These were both about how to manage it in the run-up to abolition – when and on what basis would cases have to be selectively turned away, for example – and about how new finance – mainly through increased subscriptions – might be secured in order to sustain it after abolition.[7] INQUEST was relieved to be able to put these crisis measures on hold when the GLC not only survived into 1986, but also found a legal loophole to carry on funding its voluntary groups for the best part of another year in spite of the Conservative government's attempts to block its spending powers.

While the uncertainty surrounding the abolition of the GLC during 1984–5 made forward planning difficult and seriously affected INQUEST's morale there is a certain irony here. Before the Conservative Party moved to abolish the GLC during 1984–5, Labour was not popular with London's electors and had the scheduled London-wide elections gone ahead in 1985 it is likely that the Conservatives would have been returned to power. In these circumstances the Police Committee – like the Women's Committee – would almost certainly have been immediately abolished and groups like INQUEST would have lost their grants. As it was, the perceived constitutional impropriety of abolishing the GLC enshrined in the Paving Bill (1984) forced the government – as a result of its defeat in the House of Lords on this issue – to extend the life of the GLC for a further year into 1986.

This is not to imply, of course, that a Conservative-controlled GLC in 1985 would have refused to support any London voluntary groups, but rather that the type of organizations it would have supported would almost certainly not have included radical groups like INQUEST. This analysis is supported by the politics underpinning the London Borough Grants Committee (LBGC).

The LBGC had been set up after abolition under the provisions of the Local Government Act (1985) to control across-London voluntary activity and comprised representatives from all the London boroughs. As soon as the committee got going in June 1986 the fault lines were obvious; they were almost a rerun of the wrangles that had been played out in the Police Committee and the Women's Committee with the Conservatives – occasionally supported in a half-hearted way by the Liberals – being openly hostile to gay and lesbian groups, or those groups that were believed to be associated with police monitoring. Thus, when INQUEST's grant came up for renewal before the committee a Conservative councillor said:

[he] objected on the same grounds as he objected to police monitoring committees. This organization seemed to have a particular axe to grind, it was not the concern of local authorities, and it was not the kind of group that should be supported.[8]

After a short but acrimonious exchange INQUEST's grant was voted through by 18 to 11.

While these disputes over the legitimacy of particular groups were to continue for the next few years and were a constant anxiety for INQUEST, the real danger to its continued existence came from the political tactic of blocking the entire budget process. This happened when 23 out of the 33 participating boroughs represented on the committee failed to agree the overall budget figure. Blocking the budget in this way was a tactic used by the Conservatives when they wanted to force a political change in the general direction of funding; it was not simply a question of the Conservatives wanting to reduce the size of the overall budget, although this was a legitimate (and expressed) concern.

This blocking tactic was first used early in 1987. The London Voluntary Sector Forum that had been set up to shadow the LBGC, to make it more accountable and to advise participating groups like INQUEST on how to get the best out of their organizations, reacted with dismay, commenting that:

> The whole future of the scheme is at stake. This body, set up to replace the GLC in respect of cross borough grants, is in danger of foundering . . . Without grants in April, there will be chaos for services provided by voluntary groups.[9]

The statement went on to advise participating groups to issue redundancy notices as a precaution. INQUEST was one of the many groups that followed this advice, issuing formal notices late in March.[10] The Executive took a very serious view of the impasse and drew up a detailed contingency plan to cover what it referred to as the doomsday scenario, a prolonged political stalemate, the outcome of which might all too easily lead to the effective collapse of the organization. To guard against this, the plan covered items such as the rights and duties of workers to facilitate the running of the organization on a purely part-time basis, the storing of the archive and the complex legal position covering the disposal of INQUEST's – mainly fixed – assets.[11]

This was the second time in under two years that INQUEST had to contemplate the loss of its grant under this procedure. Nor was it to be the last time. An even worse crisis was to develop in 1991 when setting the budget was delayed until April – grants were not actually paid until well into June. This caused extreme hardship. The *Guardian* reported early in March that:

Many voluntary groups in London are on the brink of collapse
because of a political deadlock over the budget for the body that
awards their grants. Some groups, ranging from arts organizations and welfare agencies, have already run out of money and
face closure. Others have issued protective redundancy notices
to staff in case the stalemate is not broken . . . Most Tory boroughs have been pressing for a reduced budget. They have been
refusing to support a standstill . . . compromise proposals by an
alliance of 21 authorities, one short of the required majority.
(*Guardian* 18 March 1991)

Again, while it is true that the Conservative boroughs were certainly keen to keep expenditure to a minimum, the politics of compromise was made more difficult by the fact that there was a clear
disagreement over priorities. The Conservatives wanted to run down
advice and information groups, giving instead more priority to those
working with the elderly, disabled young people and those suffering
from drug and alcohol addiction.[12] It was reaching a compromise on
these issues as much as the overall size of the budget that led to the
delay and that constituted the real threat to INQUEST. That is to say,
while the delay in grant would be difficult, especially in the spring of
1991 when INQUEST was running an unexpected deficit, INQUEST could
almost certainly get by. But what was obviously more worrying – and
potentially more threatening – was a possible change in the committee's priorities away from advice groups, which would clearly
threaten the very basis of its funding.

These worries were partly justified when the final budget for 1991
was agreed and INQUEST received only six months' grant, the remainder to be paid in September subject to a report to the committee on its
various activities, including fundraising and measures to regulate its
out of London work to 6 per cent. In short, INQUEST was being pushed
towards becoming what the Conservatives on the committee referred
to as an "income generating" group – it could no longer sit back and
expect to receive "handouts".[13] To keep INQUEST and other similar
groups up to the mark the committee, or rather the London Borough
Grants Unit (LBGU) that daily administered the scheme on its behalf,
later appointed a part-time advisor on fundraising.

It is easy to see an element of political malice in this decision. The
Conservatives had long been sceptical about INQUEST, and its base in
Hackney probably inclined some outer London boroughs to the view

that they were subsidizing inner London radical chic. The outer, pre-dominantly Conservative, London boroughs continually complained that too much was being spent on inner London, so much so that groups like INQUEST had already had to monitor the distribution of their metropolitan cases. On the other hand, the demands on the boroughs were enormous, priorities surely had to be questioned, whatever the shifting political climate, and new and possibly even more radical initiatives funded. And as I have implied above, INQUEST was not the only group to be put on probation in this way. To make this point is not, of course, to absolve the boroughs from the shambles and the casualties that their procrastination produced, and whether the minister most directly involved should have intervened is an open question (*Guardian* 8 February 1991). Some of the worst affected were those administrators who worked at the LBGU itself. Not only were they pressed for answers to questions by groups like INQUEST which they could not give, their own jobs were under threat. At times groups did not know who their link worker was, or at least never had sufficient time to develop a relationship with them in order to explain their work and put their case. At one point during the process an INQUEST worker reported to the Executive Committee that, "Our rep did not seem to know much more than we did."[14]

INQUEST's initial response to its six months of probation was to raise the alarm. This it did primarily by using its contacts in the quality press. The role of the *Independent* was particularly important. Its Home Affairs correspondent Heather Mills wrote a very sympathetic column under the heading, "Another worry for the bereaved; grants cuts may kill off campaign for justice at inquests". The article outlined the importance of INQUEST, its success in attaining a national profile which was now threatened by the LBGC, which was demanding that it "look elsewhere" for funds. The article also included a quotation from the General Secretary of NAPO (National Association of Probation Officers) who argued that the loss of INQUEST would "leave a gap in the voluntary sector which would be impossible to fill" (*Independent* 17 January 1992). *The Times* also praised INQUEST's work and complained that it must now waste "valuable time" making a fresh application for funds in the autumn. INQUEST's address was listed for potential donors (*The Times* 11 June 1991).

While the LBGU was stung by the implied criticism, these articles, particularly the one in the *Independent*, were of considerable importance to INQUEST as we shall see. More routinely, the LBGU kept a close oversight of INQUEST's fundraising activities during these months. Thus in May 1991 it suggested that INQUEST should: identify the sum it wished to raise; list its fundraising activities to date, and the resources it was setting aside to support such activities, including the structure and membership of a fundraising committee and, most important of all, draw up a list of potential funders.[15]

The Executive Committee found this degree of scrutiny intrusive, but the tensions it generated were partly offset by the generally helpful advice and manner of the LBGU's part-time advisor on fundraising. She reminded INQUEST that it did not have to "re-invent the wheel", that fundraising was part of the daily diet of most groups in the voluntary sector and that INQUEST should work its highly developed network to learn about the skills it required, very basic skills like what sort of materials should be sent to potential donors. LBGU also helped by providing a short but useful list of funders who might be willing to give to a non-registered charity like INQUEST. What also succeeded in reducing the tension was that INQUEST was only being asked to have a strategy in place by the autumn, to have demonstrated that fundraising was being given some sort of priority; it was not expected to have raised funds in so short a time, except perhaps by way of an appeal to its members which was made during the summer of 1991. INQUEST's strategy detailing what applications had already been made, its plans for future applications, was eventually submitted to and accepted by the committee and its grant for the remainder of the year was released.

This result raised morale and INQUEST was further encouraged by the interest shown in its work by the Barrow and Geraldine S. Cadbury Trust. Its secretary, Anthony Wilson, had been alerted to the seriousness of INQUEST's plight by Heather Mills's article in the *Independent* and he made contact with the co-directors to arrange an informal meeting. This took place in February 1991. The outcome of the meeting was very positive. Those present felt that INQUEST was being invited to push at an open door. The only difficulty was over how the grant might be used. The nub of the issue was that unlike most funds that give grants for purely charitable purposes, money from the Barrow and Geraldine S. Cadbury Trust could be used for political campaign work, and Anthony Wilson was inclined to think that this was how it should be used, rather than for casework *per se*.[16]

This at first posed something of a dilemma for INQUEST, which had always emphasized casework; grassroots legal and welfare support for poor families before and during inquests. Some members were therefore anxious that this emphasis might be lost if the organization switched to more active political campaigning around the reform of inquest procedures. On the other hand, some argued that while casework was indeed the bedrock of INQUEST's work, it had always campaigned in the political arena to secure reforms in inquest procedures, reforms that were still sadly lacking after all its efforts. Surely both types of activity were not mutually exclusive; it was only through its detailed casework that INQUEST was in a position to argue for the wholesale reform to inquest procedures. The fact that this might lead to some reduction in casework in the short term should not be seen as a problem. This line of reasoning was eventually accepted by the Executive Committee in March 1991 and shortly afterwards the Barrow and Geraldine S. Cadbury Trust voted INQUEST in the region of £20,000 for each of the following three years.[17]

This relieved the pressure on INQUEST as far as funding was concerned. The issue would not go away, but at least the grant gave some relief and allowed for the first time the appointment of a part-time administrator to relieve the full-time workers for other things, including campaigning. This feeling of security and space was reinforced when at about the same time the LBGU decided to guarantee funding for a number of groups – including INQUEST – over a three-year period.[18] Why the LBGU took this decision is not entirely clear. Perhaps it was a reaction to the débâcle surrounding the allocation for 1991–2 or, more likely, a more thought-out position about the managerial and development problems that face groups whose existence is constantly threatened in the short term. Whatever the reason, INQUEST entered the financial year 1991–2 in a more secure position than ever before. After the years of uncertainty it was in a position to plan ahead, although whether its existing management structure was sufficiently developed to grasp this opportunity is another matter, and one we shall return to.

Structure

The pressure put on INQUEST to broaden the base of its funding was to have a significant effect on its structure. This was because most of the trusts to which INQUEST, given the nature of its work, could reasonably apply would only give to groups with charitable status. The Barrow and Geraldine S. Cadbury Trust was one of the few exceptions to this, but its timely generosity was unlikely to be repeated. The logic of this position was therefore pushing INQUEST towards securing charitable status. The difficulty for INQUEST in going down this road was that it could interfere with its campaigning role. Charities are not allowed to enter the political arena. Of course, the boundary between what is political activity rather than charitable activity is a fine one and no doubt INQUEST could have applied for charitable status on the basis of its advice and welfare role. However, it would then have had to look over its shoulder to see if any of its campaign work was legal in terms of its new status. Would it not be better instead to split the organization, presenting one section as a charity, the other as a campaign group? The pros and cons of this choice were spelt out in a letter from a group of west London solicitors who specialized in these matters:

> It is certainly not impossible for you to remain one organization . . . and still apply for charitable status. If you were to choose this option you could probably present a lot of your activities as offering information to the government with a view to increasing its awareness of the issues on which legislative change might be sought. However, you may also from time to time seek to do something which could not be presented as information provision, for example, taking part in leafleting campaigns or demonstrations and would be more likely to be seen as a form of political campaigning. The problem with being all one charitable organization is that you may find yourself agonizing over each decision to take part in activities of this kind, whereas if you had a separate campaign group the decision would be easier . . . This is the argument of the most practical importance to you and favours creating two separate groups. The problem with doing a substantial amount of campaigning within the charity is that it is likely to be found to be outside of your charitable status which would be threatened and with that any tax advantages you might have obtained through being a charity and various fundraising advantages which registered charities have.[19]

As a group which was in the process of drawing up a Private Member's Bill to reform inquest procedures and therefore actively seeking to change the law the solicitor's advice left INQUEST with a simple choice; it either stayed as it was or divided itself into two separate organizations. The Executive Committee favoured the latter, but this left it with another important decision: how, or in what form, was the new charitable organization to be set up? As an incorporated company limited by guarantee or as an unincorporated association with charitable trustees? The advantage of the former was that it would limit the organization's financial liabilities and, of equal importance, it would also protect individual members of the organization from being sued in the event of a libel action. The Executive came down in favour of incorporation and was advised that this could be done in the process of preparing for registration as a charity.

It was one thing, of course, for the Executive Committee to recommend that INQUEST should seriously explore the possibility of applying for charitable status. What its members might think was another matter. It was thus decided to circulate members with an explanation of the Executive Committee's intentions and invite them to debate it at a Special General Meeting to be held in May or June 1992. The explanation gave several reasons for the proposed restructuring. First, it pointed out that INQUEST urgently needed extra funds. Its grant from the LBGU had been frozen at its previous level. The organization was therefore being asked to do the same amount of work – indeed more – on the same amount of money. Secondly, whereas the GLC had not bothered much about INQUEST's out of London work, the LBGU was now monitoring this very closely and insisting, not unreasonably as a body representing London ratepayers, that this work, or at least the bulk of it must be funded from elsewhere. The notice then went on to point out that raising this additional money for a group like INQUEST was far from easy, and that charitable status, which necessitated a restructuring of the organization in order that INQUEST's political work could continue, was the preferred way forward.[20] A thinly attended meeting gave the Executive the authority to press ahead and explore the option. The formal authorization to make the actual change came at the subsequent AGM.

The decision to consult the membership was obviously a proper one. The Executive Committee could not, in the words of Tony Ward, be seen to be "hijacking" the organization. On the other hand, attendance at the Special General Meeting had been poor and there was little formal debate about what difficulties might lie ahead. There was one well informed written contribution. This supported the proposed restructuring as probably being "inevitable" if INQUEST was to survive and expand its role, but went on to point out some of the complexities involved in being subject to external supervision by the Charity Commission.[21]

The work involved in setting up INQUEST as a charitable trust as an incorporated company – as distinct from INQUEST the campaign group

– was undertaken by a small sub-committee. It was a painstaking process, and this, combined with the lengthy time it routinely takes the Charity Commissioners to consider new registrations, meant that INQUEST did not formally receive charitable status until early in 1995. Of great help to INQUEST during this process was Mark Mullins who served on INQUEST's Executive Committee as a representative of the Inquest Lawyers' Group. It is to the work of this group and its relationship with INQUEST that we now turn.

Inquest Lawyers' Group (ILG)

It will have already become obvious that INQUEST can draw on a small group of solicitors and barristers who are expert on the conduct of inquests. It would also be true to say that many of these solicitors and barristers have developed their expertise working in cases with INQUEST. However, this contact had been organized on an entirely *ad hoc* basis until 1991 when INQUEST and a small group of those lawyers regularly involved with it floated the idea of setting up the Inquest Lawyers' Group.

To test whether there was enough support for such a group an inaugural public meeting was called at the Inns of Court in September 1991. This was addressed by Anthony Scrivener QC, a former chair of the Bar Council. In a short but powerful speech he outlined why the inquest was such an important stage in the English legal process, and then went on to argue that the "ordinary individual" was at a great disadvantage during such hearings when confronted by the great departments of state and the police, not least because of the lack of legal aid, but also because of official secrecy which "while a proud tribute to the power of the Civil Service" was a sad reflection on British democracy.[22] Dr Paul Knapman, a senior London coroner, was then invited to give his views. Tim Owen also spoke, as did a family member suggested by INQUEST.

The meeting was well attended and enough interest was shown to make the group a going concern. By 1991 a list of aims and priorities was drawn up. These included providing training sessions for solicitors on inquest law and procedures with a view to having a national pool of lawyers both able and willing to provide legal representation at inquests. This was particularly welcomed by INQUEST. All too often solicitors engaged by families understandably often know very little about how inquests work and are all too easily outmanoeuvred by coroners. To expand the network of trained lawyers it could call upon, particularly in the provinces, but also in more routine London cases which were unlikely to be taken on board by its own coterie of high profile lawyers, was a priority for INQUEST too. What also became a shared priority was the ILG's commitment to lobby and campaign for law reform, especially for the provision of legal aid and for the over-haul of the Coroners' Rules to provide for advance disclosure. As I have already noted, INQUEST had entered into a commitment with the Barrow and Geraldine S. Cadbury Trust to give more time to law reform *per se*. To co-operate on this issue would clearly be an advantage. Finally, the ILG hoped to create a regular forum – bi-monthly meetings – to discuss developments in the law, to take note of recent judgments and to swap information on inquests attended.[23] (A mechanism for storing and then disseminating such judgments and/or rulings was also discussed at a later meeting.)

While the progress of the group as measured by these priorities has been somewhat uneven – the ILG tends to move in fits and starts – much has been achieved. Meetings to report on individual cases and rulings have been held. In November 1993, for example, there was a wide-ranging discussion of *ex parte* Jamieson and the danger that by trying to stretch the "lack of care" verdict too far the higher courts might move to restrict its use. The issue here, simply put, was that lack of care verdicts stand somewhere between verdicts of misadventure and unlawful killing and imply a degree of culpability on those charged with looking after prisoners and/or patients, and as we have seen, INQUEST had often successfully pressed for such verdicts. To restrict its use might seriously restrict INQUEST's effectiveness.[24] Ed Fitzgerald also spoke about the Hillsborough ruling (see Ch. 5). Training sessions for lawyers unfamiliar with inquests have also been held. These were at first organized by the group itself, but were subsequently farmed out to the Legal Action Group. INQUEST's co-directors normally take part in these sessions. So far they have all taken place in London. Attempts to stimulate sufficient interest in major provincial cities like Leeds have so far failed. This activity has helped to raise the ILG's profile. By 1992 it had an individual and corporate membership of around 60 – mostly London based including some well known national figures such as Michael Mansfield who later became involved in the *Marchioness* inquest.

But arguably more significant in the long run has been the ILG's willingness to take on board legal reform with the drafting of a Bill to amend the Coroners' Act. This has always been on the ILG's agenda, but it was given greater priority by INQUEST's commitment to its new funders to spend more time campaigning for legal reform. This was explained to an ILG meeting in March 1993. A sub-committee with an agreed programme of work was immediately set up and by November 1993 the full text of a draft Bill was considered and agreed in full ILG committee. The principles of the Bill were discussed with members of INQUEST's Executive Committee, relayed to INQUEST's membership and at one point considered by its campaigns sub-committee; in addition, June Tweedie was fully involved in the drafting process.

November is an important month in the Parliamentary calendar. It is then that a draw takes place to select which backbench MPs will be allowed to bring forward a Private Member's Bill of their choice; to have it debated in the House and then with luck see it through all its Parliamentary stages onto the Statute Book. With its Bill now drafted INQUEST attempted to find a likely sponsor, and some MPs high up in the draw with the best chance of success showed a sympathetic interest, but none in the end were prepared to bring it forward.

In retrospect this was hardly surprising. Sounding out sympathetic MPs is not something that can be rushed. Secondly, Private Member's Bills rarely get through without a broad measure of cross-bench support and this had not been secured – even really worked at – although the need for this had been agreed at an ILG strategy meeting with Barry Sheerman MP in July 1993. But the Bill remains in place, incorporating many of the reforms that INQUEST has campaigned for over the years, such as legal aid, advance disclosure and so forth. The intention is for INQUEST and the ILG to give it a more considered, public launch early in 1996. How this will fare in the light of the government's determination to drive down the cost of legal aid remains to be seen. To put the same thing another way, whatever the level of cross-bench support, Private Member's Bills rarely succeed unless the government of the day is willing to accept them. It was in an attempt to press the government on this that, in the course of drawing up its Bill the Inquest Lawyers' Group joined with the Law Society to launch a campaign, "Victims without a Voice", which sharply opposed attempts by the government to redefine the basis for legal aid.[25]

This high level of collaboration, the fact that there is a degree of overlapping membership between the two groups, raises questions about the independence of the ILG. Is it the Inquest Lawyers' Group or INQUEST's Lawyers' Group? Strictly speaking it is the former, although it is committed to INQUEST's radical reforming agenda. This position had to be secured, since not all those who originally expressed an interest in the group were agreed on such a platform and it was left to Tim Owen to argue that:

> The ILG was formed to support and extend the campaigning work of INQUEST. It follows that membership of the ILG must in my view involve acceptance of and respect for the policy aims and objectives of INQUEST which have been developed and refined as a result of 12 years campaigning. In this sense the ILG does not have a distinct identity separate from INQUEST and we should not encourage the idea that because we are a lawyers' group we are somehow "neutral" about whose interests we are seeking to advance. The ILG does not exist to assist insurance companies, the Home Office, the police or health authorities in representing themselves at inquests. When we debate the aims of the ILG we must keep at the forefront of our minds the official aims of INQUEST.[26]

Tim Owen also had to argue INQUEST's case for reforming inquests against those in the group who felt that the inquisitorial system it employed was outmoded and that existing procedures should be scrapped altogether.[27] As I have already indicated, these arguments won "broad support" and the link with INQUEST secured. To avoid any future difficulties it was even suggested that while the ILG could of course debate and amend its aims when it thought necessary, these should be first endorsed by INQUEST's Executive Committee.[28]

In truth, this symbiotic relationship has troubled INQUEST more than it has troubled the ILG. For example, it was later reported that INQUEST had expressed "some concern" that the ILG still had no formal constitution detailing its aims and objectives, and there was some disappointment too when the ILG failed to continue with its option of sending one of its members to meetings of INQUEST's Executive Committee.[29] Notwithstanding these concerns, the groups have remained very much in step and when in gear the ILG is a useful extra limb for INQUEST, enhancing its credibility and spreading its message in an influential area of public life. It has also, I should add, given financial support to INQUEST in times of need, agreeing for example to meet some of the legal cost incurred in registering with the Charity Commission.[30]

149

Management and managerialism

To suggest that INQUEST has been "crisis managed" during the last 14 years should come as no surprise. The persistent threat to its funding, its long period of underfunding in the face of an increasing workload, these pressures must surely have taken their toll on the Executive Committee's capacity to take control of the organization and plan ahead. The pressures of simply keeping afloat during recent years are well known to most groups in the voluntary sector, not least to those who have gone under. However, INQUEST's financial worries cannot wholly explain its management failings. Indeed, in some cases the latter have been responsible for the former as grant applications have either been delayed or put off altogether. So how can I best explain INQUEST's problems? Perhaps the most obvious place to start is with the relationship between its mainly voluntary Executive Committee and its full-time workers.

When full-time workers were first appointed in 1982 fears were expressed that they might professionalize the organization. That is to say, a self-help organization that relied upon everyone making a contribution would be replaced by full-time workers who would steadily marginalize those actually involved in campaigns, those who had acquired skills from the bottom up. In this way the force, the moral force of the organization would be diluted.[31] I pointed out in Chapter 3 that these anxieties were misplaced early on, and that those involved in campaigns continued to play an important role. However, what was perhaps more justifiable was the anxiety expressed early on about the way the full-time employees ran the INQUEST office and how they related to the Executive. In a frank letter of resignation from the Executive Committee Ken Worpole complained that the INQUEST office was in "constant disarray", that the workers must learn some elementary "management" skills and that methods must be developed for communicating with the Executive Committee as a whole rather than through individuals.[32]

Many of those involved with INQUEST at this time agree that such criticisms were not without some foundation. The workers were simply "muddling through", particularly when it came to running the office, which seems to have been in such a mess that some members of the Executive were actually put off from going there. However, as Worpole himself concedes, the Executive Committee had to take some responsibility for this state of affairs. It was clearly its duty to make sure that Tony Ward and Dave Leadbetter developed the necessary office skills, and to make sure that well defined, collective policies were in place rather than, as one of the workers was to put it, to have allowed a situation to develop where:

> There seemed to be abrupt changes of view between one meeting and another. As a result we, the workers, often felt that whatever it was that we had been doing, we ought really to have been doing something else, and that something else kept changing.[33]

Granted, this is to simplify a complex situation. Some members of the Executive, Celia Stubbs for example, gave the full-time workers a lot of support, Alistair Brinkley for a time looked after the books and David Ransom kept in touch with INQUEST's Parliamentary Group. In the main, however, the Executive Committee effectively did little to iron out the group's management problems, and as often happens in these situations, the relationship between the workers – one of them was frequently out of the office campaigning – became strained and it was decided, under the slightly embarrassed but revealing heading of "Alternatives to chewing the carpet", to appoint someone from the outside "with whom the workers could discuss their work on a regular basis".[34] Typically though, the Executive left the workers to find the "someone" themselves. In some ways it could be argued that they came up with an ideal person, Roz Kane. She had both founded and worked in small voluntary organizations and was a trained psychotherapist. In retrospect, however, it is difficult to avoid the judgement that what the full-time workers really required was not psychotherapy but management, something the Executive became increasingly unwilling to take on board as the 1980s progressed.

It is easy to see how this situation arose. In the first place, while INQUEST's relationship with the GLC's Police Committee was close on issues of policy – its contact worker was in regular touch and on good terms with INQUEST's full-time workers – the GLC itself took very little interest in how its money was spent. Provided the accounts revealed no discrepancies, and money had been used strictly in accordance with the terms of the relevant local government legislation under which it had been authorized, the authority kept its distance. It was not in any discernible way interested in securing "value for money", to investigate whether groups like INQUEST were being managed to give Londoners the quality of service they deserved. In short, there was no external pressure on INQUEST to put its house in order. Nor, apart from the occasional outburst like those referred to above, was there very much internal pressure. In truth, the idea that Executive Committee members were somehow "employers" responsible for controlling their workers across the whole range of their activities was anathema to the organization. A revealing paragraph in one of the workers' responses to Worpole's critique begins by hoping that INQUEST does not try to establish:

> The sort of crummy, discredited old management structure that has caused so much grief in police monitoring circles. INQUEST has evolved a democratic structure that meets its needs reasonably well. Instead of 10 people telling two people what (and especially what not) to do, we have 12 or 13 Committee members deciding what they will do together.[35]

Of course this is a romantic picture of how INQUEST really worked, as we have demonstrated, but it well illustrates the collectivist sentiment on which INQUEST muddled through in the 1980s.

This style of management is reflected in the Executive Committee minutes, particularly in the second half of the 1980s. These are dominated by long lists of cases that formed the bulk of the workers' monthly reports. Some of these cases raised extremely important issues, many of which I have touched upon in earlier chapters. These were often discussed in great detail. In contrast, there are routine, but only brief references to financial and/or organizational matters, although on occasions what to do if funding was terminated and the organization had to continue without paid workers looms large. Apart from these exceptional moments, however, there is little about managing or developing the organization, about training, supervision, work projections or really any of the items that might routinely be expected to appear on the agenda of even a moderately efficient organization. Members of the Executive had joined INQUEST to take on and campaign around cases and argue through the issues that they raised, and that is precisely what they did.

By the early 1990s this had changed dramatically; it is almost as if the Executive Committee's priorities had suddenly been reversed. Visually, even, the minutes look quite different. Instead of long lists of cases there are dense paragraphs on managing and developing the organization. What caused this change?

External factors were highly significant. When the LBGC took over from the GLC in 1986 there was at first no real change in the relationship between groups and the grant-giving authority, other than the developing uncertainty about the scheme as a whole that I have already discussed. Basically groups were left to manage themselves much as before. Slowly, however, things began to change as the London Borough Grants Unit (LBGU) became far more interested in the management of groups, especially groups like INQUEST that had secured three-year funding. Thus, in February 1993 the LBGU wrote to INQUEST complaining that "very basic administrative tasks had not been carried out", that its duties were exercised in a very "ad hoc manner" and that this had led to a "complete breakdown" of internal communication.[36] While it is true that INQUEST had invited this particular rebuke by failing, among other things, to send in its grant application form on time, this LBGU intervention was just one of many. The unit, quite unlike the GLC before it, was becoming more interested in securing "value for money". It therefore began routinely to intervene in the day-to-day affairs of groups like INQUEST, to question whether they were using their funds in the best way possible and whether they were giving Londoners a good deal in return.

In INQUEST's case this was supposed to be guaranteed by a service agreement or contract that set out what services it offered, the levels at which they would be provided and the mechanisms by which they would be monitored. The service document was very detailed, containing eight major clauses and 26 sub-clauses.[37] It specified, for example, that the INQUEST office would be open from 9.30 a.m. to 5.30 p.m., that INQUEST must obtain feedback on the quality of its services and relay this back to the LBGU, and that postal inquiries were to be dealt with within a specified number of working days.

INQUEST was simply not used to this level of interference as most members of the Executive considered it – arguing that it would interfere with its proper work, that is, casework and campaigning. This culture shock was only partly relieved by the understanding that what was happening was part of a much wider revolution in local government. To put it simply, local government generally was now much more interested in securing "value for money" and the detailed service contract that went hand in hand with the hiving off of many local government functions was seen as one means of securing it. Service audits were far more demanding than straightforward financial audits, and voluntary bodies no less than the private service operators were

153

having to learn to live with them. It was, argued the Conservative government, a new mechanism for extending and deepening accountability. In this sense INQUEST had not been singled out, it was simply that the LBGU had now caught up with the new local government orthodoxy.

The warts that this closer inspection revealed were partly offset by the fact that INQUEST had become increasingly aware of its own deficiencies, and had at least made some preliminary moves to correct them. June Tweedie had shown a particular interest in getting in outside management advice from the Federation of Independent Advice Centres (FIAC). This is an umbrella organization for the voluntary sector. It offers a range of services to its members, including a subsidized management consultancy package. INQUEST's secretary had been instructed to contact FIAC in March 1991 and some months later an outside management consultant – through FIAC – was appointed.[38] The original consultation exercise lasted five days, but this was subsequently extended. While there was some resentment towards this exercise, primarily because of the time and energy it consumed, most members of the Executive Committee realized that it, or something like it, was necessary. Since the arrival of Deborah Coles in 1990 INQUEST had increased its public profile. The result was more referrals and ever increasing demands from elsewhere, especially the media. There were no extra resources to meet these demands and the organization began to creak ominously.

The consultant's report confirmed this pressure. Overall the review found that INQUEST had reached a watershed:

> increasing demand for its services is putting intolerable strain on workers; concentration on casework has limited and undermined the [capacity of the] agency to take on other work effectively, such as campaign and information work; and there have been few resources devoted to managing and providing an administrative base for its activities.[39]

The report went on:

> It was acknowledged that casework takes up most of the resources of the organization. This was estimated to be about 90 per cent of the work that was carried out by staff overall. It was felt that there needs to be a more even distribution between case-

work, campaigning work and information work. The emphasis placed on casework also means that little time is devoted to carrying out the support tasks of administration, finance and management. It was thought that a more appropriate allocation of time spent on these different activities would give greater emphasis to non-casework activities. For example, casework 30 per cent, campaigning and information work 30 per cent, administration and management 40 per cent. The high allocation to administration and management could be reduced after systems have been put in place.[40]

While the percentage distribution of tasks seemed a little arbitrary to some, the main thrust of the consultant's report was accepted by a majority of the Executive. The difficulty was going to be to secure this redistribution, however it was going to be apportioned in detail. The first and most obvious problem was that some members in the organization were still wedded to the absolute primacy of casework. This was very understandable. It is casework that marks out INQUEST from most other groups in the lobby; it burrows away searching out injustices, not to say on occasions, even brutalities. To suggest subordinating such activity to management tasks was always going to be resisted. Thus, and this is the second, related problem, monitoring this proposed shift, making sure that it was actually taking place was always going to be tricky for a voluntary executive, several of whose members were holding down demanding full-time jobs elsewhere. It was partly to facilitate this that it was decided – with the consultant's blessing – to constitute a smaller management committee to oversee and support this change, to oversee and assist the full-time workers more closely than it had done in the past. However, the consultant constantly made the point that there was a limit to what the Executive Committee could do and that it was incumbent on the workers to co-operate (and communicate) to make these and other changes work.

Such a realization in no way absolved the Executive Committee. It too needed to change. Reflecting on the consultant's work – then still in progress – one member of the Executive confided to the chair:

The point is that the EC has never "managed" the work or the workers; we don't even follow through/monitor the implementation of agreed work. Our style is to let things slide and depend on the workers' own effectiveness, without any structure or supportive management and then at the last minute to ask them about it, and then usually grumble because it has not been done.[41]

This is a harsh judgement, but not too far from the truth, and shows just how much needed to be done to turn the organization around as late as June 1993. Significantly, however, the same letter also gives us an insight into just how difficult this was going to be when it suggested that one of the major causes of the organization's problems was that its full-time workers enjoyed the privilege of being *ex officio* members of the Executive Committee with voting rights. It was just this point – although the emphasis was more on financial rectitude than effective management – that the LBGU had pressed on INQUEST during the previous year. This had been debated by the Executive Committee and, as a constitutional amendment to remove this privilege was required, the issue was put to the same general meeting that considered the issue of charitable status. The chair dutifully spoke about the advantages of such an amendment, that it would facilitate formal supervision and strengthen the chain of command, but also absolve INQUEST's full-time workers from any direct responsibility if the organization were to collapse; the responsibility for this should quite properly fall on the Executive Committee and not the workers.

These arguments did not prevail. Once the meeting established that the workers always acted with complete propriety, that is to say, argued about their wages and conditions when the issue arose but then withdrew, never exercising their right to vote, the meeting decided to maintain the status quo. Clearly members still preferred – almost ten years later – a situation where the 10 or 13 committee members decided what should be done collectively to a situation where ten voluntary members tell two paid workers what they can or should be doing. *Plus ça change*. Or to make the same point in a slightly different way, when Sue Slipman resigned as chairperson of the National Council for One Parent Families she was credited by a colleague as having transformed the organization from a "hotbed of radical left do-goodery" into "a strong operation with a £1m turnover, and which observers claim is a model of managerial efficiency" (*Independent* 25 February 1995). Few members of INQUEST willed a similar transformation, still less the public acclaim for having secured it!

On the basis of the limited access I have to current developments, it would not be too wide of the mark to suggest that this resistance to managerialism persists, thereby arguably inhibiting INQUEST from putting its house in order, of modernizing itself to accommodate new funding realities.

Balanced against this judgement, however, it is important to remind INQUEST's critics of just how much has been achieved and also what is at stake. As the consultant herself rightly stressed:

> The difficulties facing INQUEST are in good part the result of success. It is to the credit of the organization and the people involved that INQUEST continues to provide, despite the pressures experienced, a vital and unique service of high quality to its users.[42]

Furthermore, it is fair to point out that the opportunity cost of such highly effective casework is that even important administrative tasks sometimes have to be neglected. Distraught parents, emotionally gutted partners, cannot simply be told to call another day, or inquests re-arranged to suit a timetable drawn up by external funders. Also, small, underfunded, case-driven organizations like INQUEST where, for example, the absence of one of its two workers through illness can play havoc with administrative schedules, are never likely to be well thought of according to the tenets of the new managerialism that is being imposed on the voluntary sector. Applied insensitively and with little in mind other than squeezing still more out of an already over-stretched voluntary organization, such managerialism can be arguably counter-productive, lowering morale and limiting the capacity for change. The LBGU was sometimes guilty of such insensitivity, which did nothing to assist those trying to keep INQUEST afloat.

Finally, and arguably most important of all, it is worth reflecting on David Brindle's interview with David Gutch about the state of the UK voluntary sector in the early 1990s. He wrote:

> When he crossed the Atlantic in 1991 to specially study the impact of contracting, Gutch found a voluntary sector squeezed by local government demanding more and paying less – and often paying late – and deluged with costly and time consuming paperwork. Needing to be more managerial and businesslike, groups had appointed lawyers and accountants to their boards, often in place of users of their services, and had lost their capacity to campaign.
>
> "The organization changes from an independent body to an agent of the state," says Gutch, "the more that local authority

requirements imposes on its contractors, standards to be met, the more effectively does the organization become an arm of the authority". (*Guardian* 18 May 1994)

This trend could have a serious and debilitating effect on the quality of our civic culture, silencing protest and elevating managerialism above normative concerns and judgements. According to this reading, INQUEST's organizational problems, its perceived reluctance to modernize itself, all these things are more a matter of praise than blame. Even if this cannot excuse all of INQUEST's many inefficiencies, it contains an important kernel of truth, and one that many current members of the group adhere to.

Chapter 7

Conclusion

In this chapter I attempt an overall assessment of INQUEST's work at several levels. This begins with a fairly straightforward assessment of its contribution to the welfare of families involved in inquests and its campaigns to change various policies and practices associated with state institutions. This will draw on material from previous chapters. I then pass on to look more critically at INQUEST's part in reaffirming the role of inquests as part of the ongoing process of securing the state's legitimacy. This is something I have already touched on, but which now needs to be further developed. Thirdly, I attempt to look at its work in a somewhat unconventional way that stresses less its role as a defender of civil liberties but more its role as a pressure group that exposes the nature and limits of modern governance. Finally, there is a discussion of what implications there might be for political scientists and policy analysts in looking at INQUEST in these ways.

The balance sheet

Naturally, even when the death of a relative or friend is expected, it is likely to be hard to bear. When it happens unexpectedly, especially when it is both violent and sudden, those who are left behind, the living, are particularly vulnerable. Apart from immediate emotional support, what the bereaved want above all else is to know exactly what happened, what were the circumstances surrounding the death over which they grieve.

INQUEST has provided this emotional support for hundreds of families over the years and advised on the sometimes difficult business of discovering the truth. Inevitably the level of its involvement with families has varied. Sometimes it has just been an hour listening over the telephone, at other times it has been both listening and providing legal advice and contacts. A maximum involvement case could mean meeting and briefing solicitors and barristers; addressing campaign meetings where families have called them; liaising with the press; attending the inquest and even afterwards, perhaps advising on civil proceedings. Quite often, even where the bereaved do not become members of the INQUEST Executive Committee or its Family Support Group, friendships develop during the course of these processes and people stay in touch.

This support is often reciprocated. It is not at all unusual for INQUEST's workers to draw strength from clients. Their determination, their energy and warmth – such attributes frequently drive the workers on in what is sometimes an emotionally draining job. We have found no evidence to suggest that INQUEST exploits these relationships. A case will never be pursued without the family's consent, and there are clear guidelines, for example, covering the release of details about families to the press. Of course, we cannot deny that on one or two occasions families have felt that barristers have let them down, still less can we deny that a better managed organization might have provided an even better service for even more families. In this sense INQUEST has perhaps not always given value for money. On the other hand, the evidence suggests that, in the words of Louis Blom-Cooper, INQUEST has done "surprisingly well" on modest resources. This attention to routine casework, and the testimony of those who have benefited from it, has arguably been INQUEST's outstanding achievement and its most useful bulwark against politicians and coroners who accuse it of being "politically motivated" and who wish it would go away.

Beyond this immediate emotional and legal support for the bereaved, INQUEST has also succeeded in turning a number of individual cases into broader issues about the treatment of those held in state custody. How the police deal with those in their care, or in the process of arrest, is now a matter of public concern. Before INQUEST came on the scene no-one was much bothered about what appeared to be a peripheral issue. For example, when the Home Office was first asked about how many people died in police custody in 1979 it had to admit that it had no idea what the numbers were. Now the Home Secretary does know, and he/she should also be aware from the Police Complaints Authority if nothing else that arguably many of these deaths could, should and can be avoided. The capacity of prisons to generate suicide is also a matter of public record and concern and very significant changes from top to bottom – from the creation of the Suicide Prevention Unit at the Home Office in 1990 to the issuing of suicide prevention packs to all frontline prison officers – have been effected. It is true that other groups in the lobby can reasonably claim to have shown a recent interest in this issue; it is also true that the growing number of prison suicides – they totalled over 60 in 1994 – might have forced the Home Office to act. However, there is little doubt that, as with deaths in police custody, INQUEST in conjunction with a group of interested Opposition MPs made most of the early running, not least at the level of understanding how suicides were to be understood. INQUEST's agitation around a series of black deaths in psychiatric hospitals also helped to tease out the racial bias in certain forms of diagnosis and treatment that may have contributed to more black fatalities than there need have been.

In raising these and other issues about the treatment of those held in or around state custody INQUEST has certainly made its mark. Of course, it is another matter to claim that by simply raising this or that issue INQUEST can take credit for some of the more specific improvements that have been introduced during recent years in these areas, although we believe that the evidence of our narrative points to some strong connections. However, it might be suggested that INQUEST could have achieved even more if it had adopted a narrower focus. As it was, it seemed to have been associated with campaigns to limit prison suicides, working with the Council for the Welfare of Immigrants to secure safeguards for asylum seekers through a Charter for Immigration Detainees, campaigning for a new forum to deal with major disasters like Hillsborough and Zeebrugge and so on.

We do believe that there is something in this criticism. As a group with modest resources it possibly stretched itself too far. It was too willing to become embroiled in campaigns that were either peripheral to its main rationale of investigating controversial deaths or, alternatively, were better left to other sympathetic groups with more human and financial resources. This would have sharpened its focus and arguably increased its effectiveness but, even more important, allowed more attention to be given to its casework, its bedrock activity.

Against this, however, it would not be unreasonable to point out that its campaigning activity was in practice spread unevenly, and that although its presence can indeed be detected in a number of campaigns, its core activity was always around deaths in custody and that mostly in these campaigns, as in family campaigns around individual deaths, its role was more as facilitator than as a prime mover. It was, for example, more than willing to give legal support to the Hillsborough families and offer its AGM as a platform to talk through the issues, but it was the Hillsborough Support Group and the researchers at Edge Hill College who really took the strain. Likewise it was the rank and file trade unionists in the construction industry who picketed building sites and inquests and lobbied ministers, not INQUEST. And while INQUEST has given legal advice to the Campaign for Bedsit Rights, it is those who have suffered the loss of family or friends from carbon monoxide poisoning or in fires in multi-occupancy tenancies who have taken the campaign to Parliament and the press.[1] Finally, even INQUEST's important work over inquest procedures in Northern Ireland and its attempt to work through the European Court over the Gibraltar killings to secure reforms to the inquest system in England and Wales never took priority over its day-to-day casework, and were in any case undertaken in tandem with other groups such as Rights Watch.[2]

But did this breadth of activity distract INQUEST from working to secure Parliamentary backing for the wholesale reform of inquest procedures? After all, its achievements on this front have been fairly modest. This seems unlikely for the reason given in Chapter 4, namely, that the Parliamentary consensus for these changes has not existed since the 1980s. It is worth restating that for many other pressure groups in the civil liberties lobby the Parliamentary gains during this period were equally modest or non-existent. Indeed, some groups were not only uninfluential in Parliament, they were sometimes thrown into complete disarray by the politics of law and order, and in the process almost tore themselves apart. The most obvious example around the time of the miners' strike in 1984 was the National Council for Civil Liberties with which INQUEST worked, and to which it was affiliated.[3] (The NCCL later changed its name to Liberty.)

However, it is true that INQUEST has remained naïve about how to organize its lobby activities in this respect, about how to build a Parliamentary consensus, which is what is required, even now when it judges that the wider political climate is on the turn. In particular, its recent attempt to secure a sponsor for its Private Member's Bill, although always working against the clock it is true, did not display the commitment of resources over a sustained period that is required to secure so major a change. Either more resources for this have to be found from somewhere, or its other activities curtailed.

While the balance sheet I have drawn up does INQUEST some credit there are other ways of looking at its work, other ways of adding up the pluses and minuses. Not least among these – to confirm Dr Burton's worst fears – is to consider INQUEST's role in putting the politics back into inquests.

The politics of inquests

During the course of the James Davey Campaign (see Ch. 2) a number of academics at the University of Warwick and their students offered practical support to the family (see Ch. 3). But perhaps more significant in the long run, they also began to look more critically at INQUEST's work and the role of coroners. In a subsequent article arising out of this research they argued that:

> Any death arising from the behaviour of police officers has implications beyond the morale of the force or the tragedy of the individual death. It raises uncomfortable issues about the nature of police force and the degree of accountability, quite apart from the public intrusion into the cell block and the rule book that follows such an event. Behind these suspicious deaths with their rumours of excessive force and innuendoes of unlawful violence, lies the taint of arbitrary power and unthinkable aspersions on the rule of law.[4]

What is true of deaths in police custody is also true of deaths in prisons and psychiatric hospitals. In his report on prison suicides, for example, Judge Tumim spoke of such deaths giving rise to "all manner of prejudices".[5] In the Ashworth report, Blom-Cooper argued that deaths in psychiatric hospitals "instinctively" excite "the notion that the death was unnatural".[6] It is just as important that suspicions about these deaths be allayed as those that have occurred at the hands of police. When we lock people away in liberal democratic societies we do not throw away the rule of law at the same time.

Looked at in this way inquests into custodial deaths have a propaganda purpose. The state agency involved wishes to demonstrate that the rule of law has been upheld, that the actions of its officials have been anything but arbitrary, while others like INQUEST seek to test this assertion. The media and influential elites are usually in attendance. It is important what the jury decides. If the state agency involved gets a bad result then it will seriously consider judicial review, since what is at stake here is its authority, its legitimacy. As a safeguard to our liberties then, these inquests are not unreasonably seen as important, as highly political events. They reaffirm the power ratio between the state and the individual.

The problem, of course, as this book has demonstrated is that the parties at the inquest are hardly on an equal footing, and it is not in the interests of the state to initiate reforms to see that they are, to see its own propaganda advantage in any way diminished. Indeed, it has been argued that the state has even recently moved to strengthen its position. Briefly put, the argument is that inquests could well be conducted without juries, as the Broderick report pointed out, but to do so would throw suspicion on the state and eliminate a crucial democratic element from the process of investigating controversial deaths.[7] They have therefore been kept in place, and on the surface at least their neutrality strengthened by INQUEST's initiative to secure their random selection. However, other changes to the Coroners' Rules in recent years have attempted to limit the range of critical verdicts that can be reached, and have abolished the right of juries to issue riders. In other words, the legitimizing stamp of the jury is required by the state, but definite limits must be set on its powers to criticize and initiate.

To pursue this point it is perhaps worth recalling that the state enters an inquest with an enormous advantage anyway because all inquests begin with the assumption that it, or rather its employees, has no clear-cut case to answer. If there had been *prima facie* evidence of wrong-doing then either the Crown Prosecution Service or the DPP would have prosecuted, with an inquest perhaps to follow once the criminal trial had taken place. True, the inquest might throw up such *prima facie* evidence of wrongdoing, but the state has removed the right of inquests to name guilty parties and initiate criminal proceedings following a verdict. It is now up to the DPP to initiate criminal proceedings, which as we have seen he or she rarely does, even when a jury returns a verdict of unlawful killing. The DPP is thus in control at the beginning and the end of the process; all he or she really has to do is sit back and hope that juries and/or, as in the case of Oliver Pryce,

INQUEST or some other august body like the Bar Council, will not rock the boat.

But the DPP's confidence is not shared in other branches of the state apparatus which are in no position to leave such delicate matters to chance. For example, Boards of Visitors, who are appointed to oversee the administration of our prisons and to be the "eyes and ears" of the Home Secretary, issue detailed advice to their members through their Association (AMBOV) about how to manage inquests. These include advice about what should be in press releases. In the case of a suicide, for example, the existence of a suicide prevention group in the prison should be mentioned. There is also advice about how and when press releases should be written – e.g. in longhand to suggest spontaneity if the statement is to be issued after an inquest and written in good time to meet editorial deadlines.[8]

The work of INQUEST and its supporters in reaffirming the symbolic and politically sensitive role of inquests is arguably another outstanding achievement, different in kind from the emotional and legal support it has offered to families over the years, but, at another level, surely equally important. The modern liberal democratic state exercises powers over us all, quite considerable powers, but the exercise of such power has to be continually legitimized; it is not something that we either give up once and for all as some political theorists would have us believe, or allow to be taken for granted as every controversial inquest affirms. If this makes certain coroners uncomfortable then this is a great pity, since it suggests that as independent judicial officers they are key participants in a process they only partly understand. But as we have already seen, not all coroners are as naïve or as uncritical as this suggests, nor for that matter are the different state agencies always sufficiently at one to secure victory. In these cases governance is challenged. INQUEST and the families they represent win cases, and even where prosecutions are not forthcoming as in the Blair Peach case, for example, compensation is sometimes paid in tacit admission that a wrong has been committed.

The rhetoric and practice of opposition

It might be reasonably argued that all this talk about the state is to simplify a somewhat complex phenomenon. We do not dissent from this view and, in particular, acknowledge that much of INQUEST's anti-state rhetoric is something of a blunt instrument. It is not necessary to subscribe to the more extravagant tenets of postmodernism to appreciate that the state is an ensemble of institutions and that the business of what these days is called governance suggests a number of locales or networks that exercise power in the guise of the state in sometimes semi-autonomous, even contradictory ways. In the words of Nikolas Rose & Peter Miller:

> The entities and agents within governmental networks are not faithful relays, mere creatures of a controller situated in some central hub. They utilize and deploy whatever sources they have for their own purposes, and the extent to which they carry out the will of another is always conditional on the particular balance of force, energy and meaning at any moment. Each actor, each locale, is the point of intersection between forces, and hence a point of potential resistance to any one way of thinking or acting, or a point of organization and promulgation of a different or oppositional programme. Entities may defect from a network, may refuse to be enrolled, or may bend its operations at certain points beyond all recognition. Budget holders will refuse to release sufficient funds . . . Experts and academics will seize upon the tactical possibilities open to them and seek to deflect them to their own advantage. And professional groups will bargain, bicker and contest on the basis of quite different claims and objectives instead of meshing smoothly and with complete malleability in the idealized schemes of a programmatic logic. Government is a congenitally failing operation; the sublime image of a perfect regulatory machine is internal to the mind of the programmers. The world of programmes is heterogeneous, and rivalrous.[9]

This is not to deny the existence of the state, or deny that as an apparatus it has grown as the business of governance has increasingly spread into many hitherto autonomous areas of social life. On this point, if on nothing else, Foucault and his disciples like Donzelot are surely right.[10] However, what it does suggest is that the strategies it adopts are negotiated at various levels and that their outcomes are far from certain, sometimes quite at odds with what is intended, not least by those politicians and senior civil servants who devise them and who are accountable to Parliament for their implementation.

The relevance of this to INQUEST is that its anti-state rhetoric contin-ues to suggest that we are still dealing with the all-seeing, all-power-ful Great Leviathan of political science. The truth of the matter is very different. Power is dispersed and fragmented. Of course, it is possible, and we would contend, proper, to hold politicians and senior civil servants responsible for their strategies, but they are hardly masters of the social body on which these strategies are inscribed. Such an idea would endow them with power they might like, but which they clearly do not have.

INQUEST's own practice reveals this to be the case, to take some examples from previous chapters. The prison department issued very clear guidelines about establishing suicide prevention management teams. No such teams were in place when the Chief Inspector brought forward his inspection of Risley in 1988 following a spate of suicides. The transfer of mentally ill patients in prison to hospitals was pro-vided for by legislation, but it became clear from the Chief Inspector's report on Brixton prison that the Health Service was impeding such transfers. The Minister for Social Services accepted the Ritchie report's recommendation on the supervision of mentally ill patients following sedation, but these were ignored by administrators and expert clini-cians at Broadmoor who backed their own professional judgement and took a different view.

In burrowing away in the interstices of the state apparatus, pointing to its failures and abuses in this way, INQUEST is as much demonstrat-ing the congenital failure of governance as it is defending our civil lib-erties by forcing the state to justify its exercise of authority. These ways of looking at its role are not contradictory, but rather ways of con-ceptualizing INQUEST's work from different viewpoints. However, the former arguably has an advantage because it is less conspiratorial and, following Rose & Miller, is less dependent on the discourse of civil lib-erties that, while it remains an extremely useful political shorthand against authoritarianism, rests on a distinction between civil society and the state that is very difficult to sustain as increasing regulation engulfs us.

The idea of governance cannot itself tell us much about when and why the present state apparatus developed in the particular form that it has done, a limitation that does not seem to trouble Rose & Miller who show little concern with history. Nor for that matter does it tell us much about whose interests its strategies might be devised to protect, although it is doubtful that those interests are simply reducible to a single component such as class or race. In these important respects then, its explanatory potential is limited. However, by stressing complexities and closures it suggests tactics for opposition which groups like INQUEST all too easily ignore in their preference for an anti-state rhetoric. Such rhetoric not only denies their daily experience, but also suggests an instrumentalist view of the state that links issues like policing race, gender and mental health together in a mutual framework which we believe is difficult to sustain.[11] To take this position in no way denies that INQUEST has been mostly involved with defending marginal and disadvantaged groups during turbulent political times, or to disagree with commentators such as Foucault that most elements of social regulation stem from the state, nor that in some ways or at some levels they are connected, as I trust this study has shown.[12]

Pressure groups, INQUEST and the limits of political science

It is more than a decade since it was observed, somewhat wryly, that the classification of pressure groups had become a "cottage industry".[13] It is not the intention here to add to this industry, which in the intervening years has multiplied as process-driven policy analysts have joined more value-orientated political scientists in extending and refining classifications. Rather, the intention is to take on board some existing, and arguably useful definitions and classifications, to illustrate through INQUEST some of the limitations of political science.

In an earlier chapter I referred to the fact that INQUEST operated across a number of lobbies or policy networks. The characteristics of these are variable, some are what policy analysts would call policy communities, others would be defined as issue networks. To simplify matters, a policy community is likely to involve single, or perhaps at most, two or three pressure groups operating directly to a single government department. These communities are relatively stable, with all the participants sharing core assumptions. Differences where they occur are likely to be settled by discussions behind closed doors, certainly never in the glare of publicity or as the consequence of a strident public campaign. The pressure groups concerned will have regular access to decision-makers, will sit on government working parties and so forth. Group leaders are assumed in such communities to represent their members and to be in a position to deliver their consent to any negotiated position. In issue networks on the other hand, consensus is unlikely. There will be many groups with competing policy paradigms. Continuity cannot be assumed as groups will come and go. Contacts between groups and government officials are therefore likely to be uneven, even acrimonious.[14]

It is important to stress that these classifications of lobbies or policy networks are presented here as ideal types, and it is therefore unlikely that pure policy communities or pure issue networks will occur in most areas of public policy. Furthermore, lobbies and policy networks do change. For example, in the 1950s and 1960s the penal lobby could reasonably be said to approximate a policy community with the Howard League and its well connected leadership interconnecting and overlapping with Civil Service and political elites in a closed – deliberately closed – dialogue.[15] The Magistrates Association perhaps constituted what is known as a secondary community. By the 1970s and into the 1980s, however, this situation had changed dramatically. The League was not only joined by the government, sponsored National Association for the Care and Resettlement of Offenders (NACRO) and the Prison Reform Trust, but also by groups like the prisoners' union, PROP, Radical Alternatives to Prison (RAP) and Women in Prison (WIP) who took very different views about the nature and purposes of the penal system, and who were definitely not going to be bound by the "rules of the game". Here was an issue network with a vengeance! (Sabatier's call for more longitudinal studies of policy networks might yield some important insights if applied to this example.[16])

It would require far more detailed research to define with complete accuracy where the various lobbies in which INQUEST operates should be placed along the community network continuum. However, if we consider what we take to be its defining issues, that is, its activities in the penal and civil liberties lobbies, then it would appear to be mostly active in issue networks rather than policy communities, although we concede that the mental health lobby is somewhere in between. From this we would expect, and indeed our narrative has confirmed, that INQUEST's contacts with policy-making elites are fitful, and at times, even antagonistic.

If policy analysts are to be taken seriously about the limits of ideal types, and they should be, then it should not be surprising to find that even within issue networks some groups are reasonably well

169

plugged into government. This is certainly the case in the penal and civil liberties lobbies. But INQUEST is not one of these. In this context Wyn Grant's well tested classification of insider and outsider groups is useful.[17] According to this, INQUEST would be most appropriately placed among "ideological outsider" groups; that is, among those groups whose objectives are at odds with many of the basic social and political assumptions of the current political system. The evidence suggests that INQUEST is mostly concerned with those on the border between legality and illegality, the mentally ill, often the poor or the casually employed, those marginal and disadvantaged groups who are subject to state regulation and whose lot is unlikely to be considerably improved without fundamental political change.

This location does not render INQUEST entirely powerless. I have demonstrated elsewhere that ideological outsider groups can and do exert influence on policy.[18] This may be at an ideological level and/ or at a practical level. For example, INQUEST had a very real impact on the way prison suicide was understood and how suicide prevention is now practised in our prisons. Those outside the tent then, to adapt President Johnson's colourful phrase, can have an impact on those inside the tent. However, we do not take it entirely for granted that INQUEST's outsider status is given and fixed. For example, in the 1960s and 1970s what might loosely be defined as the liberal penal lobby in Britain very definitely had the ear of government. But with the advent of the New Right this changed quite dramatically. Groups like the Howard League, the Prison Reform Trust, even NACRO, which is partly sponsored by government, were defined to the edges. Far more influential were groups like the Magistrates Association, which has been credited with helping to revoke those clauses in the Criminal Justice Act (1991) that had helped to reduce the prison population, and think-tanks like the Adam Smith Institute which lobbied hard for prison privatization.[19] In the civil liberties lobby the National Association of Freedom was more influential than the NCCL in the struggle over the rights of trade unionists.

While there is more that could be said about INQUEST's position in the frameworks under consideration, the evidence suggests that political scientists and policy analysts have provided us with a flexible and interpretative set of tools to understand how pressure groups operate. Up to a point I would not dispute this, and by way of an auto-critique I would acknowledge that in stressing relational perspectives policy analysts have in some respects improved on what has gone before.

What then is the problem? In simple terms it is that political scientists and policy analysts restrict the site on which they ply their trade; their boundaries are so narrowly drawn that they cannot fully appreciate the contribution that many pressure groups make to sustaining democracy, even although they mostly emphasize and, indeed, praise, this contribution. To illustrate this point I will be referring to two textbooks. The first is well regarded as a comprehensive guide to British government and politics for undergraduates which has been reprinted and revised numerous times; the second is a recent, specialist book on pressure groups that lucidly summarizes current theoretical perspectives and adds some original detail from the mid-1980s.

In *Contemporary British politics*, Bill Coxall & Lynton Robins ask, "At which points in the political system do pressure groups seek to exert influence?" To which they reply:

> British pressure groups have four main target areas; the "core executive" – Government ministers (including the prime minister) and civil servants (Whitehall); Parliament (both Houses); public opinion (mainly through the media); and increasingly in the 1980s and 1990s – the European Community/Union.[20]

Leaving aside the European dimension which is not directly relevant to the thrust of our argument, this analysis of the sites on, or through which pressure groups operate is, broadly speaking, replicated in most other standard texts on British government and politics. Of course, these sites need to be refined. Bob Baggott in his specialist text, *Pressure groups today*, reminds us, for example, that:

> The Executive is not monolithic, but a collection of institutions each with different pattern of influence and accountability Recent reforms such as "Next Steps" have if anything, fragmented the Executive even further. It is not enough that a pressure group has access to parts of the Executive. In order to have influence it must have access to those institutions within the Executive which exercise a critical influence over the policy issues which affect it.[21]

This all seems very straightforward, not to say comfortably familiar. So in the case of INQUEST, for example, it could be said, indeed, I have claimed, that it secured modest legislative changes, forced the Prison

Department, or the Prison Service Agency as it became under Next Steps, to change its understanding of prison suicides and adapt its procedures on suicide prevention accordingly, and so forth.

The difficulty is that this focus almost completely ignores what INQUEST mostly does! It also ignores, I would argue, what constitutes its real contribution to sustaining democracy, which is its capacity through detailed casework to burrow away in the crevices of the state in search of abuses of power by those who exercise control in our name, and through the public ritual of inquests, forcing the state to reaffirm its authority, its claim, as Weber put it, to the legitimate exercise of force.

INQUEST's key sites of operation are the coroner's court and, through it, the prison cell, the hospital ward, sites that are of little interest to political scientists and policy analysts. At one level this might hardly be construed as a criticism. Political scientists and policy analysts are only interested in such groups as they impact on the political system, albeit bringing with them the information and knowledge that they acquired elsewhere. And there is surely nothing wrong with such a narrow focus. After all, most academic disciplines define themselves not only through their method, but also partly through the object of their study, in this case, the political system.

This may seem a strong line of defence, and up to a point it is. However, it does not alter the fact that by largely confining its attention to the role of pressure groups in the formal political system the *discourse* of political science seriously undervalues the significance of pressure groups like INQUEST that engage state power elsewhere.

This is critical in our view because it tends to give the impression that power, the exercise of which we take to be one of political science's enduring concerns, is most tellingly located in the political system, on or around the various sites that Coxall, Robins and Baggott have indicated. While it would be foolish to deny that power relationships exist on such sites, the consequences of which have a significant impact on wider society, the truth of the matter is that power is dispersed throughout society, in the nooks and crannies of the fragmented state apparatus and, as I trust I have demonstrated, its exercise is sometimes quite outside the control of the formal political system, sometimes covering up, but more often than not, fouling up. It seems that as long as political scientists, or at least those concerned with political institutions, continue to write as if the Great Leviathan is still writ large then they will continue to elevate the centrality of the political system above and beyond what is justified to understand the exercise of power in modern societies and the realities of policy implementation, and in that process, limit our appreciation of the part played by some, though admittedly not all, pressure groups in engaging that power, an ongoing process that has no end if our liberties are to be secured.

Notes

Chapter 1

1. M. J. Smith, *Pressure, power and policy* (London: Harvester, 1993).
2. Home Office, *Statistics of deaths reported to coroners; England and Wales* (London: HMSO, 1994), p. 1.
3. Ibid., p. 1.
4. The right of families or other interested parties to a second postmortem was challenged by a coroner in 1985, but thanks to INQUEST acting on behalf of the family involved this right was soon reaffirmed (*ex parte* Ridley).
5. Home Office, *Statistics of deaths reported to coroners*, p. 1.
6. Ibid., p. 7.
7. Ibid., p. 1.
8. T. Ward, "Speaking for the dead", *Legal action* (August 1984), 9–11.
9. P. Scraton & K. Chadwick, *In the arms of the law* (London: Pluto, 1986), p. 46.
10. JUSTICE, *The coroners courts in England and Wales* (London: JUSTICE, 1986), p. 10.

Chapter 2

1. P. Scraton & P. Gordon, *Causes for concern* (London: Penguin, 1984), ch. 1.
2. T. Jefferson, *The case against paramilitary policing* (Milton Keynes, England: Open University Press, 1990), ch. 2.
3. T. Ward, *Death and disorder* (London: INQUEST, 1986), ch. 2.
4. NCCL, *The report of the unofficial committee of enquiry into the disturbances in Southall 23 April 1979* (London: NCCL, 1980), ch. 3.
5. D. McNee, *McNee's law* (London: Collins, 1983), pp. 84–5.
6. NCCL, *The death of Blair Peach. The supplementary report of the unofficial committee of enquiry* (London: NCCL, 1980), p. 31.
7. Ibid., p. 30.
8. Ibid., p. 39.

175

9. Ibid., p. 40.
10. Ibid., p. 41.
11. D. Ransom, *Licence to kill* (London: Friends of Blair Peach Committee, 1980), p. 21.
12. NCCL, *Death of Blair Peach*, pp. 42–6.
13. Scraton & Gordon, *Causes for concern*, ch. 2.
14. T. Banks, "The death of Jimmy Kelly" (undated manuscript), ch. 2.
15. Ibid.
16. Scraton & Gordon, *Causes for concern*, p. 56.
17. Ibid., p. 59.
18. Banks, "Death of Jimmy Kelly", ch. 3.
19. P. Scraton, Interview (Padua, September 1992).
20. Ibid. This research later formed the basis of *In the arms of the law* (London: Pluto, 1986).
21. Banks, "Death of Jimmy Kelly", ch. 4.
22. Ibid., ch. 4.
23. P. Scraton (ed.), *Law, order and the authoritarian state* (Milton Keynes, England: Open University Press, 1987), ch. 2.
24. Michael Meacher's attention was first drawn to the Liddle Towers case by a peace campaigner in the northeast. Personal communication with the author 22 July 1992.
25. Home Affairs Select Committee, *Deaths in police custody* (Sessional Papers, 1979).
26. Banks, "Death of Jimmy Kelly", ch. 9.
27. This is a handwritten note. INQUEST Executive Committee files 1981–5. Interestingly, the note makes no mention of the provision of legal aid at inquests. It was possibly taken for granted.
28. G. Coggan & M. Walker, *Frightened for my life* (London: Fontana, 1982).
29. This high-profile case involved Stanley Clinton Davis MP who raised it in Parliament on a number of occasions, including an adjournment debate.
30. Matthew O'Hara Committee, press release (November 1980).
31. Ibid.
32. GLC, *Verbatim reports of proceedings*, vol. 6 (London: GLC, 28 May 1991), col. 18.
33. Ibid., col. 18.
34. Ibid., col. 19.
35. GLC Police Committee, *Policing London* (London: GLC, 1982).
36. P. Scraton, Interview (Padua, September 1992).
37. GLC Police Committee, concurrent reports 2/3 (1 July 1982).

Chapter 3

1. G. Coggan & M. Walker, *Frightened for my life* (London; Fontana, 1982), p. 115.
2. The James Davey Campaign complained about this to the Home Secretary in a letter dated 23 October 1983. The Home Secretary refused to

intervene, arguing that coroners are under no legal obligation to preserve a dead body in deep-freeze conditions. A similar reply was received from the Prime Minister dated 13 March 1984.

3. James Davey Campaign, *West Midlands police: let's have a public inquiry* (Coventry: University of Warwick Students Union, 1984).

4. INQUEST/James Davey Campaign correspondence (undated), and between INQUEST and Gareth Peirce, the Davey family's solicitor, 22 April 1984.

5. James Davey Campaign, press release (July 1994).

6. INQUEST, *Annual report* 1983/4.

7. James Davey Campaign. March 1984. "Which way forward for the Davey campaign?" memorandum.

8. T. Ward, Interview (London, July 1992).

9. T. Banks, "The death of Jimmy Kelly" (undated manuscript), ch. 4.

10. *Policing in Hackney 1945–1984, a report commissioned by an independent committee of inquiry* (London: Karia Press and the Roach Family Support Committee, 1989), p. 261.

11. It was reported that "a very explosive situation now exists in respect of Hackney policing ... and Stoke Newington in particular". INQUEST, *Workers' report* (January 1993).

12. *Policing in Hackney 1945–1984*, p. 80.

13. INQUEST/Barnor Hesse (Roach Family Support Group) correspondence 21 March 1984.

14. *Policing in Hackney 1945–1984*, p. 104.

15. INQUEST, *Bulletin* (no. 7. 1985).

16. R. Geary, *Deaths in prison* (London: NCCL, 1980).

17. Coggan & Walker, *Frightened for my life*.

18. A. Sivanandan, "Challenging racism: strategies for the eighties", *Race and Class* **25**(2), 1–11, 1983.

19. Grant application for INQUEST's northern worker, p. 4 (INQUEST archive, Misc. file).

20. INQUEST/Urbanowicz correspondence 23 November 1984 (INQUEST archive. Misc. file).

21. P. Scraton, Interview (Padua, September 1992). The charge of metropolitan bias was later to sour the relationship between INQUEST and Prison Watch, the East Midlands group set up by Peter Moore. A former member of the Hayes police-monitoring group who had also served on INQUEST's Executive Committee in the early 1990s, Peter Moore worked with a former young offender, Tim Taggett, to successfully harry local prison governors over a range of issues, including deaths in custody.

22. INQUEST, "Report to the GLC Police Committee" (undated). INQUEST asked the GLC to remove the Southwark coroner but was told that this was beyond the council's authority. GLC/INQUEST correspondence 17 May 1985.

23. Letter to Tony Ward from Neera Sharma on behalf of Camden's Chief Executive.

24. These recommendations were endorsed by the Community and Police Committee 924, March 1987 and passed on to the council.

25. INQUEST, Financial statement (November 1983).

26. INQUEST, Executive Committee minutes (May 1985). Ken Worpole had resigned 18 months before in November 1983.
27. Some of these high-profile campaigns continued for several years. The Friends of Blair Peach, for example, only formally wound itself up in 1990 and transferred its by then modest assets to INQUEST.
28. Referred to in a letter from Phil Scraton 1981.
29. INQUEST, "Unlawful killings" (December 1981). Drafted by Ken Worpole.
30. INQUEST, "Reform of inquest procedures" (February 1982). Probably drafted by Phil Scraton.
31. Ibid.
32. C. Stubbs, Interview (London, April 1992).
33. *House of Lords debates*, vol. 435 (27 October 1981–2), cols 573–4.
34. T. Ward, Interview (London, July 1992).
35. *House of Commons debates*, vol. 41 (29 April 1983), cols 1138–62.
36. Christopher Price/Home Office correspondence March 1993. INQUEST archive, Parliamentary file.
37. *House of Commons debates*, vol. 41 (29 April 1983), col. 1146.
38. Home Secretary/Christopher Price correspondence 26 April 1983, p.1. INQUEST archive, Parliamentary file.
39. Ibid., p. 1.
40. Christopher Price/Home Secretary correspondence 6 May 1983, INQUEST archive, Parliamentary file.
41. L. Christian, *Policing by coercion* (London: GLC, 1983), cols 225–8.
42. *House of Commons debates*, Standing Committee E, *Police and Criminal Evidence Bill* (6 December 1983), cols 225–8.
43. *House of Commons debates*, Standing Committee E, *Police and Criminal Evidence Bill* (7 February 1984), col. 1106.
44. *The Abolitionist* (no. 16, 1984), p. 24.
45. INQUEST, *Deaths in custody and the Police Bill* (London: INQUEST, 1983).
46. T. Ward, Interview (London, July 1992).
47. INQUEST, "Comments on the Home Office Consultation Paper on the Coroners' Service" (London: INQUEST, 1984). For confirmation that this briefing was sent to Clive Soley, HM Opposition spokesperson on this issue, INQUEST Executive Committee minutes (April 1987). Tony Ward, who drafted this brief, was also a member of the Labour Campaign for Criminal Justice which Clive Soley chaired. Contacts between the two were therefore close and regular.
48. *House of Commons debates*, Standing Committee G (31 January 1985), cols 949–50.
49. Ibid., col. 1954.
50. INQUEST, Executive Committee minutes (December 1987).
51. INQUEST/NAPO. May 1994. "Health Care of Prisoners Bill". Press release (May 1994).
52. Ransom/Meacher correspondence 11 June 1982. Meacher's reply apologizing for the delay, 6 September 1982. INQUEST archive, Parliamentary file.
53. R. Baggott, *Pressure groups today* (Manchester: Manchester University Press, 1995).
54. JUSTICE, *Coroners courts in England and Wales* (London: JUSTICE, 1986).

55. Ibid., p. 10.
56. INQUEST, *Annual report* 1985–6.

Chapter 4

1. *The Abolitionist* (no. 22, 1986), p. 22.
2. INQUEST, *Annual report* 1986–7.
3. Ibid.
4. Ibid.
5. *The Abolitionist* (no. 17, 1984), pp. 25–6.
6. Ibid.
7. Ibid., pp. 12–13.
8. Ibid., p. 26.
9. *The Abolitionist* (no. 19, 1985), p. 29.
10. British Medical Association Medical Ethics Committee, *Health care of detainees in police stations* (London: British Medical Association, 1994), p. 28.
11. Police Complaints Authority, *Annual report* (London: HMSO, 1994–5), p. 32.
12. INQUEST, *Northern workers' report* 1982–3.
13. INQUEST, *Annual report* 1983–4.
14. INQUEST, *Annual report* 1991–2.
15. Police Complaints Authority, *Annual report*, (London: HMSO, 1994–5), p. 31.
16. T. Ward, *Death and disorder* (London: INQUEST, 1986), pp. 58–9.
17. INQUEST, Executive Committee minutes (7 June 1986).
18. Lord Gifford, *The Broadwater Farm inquiry* (London: Borough of Haringey, 1986).
19. D. Coles, Interview (London, March 1992).
20. INQUEST, *Newsletter* (Summer 1995), and *Guardian* 26 January 1996. The CPS is also believed to be looking again at the case of Richard O'Brien. A Southwark jury recently found he had been unlawfully killed by the police during his arrest in south London during 1994 (*Guardian* 13 February 1996). INQUEST worked closely with the O'Brien family both before and during the inquest.
21. *Voice*. 17 August 1993.
22. Winston Rose's family only heard about the decision in the press. (See INQUEST's submission to the Justice Committee on Coroners, p. 26.)
23. It is also significant that the PCA joined INQUEST in calling for changes to allow for advance disclosure following the controversial inquest into the death of Brian Douglas who died after being hit by police with a long-handled, American-style baton during his arrest in Clapham in May 1995 (Channel 4 news bulletin, 8 August 1996). In this case the jury returned a majority verdict of misadventure.
24. INQUEST, *Bulletin* (August 1993), and M. Benn & K. Worpole, *Death in the city* (London: Canary Press, 1986).

25. This book was funded as part of the GLC's campaign against the Public Order Bill.
26. INQUEST, *Bulletin* (August 1993).
27. Ibid.
28. Police Complaints Authority, *Annual report* 1994–5, p. 56.
29. Ibid., p. 40.
30. Gifford, *Broadwater Farm inquiry*, p. 60.
31. Police Complaints Authority, *Annual report* 1994–5, p. 44.
32. J. Sim, *Medical power in prisons* (Milton Keynes, England: Open University Press, 1990), pp. 114–15.
33. Ibid., pp. 114–15.
34. INQUEST, "Coroners inquests" (Submission to Justice Committee on coroners), Appendix 1.
35. INQUEST, *Bulletin* (no. 3. May/June 1984).
36. *House of Commons debates*, vol. 31 (8 November 1982), col. 31.
37. *House of Commons debates*, vol. 34 (16 December 1982), cols 470–71.
38. *House of Commons debates*, vol. 37 (23 February 1983), col. 392.
39. INQUEST, *Bulletin* (no. 3. May/June 1984).
40. Ibid.
41. INQUEST, *Annual report* 1985–6.
42. INQUEST, *Workers' report* (May 1986).
43. INQUEST, *Annual report* 1985–6.
44. *The Abolitionist* (no. 14, 1983) 14.
45. HM Chief Inspector of Prisons, *Report on suicides in prison* (London: Home Office. May 1984), p. 13.
46. Ibid., p. 15.
47. Ibid., p. 30.
48. INQUEST, *Bulletin* (no. 5. December 1984).
49. Ibid.
50. Home Office, press statement (5 September 1986).
51. INQUEST, *Bulletin* (no. 2. 1984).
52. *Deaths in custody; follow up action* (Circular Instruction 33/1984. Standing Order Amendment 376).
53. HM Chief Inspector of Prisons, *Report on HM Remand Centre Risley* (London: HMSO, 1988), para. 4: 14.
54. A. Liebling, "Suicide and self injury among young offenders in custody", paper presented at British Criminology Conference, Bristol, 1989, p. 828.
55. *House of Commons debates*, vol. 147 (24 February 1989), cols 830–35.
56. Barry Sheerman, press release (4 April 1989).
57. *House of Commons debates*, vol. 164 (20 December), col. 270.
58. The coroner was empowered to make these recommendations under Rule 43 of the Coroners' Rules 1984.
59. HM Chief Inspector of Prisons, *Report on HM Prison Brixton* (London: HMSO, 1990), p. 1.
60. Ibid., p. 108.
61. Ibid., pp. 105–6.
62. Ibid., pp. 110–12.
63. Ibid., pp. 118–20.

64. Home Office, press release (14 December 1990).
65. *House of Commons debates,* vol. 166 (1 February 1990), cols 298–9 and col. 384.
66. HM Inspector of Prisons/INQUEST correspondence 20 February 1990. INQUEST archives, Brixton file.
67. INQUEST submission to HM Chief Inspector of Prisons, "Inquiry into suicide and self-harm in prisons" (*c.* March 1990).
68. HM Chief Inspector of Prisons, *Suicide and self-harm in prison service establishments in England and Wales* (London: HMSO, 1990), Cm 1383.
69. D. Coles, Interview (London, March 1992).
70. T. Ward & D. Coles "Failure stories; prison suicides and how not to prevent them", in *Deaths in custody: international perspectives,* A. Liebling & T. Ward (eds) (London: Whiting & Birch, 1994).
71. *Independent* 11 October 1991.
72. Ibid.
73. *Guardian* 30 December 1991.
74. A. Liebling, "Suicide and suicide attempts among young prisoners; the UK experience" in *Deaths in custody: international perspectives,* A. Liebling & T. Ward (eds) (London: Whiting & Birch, 1994), p. 109.
75. P. Scraton, Interview (Padua, September 1992).
76. P. Scraton & K. Chadwick, "The experiment that went wrong", *The Abolitionist* (no. 20, 1985), pp. 28–33.
77. Ibid., p. 32.
78. Howard League, *Dying inside; suicide in prison* (London: Howard League, 1992), p. 2.
79. Liebling, "Suicide and suicide attempts", p. 110.
80. INQUEST, Executive Committee minutes (November 1990).
81. INQUEST, "Youth deaths in custody" *Bulletin* (1992).
82. Howard League, *Suicides in Feltham* (London: Howard League, 1993).
83. Ibid., p. 41.
84. Ibid., pp. 3 and 4.
85. Ibid., p. 12.
86. Ibid., p. 7.
87. Ibid., p. 6.
88. Ibid., p. 71.
89. Ibid., p. 7.
90. *Independent on Sunday* (22 March 1992).
91. Howard League, *Suicides in Feltham,* pp. 9–11
92. Liebling, "Suicide and suicide attempts", p. 119.
93. A. Liebling, *Suicides in prison* (London: Routledge, 1992), p. 231.
94. Liebling & Ward, *Deaths in custody,* p. 76.
95. INQUEST/MIND research project relating to deaths of patients who are receiving psychiatric treatment in hospital submitted to the King's Fund, 1987, p. 5.
96. Ibid., p. 6.
97. Ibid., pp. 7 and 8.
98. Department of Health and Social Security, *Report to the Secretary of State for Social Services concerning the death of Michael Martin at Broadmoor*

Hospital on 6 July 1984 (London: DHSS, April 1985), pp. 5 and 6.
99. INQUEST, *Annual report* 1983–4.
100. Ibid.
101. *The Abolitionist* (no. 18. PROP insert (unnumbered)).
102. Department of Health and Social Security, *Report concerning the death of Michael Martin*, pp. 14, 15.
103. *Daily Telegraph* (31 August 1985).
104. *The Times* (1–3 July 1985).
105. INQUEST, *Bulletin* (June 1989).
106. *The report of the committee of inquiry into the death in Broadmoor Hospital of Orville Blackwood and review of the deaths of two other Afro-Caribbean patients* (London: Special Hospital Service Authority, 1993), p. 30.
107. Ibid., p. 1.
108. Ibid., p. 3.
109. Ibid., p. 74.
110. Ibid., p. 32.
111. Ibid., p. 71.
112. Ibid., p. 47.
113. Ibid., p. 47.
114. INQUEST, press release (31 August 1993).
115. INQUEST, "Oral evidence to the committee of inquiry into complaints about Ashworth Special Hospital" (2–3. Stage 11. 17 March 1992).
116. INQUEST, *Written evidence to the committee of inquiry into complaints about Ashworth Hospital* (London: INQUEST, n. d.), pp. 44–52.
117. *Report of the committee of inquiry into complaints about Ashworth Hospital* (London: HMSO, 1992), vol. 1. Cm 2028–1. ch. XXV, p. 211.
118. Ibid., p. 212.
119. Ibid., p. 213.
120. Ibid., p. 212.
121. Ibid., p. 216.
122. Ibid., p. 217.
123. INQUEST, *Annual report* 1991.
124. *Report of the committee of inquiry into complaints about Ashworth Hospital* vol. 1. Cm 2028, pp. 233–4.
125. *New Statesman and Society* (26 May 1995. Fortress Europe supplement), xi.
126. INQUEST, *Annual report* 1986–7.
127. Ibid.
128. Ibid.
129. This suggestion is often made. For example, Louise Pirouet. "Suicide and attempted suicide of asylum seekers detained by the UK", in *Deaths in custody: international perspectives*, A. Liebling & T. Ward (eds), (London: Whiting & Birch, 1994), pp. 143–60.
130. Ibid., p. 156.
131. C. Moraes, "Immigration detainees in prison", *Criminal Justice* **13**(1), 5–6, 1995.
132. *New Statesman and Society* (26 May 1995. Fortress Europe Supplement), xi.
133. *Statewatch* (November/December 1992), 1; *Statewatch* (September/October 1992), 1.
134. *Statewatch* (January/February 1995), 1.

135. INQUEST, *Annual report* 1994.
136. Ibid.
137. *Guardian* 28 July 1993.
138. Chris Smith MP/Home Office correspondence 18 July 1994. INQUEST archive, asylum seekers' file.
139. Early Day Motion 640 (22 February 1994).
140. Amnesty International/Home Office correspondence July 1994. INQUEST archive, asylum seeker's file.
141. INQUEST/Joint Council for the Welfare of Immigrants, Charter for Immigration Detainees (May 1994).

Chapter 5

1. P. Scraton, A. Jemphrey, S. Coleman, "No last rights; the denial of justice and the promotion of myth in the aftermath of the Hillsborough disaster" (unpublished manuscript), p. 29. (Published in 1995 by Liverpool City Council.)
2. Ibid., p. iv.
3. Ibid., p. 46.
4. Ibid., p. 46.
5. Ibid., p. 47.
6. Ibid., pp. 63–72.
7. Ibid., p. 74.
8. Conversation with June Tweedie. June 1995. As a friend of one of those who died in the *Marchioness* tragedy, June Tweedie naturally took a special interest in this campaign.
9. Scraton et al., "No last rights", pp. x–xi.
10. Ibid., p. 192.
11. Ibid., p. 199.
12. Ibid., p. iv.
13. D. Bergman, *Disasters: where the law fails* (London: Herald Charitable Trust, 1993), pp. 4–5.
14. Scraton et al., "No last rights", p. xxii.
15. INQUEST, "Oral evidence to the committee of inquiry" (para. h. Stage 2 17 March 1992).
16. P. Scraton, Interview (Padua, September 1992).
17. *Independent* (8 April 1995).
18. *House of Commons debates*, vol. 211 (9 July 1992), col. 695.
19. *The Times* (5 July 1994).
20. *The Times* (19 October 1994).
21. *Independent* (8 April 1995).
22. London Hazards Centre/INQUEST, *Deaths at work. Accidents or corporate crime* (London: Workers' Educational Association, 1991), p. 28. See also C. Wells, *Corporations and criminal responsibility* (Oxford: Clarendon, 1993).
23. Ibid., pp. 7–14.

24. Health and Safety Commission, *Annual report* 1988–9 (Summary), p. 7.
25. *Construction News* (2 March 1989).
26. Ibid.
27. UCATT strongly resisted this policy. See, for example, Finsbury Park UCATT/Minister of Trade correspondence 9 September 1985. INQUEST archives, deaths at work file.
28. Finsbury Park UCATT/INQUEST correspondence 7 January 1989. INQUEST archives, deaths at work file.
29. London Hazards Centre, *Hazards* 22. (London: Hazards Publications, 1989).
30. Construction Safety Campaign flysheet, London 1989.
31. *Irish Times* (22 October 1988).
32. Construction Safety Campaign, *Policies and organization of the construction safety campaign* (London: Construction Safety Campaign, n.d.), p. 1.
33. INQUEST/Heather Swales (Rowntree Trust) correspondence 31 July 1991.
34. London Hazards Centre/INQUEST, *Deaths at work*, p. 4.
35. Ibid., p. 33. Whether the Law Reform Commission's recent proposals on corporate manslaughter will offer sufficient protection to employees is a matter of debate. (See, for example, *Independent* (6 March 1996).)
36. *Independent* (1 October 1991).
37. Institute of Race Relations, *Deadly silence. Black deaths in custody* (London: Institute of Race Relations, 1991), p. 3.
38. Department of Health and Social Security, *Report to the Secretary of State for Social Services concerning the death of Michael Martin at Broadmoor Hospital on 6 July, 1984* (London: DHSS, April 1985), par. E 1.
39. *Report of the inquiry into the circumstances leading to the death in Broadmoor Hospital of Joseph Watts* (London: Special Hospitals Service Authority, 1990), par. 123.
40. *Report of the committee of inquiry into the death in Broadmoor Hospital of Orville Blackwood and a review of the deaths of two other patients* (London: Special Hospitals Service Authority, 1993), p. 53.
41. Ibid., p. 51.
42. Ibid., p. 52.
43. Germain Alexander died during a struggle in Brixton prison in 1989. A member of his family joined the INQUEST Executive during the campaign.
44. *Report of the committee of inquiry into complaints about Ashworth Hospital* (London: HMSO, 1992), Cm 2028–1, pp. 148–50.
45. INQUEST, *Annual report* 1988–9.
46. *Report on black deaths in police custody (1970–1988)* was incorporated into INQUEST's *Annual report* 1988–9.
47. Ibid.
48. Institute of Race Relations, *Deadly silence*, pp. 65–6.
49. *Independent* (28 August 1985). The reply was sent direct to INQUEST, but was undated and unsigned.
50. *New Statesman* (9 December, 1983).
51. INQUEST, *Annual report* 1982–3.
52. *New Statesman* (9 December, 1983). Melissa Benn was formally co-opted onto INQUEST's Executive Committee in June 1993.

53. *Venue* no. 79 (May 1985).
54. Circular to members 12 January 1986.
55. INQUEST, *Annual report* 1985–6. See also, *The Abolitionist* (no. 1, 1986), p. 19 and p. 26.
56. *New Statesman* (9 December, 1983).
57. *The Abolitionist* (no. 21, 1986), p. 19.
58. The most authoritative academic research in this area in the 1980s came from Pat Carlen who was closely associated with Chris Tchaikovsky and others in the writing and production of *Criminal women* (Cambridge: Polity, 1985).
59. P. Scraton & K. Chadwick, *In the arms of the law* (London: Pluto, 1986), p. 131.

Chapter 6

1. Mark Urbanowicz was listed as INQUEST's Hon. Treasurer with a London address in the group's original application to the GLC in May 1992.
2. INQUEST, Workers' report to Executive Committee on financial position 22 November 1982.
3. INQUEST, Executive Committee minutes. November 1982.
4. Ibid.
5. INQUEST, Workers' report to Executive Committee on financial position 2 November 1983.
6. INQUEST, Executive Committee minutes. November 1983.
7. INQUEST, Executive Committee minutes. July 1985.
8. Verbatim minutes of London Borough Grants' Committee 10 June 1986 taken by observers from the London Association of Community Relations Councils.
9. London Voluntary Sector Forum, Circular to all applicants to LBGU, 2 March 1987.
10. INQUEST, Executive Committee minutes. March 1987.
11. Ibid.
12. LBGU/INQUEST correspondence December 1990.
13. Ibid.
14. INQUEST, Executive Committee minutes. May 1991.
15. LBGU/INQUEST correspondence 22 May 1991.
16. He expressed this view in the meeting with the co-directors and chair in February 1991.
17. INQUEST, Executive Committee minutes. April 1992.
18. INQUEST, Executive Committee minutes. February 1982.
19. Sinclair, Taylor & Marks/INQUEST correspondence 5 February 1992.
20. The issues on the agenda that day were discussed and voted upon by members only. The remainder of the time was given over to a public meeting which addressed other issues.
21. Ian Ray – Todd/INQUEST correspondence 18 May 1992.

22. A. Scrivener, "Cause for concern; the law and deaths in custody". (Unpublished paper, 1991).
23. These priorities were discussed at an ILG meeting. 9 October 1991.
24. For a wide ranging discussion of *ex parte* Jamieson, see P. Scraton, A. Jemphrey, S. Coleman. *No last rights; the denial of justice and the promotion of myth in the aftermath of the Hillsborough disaster*.(Liverpool: Liverpool City Council, 1995).
25. *Legal aid now. Journal of the Legal Aid Association*. October 1993.
26. Paper circulated to ILG February 1992
27. The differences between adversarial and inquisitorial procedures are not quite as clear-cut as some would make out. See, for example, R. Burridge, A. Paliwala, S. Morris, "The inquest as a theatre for police tragedy", *Journal of Law and Society* **12**, 35–61, 1985.
28. ILG Committee meeting February 1992.
29. ILG Committee meeting April 1992.
30. ILG Committee meeting July 1963.
31. These fears were expressed most clearly in Ken Worpole's resignation letter, 25 November 1983.
32. Ibid.
33. INQUEST, *Workers' report to the Executive Committee* (Leadbetter) November 1983.
34. INQUEST, Executive Committee minutes February 1984.
35. INQUEST, *Workers' report to the Executive Committee* (Leadbetter) November 1993.
36. LBGU/INQUEST correspondence 17 February 1993.
37. Long term funding arrangements between LBGC and INQUEST for the period 1 April 1992 – 31 March 1992 (undated).
38. INQUEST, Executive Committee minutes March 1991. For discussions on the consultancy initiative, see INQUEST, Executive Committee minutes May 1992.
39. P .Waterhouse, INQUEST. *Final report on the organizational development programme* (1992), p. 2.
40. Ibid., p. 11.
41. Personal communication to the chair 5 April 1993.
42. Waterhouse INQUEST, *Final report*, p. 1.

Chapter 7

1. Likewise, INQUEST has given advice and sympathetic support to Roadpeace, which investigates deaths in road accidents, but no more. Further afield, INQUEST's successful campaigns led to the creation of a parallel group in Sydney based around the Law Faculty at the University of New South Wales.
2. INQUEST did not achieve much joy from the European Court which, in the context of the Gibraltar killings, ruled that inquests were a suitable means of investigating deaths (*Guardian* 28 September 1995).

3. In the debate over the NCCL's future following its offer of advice to a right-wing group in the mid-1980s, INQUEST's delegates were mandated to vote in favour of holding the group together.

4. R. Burridge, A. Paliwala, S. Morris, "The inquest as a theatre for police tragedy", *Journal of Law and Society* **12**, 35–61, 1985.

5. HM Chief Inspector of Prisons, *Suicide and self-harm in prison service establishments in England and Wales* (London: HMSO, 1990), Cm 1383, para. 5.09.

6. *Report of the committee of inquiry into complaints about Ashworth Hospital* vol. 1 (London: HMSO, 1992), p. 211.

7. Burridge et al., "The inquest as a theatre". For more on this line of interpretation, though in a historical context, see J. Sim & T. Ward, "The magistrates of the poor? Coroners and deaths in custody in nineteenth century England", in *Legal medicine in history*, M. Clarke & C. Crawford (eds) (Cambridge: Cambridge University Press, 1994).

8. The Association of Boards of Visitors, "Inquests and the press" (circular, 1992).

9. N. Rose & P. Miller, "Political power beyond the state: problematics of government" *British Journal of Sociology* **43**(2), 172–205, 1992.

10. M. Foucault, *Discipline and punish* (London: Allen Lane, 1977); J. Donzelot, *The policing of families* (London: Hutchinson, 1980).

11. M. Ryan & T. Ward, "From positivism to postmodernism; some theoretical and strategic reflections on the evolution of the penal lobby in Britain", *International Journal of the Sociology of Law* **20**, 321–35, 1992.

12. M. Foucault, "Afterword: the subject and power", in *Michael Foucault: beyond structuralism and hermeneutics*, H. Dreyfus & D. Rabinow (Brighton: Harvester, 1992).

13. G. Alderman, *Pressure groups and government in Great Britain* (Harlow, England: Longman, 1984).

14. R. Baggott, *Pressure groups today* (Manchester: Manchester University Press, 1995); M. J. Smith, *Pressure power and policy* (Brighton: Harvester Wheatsheaf, 1993); A. G. Jordan & J. J. Richardson, *Government and pressure groups in Britain* (Oxford: Clarendon Press, 1987).

15. M. Ryan, *The acceptable pressure group. Inequality in the penal lobby, a case study of the Howard League and radical alternatives to prison* (Farnborough: Saxon House, 1978).

16. P. Sabatier, "Toward better theories of the policy process", *Policy Science and Politics* (June 1991), 147–56.

17. W. Grant, *Pressure groups, politics and democracy* (Hemel Hempstead: Philip Allan, 1989).

18. D. Marsh (ed.), *Pressure groups in Britain* (London: Junction Books, 1983), section 11.

19. M. Ryan & T. Ward, *Privatization and the penal system: the American experience and the debate in Britain* (Milton Keynes, England: Open University Press, 1989).

20. B. Coxall & L. Robins, *Contemporary British politics* (London: Macmillan, 1994).

21. Baggott, *Pressure groups today*, p. 87.

Index

189

INDEX

arrest   51–2, 130, 163, 177*n*, 179*n*
prisons   163
psychiatric and Special Hospitals
88, 163
Deaths in custody; follow up action   68,
180*n*
Director of Public Prosecutions (DPP)
16, 26, 50, 58–9, 109–10
Disaster Action   107
Disasters. Where the law fails   124
Divisional Courts   12, 52, 62–63, 70, 92,
102–3, 110, 112
Doncaster prison   101
Donzelot, J., *The policies of families*
187
Douglas, Brian   179*n*
Douglas, Wayne   61
Downing Street, petition   27
Dubbs, Alf MP   32, 43
Ducatt, Paul   65

Eastwood and Partners   110
Edge Hill College   27, 34, 162
EEC
countries, immigrants   100
health and safety standards   125
Emergency Services   111
Environment, Department   114
European Commission, proposals on
immigration   101
European Court, Gibralter killings   162
Ewin, David   60

F-marking system   64–8
Fairleigh Hospital   88
Federation of Independent Advice
Centres (FIAC)   154
Feltham prison   82–7, 181*n*
Feltham Youth Custody Centre   83
Fitzgerald, Ed   19, 90, 92, 99, 133, 147
Foot, Michael   38
Football Association   108
Foucault, M.   166, 187*n*
Frightened for my life (PROP)   62, 132

Gardner, Joy   59, 101
Gately, Kevin   10
Gateshead   17
Gatwick airport   99
Geary, Richard   32
Deaths in prison   177*n*
General Election campaign (1979)   10
Gerry, David   15
Gerty report   16
Ghenochil, Scotland   79–80
Gibraltar killings   162, 186*n*
Gifford, Lord   57, 61
The Broadwater Farm inquiry   179*n*,
180*n*
Glasgow, Gateway Exchange project   79

Glen Parva Young Offenders
Institution   81
Goggan and Walker   25
Gordon, Ian   60
Grace, Gary   56
Grant, Bernie MP   57
Grant, W. *Pressure groups, politics and
democracy*   187*n*
Great Leviathan   167, 172
Greater London Council (GLC)
20–22, 35, 42–5, 138–9, 153 *see also*
London Hazards Centre
Police Committee   20–23, 30–31, 33,
43, 45, 56, 131, 137–8
Concurrent reports 2/3   176*n*
Policing London   176*n*
Support Unit   22, 33, 57, 60
Verbatim reports of proceedings   176*n*
Women's Committee   131, 138
Griffith, Eldon   44
Guardian   61, 71–2, 77, 117, 139–41, 158,
179*n*, 181*n*, 182*n*, 186*n*
Gutch, David   157–8

Hackney   30–31, 140
Black People's Association   30–31
Workers' Educational Association
(WEA)   19
Hall, Professor Stuart   17, 31
Hammersmith
Council, community and police
committee   36, 177*n*
police cells   34
Harmondsworth immigration centre
100
Harringey Police Research Unit   57
Hasler immigration centre   100
Hayes, John (report)   114–15
Hayes police-monitoring group   177*n*
Health, Department   71
Health and Social Security, Dept, *Report
concerning death of Michael
Martin*   181*n*, 101, 184*n*
Health care of detainees in police stations
179*n*
Health and Safety Commission, *Annual
report* (1988–9)   183*n*
Health and Safety Executive (HSE)
118–24
Health Service, transfer of mentally ill
patients in prison   167
Heather-Hayes, Jim   62–65, 81–3, 90
Heather-Hayes, Shelia   37
Helm, David   13
Herald Families Association   107 *see also*
Zeebrugge ferry disaster
High Court   30, 47
Ashworth inquiry   94
Highpoint prison   78
Hillsborough project   107–12, 117–18,

191

INDEX

Police Federation 28, 44, 48
Police shootings 60–61
Policing in Hackney (1945–1984) 177*n*
Policy Studies Institute (PSI) Report 130
political science 168–73
Popper (coroner) 109, 111–12
Preservation of the Rights of Prisoners
  (PROP) 7, 32, 62–3, 89–90, 127–8, 169
Price, Christopher MP 40–41, 46–7, 62–4
  Home Office correspondence 178*n*
Prime Minister, letters 26
Prins, Hershel (report) 126–7
Prison
  Department 75, 78–9, 87, 103–4, 171
  Her Majesty's Inspector 52, 64–6, 69
  suicides 62–3, 170
Prison Medical Health Officers 64, 71,
  75
Prison Medical Service 5, 19, 42, 46–7,
  65–7
Prison Officers' Association 5, 92–4, 96,
  127
Prison Reform Trust 2, 105, 169–70
Prison Service Agency 172
Prison Watch 177*n*
prisoners 62, 94–6
Prosser, Barry 62–3
Pryce, Oliver 57–8, 61, 164
psychiatric hospitals 4, 51, 71, 88, 163
psychiatrists 76
Public Order Act (1936) 21
Pucklechurch Remand Centre, Bristol
  132

R v. HM Coroner for East Kent ex parte
  Spooner and others 103
Race and Class 33
Radical Alternatives to Prison (RAP) 7,
  32, 62, 169
Rampton 89
Ransom, David 37, 48, 151
  Licence to kill 176*n*
  Meacher, Michael MP correspondence
  178*n*
Rastafarian religion 127
Ray, Ian/Todd/INQUEST
  correspondence 185*n*
Red Lion Square 10
Rees, Merlyn MP 10
Registrar of Births, Marriages and
  Deaths 2
Reid, Errol 36
Reilly, Steve 123
Report on black deaths in custody
  (1970–1988) 128–9, 184*n*
Report on suicide prevention and self injury
  (1990) 86, 167
Responding to criticism 67–79
Rice, Christopher 42
Rickets, Caroline 57

Rights Watch 162
Risley remand centre 69–79, 167
Ritchie, Shirley QC (report 1992) 90–93,
  126, 167
Roach, Colin 27, 30–33, 42, 177*n*
Roadpeace 186*n*
Roberts, Ernie MP 31
Rochester prison 101
Rose, Nikolas 166–7
  & P. Miller, *Political power beyond the*
  state 187*n*
Rose, Winston (1981) 58–9, 179*n*
Rouse, Sidney 119–20
Royal College of Psychiatrists 93
Royal Free Hospital 53
Ruddock, Joan MP 115
Ryan, M.
  The acceptable pressure group 187*n*
  & T. Ward
    From positivism to postmodernism
    187*n*
    Privatization and the penal system
    187*n*

Sabatier, P. 169
  Toward better theories of the policy process
  187*n*
St Pancras coroner's court 123
Sancto, Mark 132–3
Scarman, Lord (report) 10, 30
Scotland, nationalism 9
Scott, Christine 133
Scraton, Phil 16–17, 22, 27, 34–5, 44,
  79–80, 105
  draft letter from INQUEST to MPs 178*n*
  Hillsborough case 108–9, 113
  Interview 176*n*, 177*n*, 181*n*, 183*n*
  link between WIP and INQUEST 134
  major disasters 131
  "Reform of inquest procedures" 178*n*
Scraton, Phil & K.Chadwick, *In the arms*
  of the law 175*n*, 185*n*
Scraton, Phil & P. Gordon
  Causes for concern 175*n*, 176*n*
  Law, order and the authoritarian
  state 176*n*
  The experiment that went wrong 181*n*
Scraton, Phil et al, *No last rights*
  109–10, 112–13, 117, 183*n*, 185–6*n*
Scrivener, Anthony QC 146
  "Cause for concern: the law and deaths
  in custody" 185*n*
Sefton Trades Council 29
Sheerman, Barry MP 46, 69, 128, 148,
  180*n*
Sheffield 108–10
Sim, J.
  Medical power in prisons 180*n*
Sinclair, Taylor and Marks/Inquest
  corespondence 185*n*

195